WORK IN CRISIS

WORK IN CRISIS

The Dilemma of a Nation

ROGER CLARKE

THE SAINT ANDREW PRESS
EDINBURGH

First published in 1982 by
THE SAINT ANDREW PRESS
121 George Street, Edinburgh EH2 4YN

Copyright © Roger Clarke, 1982

ISBN 0 7152 0540 4 (CASED)
ISBN 0 7152 0543 9 (LIMP)

Printed in Great Britain by
CWS Printers,
35 Bogmoor Place, Glasgow

What men desire is, not paragraphs in constitutions, but results, in the form of arrangements which ensure them the essentials of a civilised existence and show a proper respect for their dignity as human beings. If they do not get them in one way, they will try to get them in another.

R.H. Tawney *We Mean Freedom*

The debate needs to be about how the work that is available should be distributed. . . . We need to discuss the principles of justice and equity that should apply in the allocation.

Brian Showler and Adrian Sinfield *The Workless State*

THE PRESENT CRISIS OVER UNEMPLOYMENT
AND THE FUTURE OF WORK

THE QUANTITATIVE ISSUE
Is Full Employment
likely to be attainable
this decade?
Section I

THE QUALITATIVE ISSUE
What kind of society
do we want?

**ASSESSING THE IMPACT OF
CONTINUING HIGH
UNEMPLOYMENT**

**ASSESSING THE POSSIBILITIES
OF CONSTRUCTIVE CHANGE**

**ON
INDIVIDUALS**

What does it mean
in personal terms
to be without work
in a work-centred
society?
Section II

ON SOCIETY

What social ills
emerge when work
opportunities are
inequitably dis-
tributed?
Section III

**THE
DISTRIBUTIVE
PROBLEM**
If work is now a
scarce resource:
(1) How do we pre-
vent the unem-
ployed and their
dependants falling
victim to poverty?
Section III

(2) How can we
distribute work op-
portunities more
equitably among so
many claimants?
Section IV

**THE
CULTURAL
PROBLEM**
(1) What accom-
modations in at-
titude, value
systems and
lifestyle are having
to be made in the
face of the new
realities?

(2) What work can
we positively
affirm?
Section V

CONTENTS

ABBREVIATIONS

CBI   Confederation of British Industry
DE   Department of Employment
DHSS   Department of Health and Social Security
DIY   Do-it-yourself
DMC   District Manpower Committee
EEC   European Economic Community
EOC   Equal Opportunities Commission
ERS   Earnings related supplement
MSC   Manpower Services Commission
OECD   Organisation for Economic Co-operation and Development
PEP   Political and Economic Planning
PSBR   Public Sector Borrowing Requirement
PSI   Policy Studies Institute
SBC   Supplementary Benefits Commission
TUC   Trades Union Congress
YOP   Youth Opportunities Programme

PREFACE

At this present time many responsible and caring people are asking penetrating questions about the future of work and unemployment. The swaggering confidence which characterised our approach to employment issues during the post-war years of growth has faded and in its place one now encounters perplexity, anxiety and a growing social concern. That concern focuses especially upon the young and the long-term adult unemployed for whom the whole structure of opportunities is in grievous disarray. From the mid-1960s the number out of work has risen steadily and in recent years it has risen dramatically.

The knowledge that so many capable men and women cannot secure employment at this point of time and are forced to stand idle is deeply disturbing. Gifts and talents which could be put to more purposive use are being squandered, motivation decays and hope dwindles as the months and the years pass and still no opportunities of recruitment are found.

This book challenges that state of affairs and argues the moral case for changes that would bring about a redistribution of work. As such I hope that it might be read by a very broad cross-section of the community. Its comments on the social order and its concerns are addressed to those in employment and to those presently without work; to employers and to the trade unions; to the concerned and intelligent ordinary citizen wishing to think a little more deeply about some of the great issues of our time; to the politician and those responsible for the framing of appropriate social and employment policies in the difficult years that lie ahead; to the opinion formers and the agents of creative change wherever they may be within the structure of society; above all, to men and women of goodwill who are concerned to see justice and compassion prevail within the contemporary social order.

ROGER CLARKE
Dundee

ACKNOWLEDGEMENTS

This book emerges as a result of three years of study undertaken in conjunction with the University of Manchester and the William Temple Foundation. To my tutor during this period, Dr John Atherton, I owe a particular debt of gratitude for all his helpful encouragement, criticism and assistance. I wish also to thank the Trustees of the Industrial Mission Trust and the Department of Home Mission within The Church of Scotland for their financial support and for their continued interest in this project.

During these three years my thoughts have been stimulated by a great number of people. They are so many it would be impossible to name them all. But of particular significance in the formulation of my thesis have been the insights gained while a member of the Scottish Theological Development Group which was set up in 1980 with the intention of bringing Christian faith to bear more effectively upon the problems posed by rising unemployment. My thanks also go to the library staff of the University of Dundee and to my many working colleagues within the Manpower Services Commission who have supplied me with much valuable research material. I would also want to place on record my particular thanks to those who have helped me put this book together; to Mr Douglas Law and his staff in The Saint Andrew Press; to Nancy Markham, who typed some of the early drafts; and especially to Delphine Newsome for all her hard work in helping me prepare the final manuscripts. Finally, my love and thanks go to my family who for many a long month have lived with forbearance amid a great assortment of books and papers and who have shared with me in the agony and the ecstasy of the writer's craft.

The author and publishers are grateful for permission to use copyright material from the following sources and are happy to make acknowledgement to the authors, publishers and agents listed below:
George Allen and Unwin for extracts from *The Attack and Other*

Papers by R.H. Tawney; *Full Employment in a Free Society* by
W.H. Beveridge; *The Protestant Ethic and the Spirit of Capitalism*
by Max Weber; and *Philanthropy in England* by W.K. Jordan.
A.H. Halsey (1978), *Change in British Society* by permission of
Oxford University Press. Arnold Wesker for an extract from his
play *I'm Talking About Jerusalem,* published by Jonathan Cape.
Secker and Warburg for permission to quote from George Orwell's
The Road to Wigan Pier. James Nisbet and Co. for kindly allowing
me to use two extracts from E.W. Bakke's classic account *The
Unemployed Man.* Chris Cook and John Stevenson for permission
to quote material from their book *The Slump: Society and Politics
during the Depression,* published by Jonathan Cape. The
Controller of Her Majesty's Stationery Office for permission to
reproduce extracts from the *Employment Gazette* and the
Supplementary Benefits Commission 1979 Report Comnd 8033.
Granada Publishing for allowing me to use a passage from *The
Conditions of the Working Class in England* by F. Engels, and
Hodder and Stoughton for permitting me to use an extract from
God on Monday by Simon Phipps. *The Harvard Theological
Review* for permission to reprint material from *Protestantism and
Capitalism: The Weber Thesis and its Critics* by Robert W. Green.
Cassell Ltd. for passages from *A Sociology of Work in Industry* by
Alan Fox.

I would wish also to express my thanks for permission to use a
passage written by my colleague Paul Brett and reproduced from
Work and the Future, published by CIO Publishing, 1979,
copyright Central Board of Finance of the Church of England. I
am grateful that I have been allowed to use some extracts from the
preface of *Useful Toil,* edited by John Burnett (Pelican Books,
1977), Copyright John Burnett, 1974, which is reprinted by permission of Penguin Books Ltd., and also a passage from Jeremy
Seabrook's book *City Close-up* (Penguin Books, 1973), Copyright
Jeremy Seabrook, 1971, again reprinted by permission of Penguin
Books Ltd. Martin Robertson and Co. Ltd. have kindly granted me
permission to use extracts from Adrian Sinfield's book *What Unemployment Means* and from *The Workless State* by Brian
Showler and Adrian Sinfield. John Murray (Publishers) Ltd. have
permitted me to use a passage from *Religion and the Rise of
Capitalism* by R.H. Tawney, and T. and T. Clark Ltd. have
allowed me to use one extract from Williston Walker's *History of
the Christian Church.* Tavistock Publications Ltd. have kindly

allowed me to use material from *The Ideology of Work* by P.D. Antony and a very helpful paper on the formative influence of the Charity and Sunday Schools written by M.W. Flynn and contained in *Social Theory and Economic Change*, edited by Tom Burns and S.B. Saul. I am grateful to *Resurgence* for allowing me to use material from a thought-provoking article by Sheila Rothwell on 'Women and Work'. I have also been permitted to use certain extracts from John Hill's article on 'The Psychological Impact of Unemployment' and Marie Jahoda's article on 'The Psychological Meanings of Unemployment'. I am happy to acknowledge that both these articles are copyright of *New Society* and reprinted by permission of the Editor.

I would also wish to thank SCM Press Ltd. for allowing me to use short extracts from *The Secular City* by Harvey Cox, *The Contradiction of Christianity* by David E. Jenkins, *The Biblical Doctrine of Man in Society* by G. Ernest Wright, and *Work in Modern Society* by J.H. Oldham; Maurice Temple Smith Ltd. for permission to reprint extracts from *Stories from the Dole Queue* by Tony Gould and Joe Kenyon (1972) and *The Workhouse* by Norman Longmate (1974); Longman Group Ltd. for permission to quote from *Poverty and Vagrancy in Tudor England* by John Pound; the Policy Studies Institute for allowing me to include a passage from the 1977 PEP report entitled 'Where are they now?' and the Writers and Readers Co-operative who have allowed me to use two passages from *Down the Road* by Sarah Cox and Robert Golden.

In the preparation of my manuscript I have also made use of a number of unpublished papers, many of which have provided me with valuable insights into my thesis theme and I have incorporated a list of these within the Bibliography. However, I have quoted at some length from three of these papers and I would want to express my thanks to the following authors for allowing me to use their material in my text. To Sandy Cowie for permission to quote from his paper on 'Work-Sharing', Professor Robert Davidson for allowing me to use material from his unpublished paper 'Work and Unemployment: a Biblical Approach'; and to my colleague David Welborn, who has allowed me to quote a passage from his stimulating lecture on 'New Attitudes for a New Age', my very particular thanks.

INTRODUCTION

There is a sterility about much of the present debate over the high
levels of unemployment which afflict Britain and the other advanced industrialised nations. The discussion ranges over well-trodden
ground. The clichés and the conventional statements of position
begin to cloy and in response to one of the great issues of the day
precious little creative thinking appears to emerge. As I write I am
conscious that much of the current debate seems to have become
boxed into two seemingly opposing camps. One school of thought,
characterised by the technocrats and those who sit at their feet,
asserts that, given the present economic, demographic and global
circumstances, very high levels of unemployment are inevitable.
The opposing school of thought is characterised by the man on the
Unemployment Rally: He is there to protest that, in the words of
the United Nations Charter, 'Everyone has the right to work.' He
stoutly resists what the technocrat is saying, asserting with some
fire in his belly that unemployment and particularly long-term unemployment is iniquitous and morally unacceptable. Between the
two camps there seems to be a great divide. They seem to be saying
quite contradictory things and the general public in the middle is
perplexed and uneasy—uncertain as to whether the appropriate
course is to accommodate to the inevitable or to resist the propagation of the unacceptable.

The man with the banner feels that the technocrat has
capitulated in accepting that job market forecasts for the remainder
of the 1980s are now bleak in the extreme. Meanwhile the
technocrat with his detailed knowledge of the multiplicity of constraints operating within the economic system and reinforced by
cabinet files full of statistics, comparative figures, trends and
predictions, sadly shakes his head and muses on the stubborn
refusal of others to face the facts. So the impasse continues. Two
parties looking out on the same world, genuinely stating what they
believe in their hearts to be true but not engaging in real creative
dialogue.

When two parties disagree so passionately it is not always that one is pigheadedly wrong and that the other was right all the time. It may be, if you listen carefully enough, that there are precious insights hidden within what both parties are attempting to say to each other. Thus I believe that the technocrat is right when he points to the enormity of the problems which now confront us in attempting to re-establish a situation of Full Employment. But the man with the banner on the Right to Work demonstration also speaks the truth when he asserts that a society in which mass unemployment remains as a continuing feature is a society which is very seriously flawed.

In evaluating the present crisis over work and unemployment we must begin by carefully assessing the prospect now before us. As I write, unemployment teeters on the edge of the three million mark and the short-term forecasts point to even that unprecedented level being exceeded. But what of the longer term? Is a return to full employment achievable and, if so, within what time-span? Is the ending of mass unemployment merely a matter of economic priorities and political will or have the prevailing economic realities undergone a fundamental change? In particular, are the current global, technological and internal economic constraints such that we must concede that a major quantitative increase in the total number of jobs is now unlikely in the mid-term and that a return to our previous patterns of full employment will continue to be frustrated during the foreseeable future? These quantitative issues form one strand of the present debate over unemployment and form the basis of Section I of the book.

The quantitative issue of the number of sustainable jobs which the economy is capable of generating is an important starting point in our analysis of the current crisis over work. It is a discussion which operates within the arena of economics, though it has strong political overtones. However, the quantitative issue which deals with future manpower requirements and the state of the economy is only one strand in what is now emerging as a more complex debate over the future of work. For if we conclude in our careful assessment of future manpower trends that the technological revolution and increased foreign competition will be likely to combine with other factors to seriously curb the generation of new jobs during the 1980s then the nation is impelled to search out other means by which the social ills which follow in the wake of high unemployment are to be resolved. Sections II and III identify respectively the personal and the social consequences of failing to achieve the ideal of Full Employment. For the individual caught into a situation of long-term unemployment there is not only financial privation but also the psychologically corrosive impact of living without work. Meanwhile, within the social order the sharp division of incomes and lifestyles between the community of the employed and the community of the unemployed makes for stressful and embittered social relationships.

Out of the material contained in Sections II and III two major distributory problems emerge. The first centres around the financial implications of running a two-nation society in which one group maintains its position of relative affluence because it has access to earnings within the paid economy, while the unemployed live a considerably more impoverished existence because they can only draw on fairly minimal state benefits. The issue is one which centres upon the adequacy of present benefit levels and the collective responsibility of those in employment for those who are not. As such, it forms part of the ongoing debate over the persistence of poverty in the midst of comparative affluence and appropriate mechanisms for the distribution of wealth within a nation. But the loss of work involves much more than a consequent loss of income. The debate therefore leads on to an additional distributory problem. I refer here to the problem of fairly distributing such work as there is among so many potential claimants. The problem is an acute one because market forces on their own are unlikely to bring about a sharing of job opportunities in a fairly even-handed way across the whole nation and the unemployed are likely to remain locked out of work.

As I shall indicate in Sections II and III, work plays a very important part in our lives. The loss of work affects our status within society and inevitably brings in its wake many accommodations in lifestyle. The affected individual is denied the social satisfactions which come from being a member of a work group and frequently experiences profound social isolation. Further, their sense of purpose and life direction is seriously challenged when people are exposed to prolonged unemployment. They feel themselves unmanned and ill at ease in a social situation where they can no longer make a contribution to the society of which they are a part. What is being disturbed here is a series of expected role relationships which have emerged down through the years with respect to work and the maintenance of a community's economy. Thus in order to under-

stand some of the changes that are taking place in our time we shall
have to speak not only in economic and financial terms but also in
the language of relationships and enter into the world of social, psychological and ethical considerations. In making my case for the
adoption of those social arrangements which might serve to distribute the available work opportunities more equitably across the
whole nation I shall want to speak about human needs and the
human condition, of wholesome patterns of participation in community life and the significance of work in the life of man.

I believe that the need to feel that we belong, that we have an accepted place within the community and that in turn we are provided
with opportunities to make a contribution through work to the
community of which we are part, are all fundamental features of a
wholesome social existence. In Section IV I therefore wrestle with
the problem of moving from the present unsatisfactory position
towards one where such work opportunities as there are available
are more equitably distributed. This leads us into a discussion of a
variety of work-sharing initiatives and an assessment of their merits
and their costs. The discussion here is about the cost of sharing, the
challenge to vested interests and the practical problems of achieving those social arrangements which might remove some of the
deep divisions of our present two-nation state.

Finally in Section V I turn from the distributive problems posed
by a scarcity of job opportunities and look instead at the cultural
accommodations that are having to be made at this time. Together
with the family, work has formed one of the stable bases of our life.
The loss of the ideal of Full Employment therefore poses a serious
challenge to anticipated lifestyles. The inherited work ethic, with its
adulation of the worker and its moral condemnation of those who
do not work, is becoming increasingly anachronistic and unhelpful
in an age where jobs have become a scarce resource. Because past
value systems are in question and work looks like assuming a more
subordinate place in our lives, I spend some time in analysing our
inherited attitudes towards work and make some suggestions with
regard to a more appropriate ethic for our times.

I have tried to arrange my material in such a way that the five
principal sections outlined above will give the reader the opportunity to examine the present unemployment crisis from five
slightly different angles. These five arenas, as I have termed them,
allow us to make a multidisciplined assessment of the human
predicament over work which has many facets to it. I hope using

this broad range of analytical skills we are enabled to build up a comprehensive and adequate understanding of the issues that now confront us and be led towards a more adequate and constructive social response. As a further guide to readers, a simple diagrammatic model identifying the sort of issues which will be dealt with in the course of the book is set out opposite the Contents page.

Throughout the book my primary concern is with those arrangements which make for well-being both within the social order and within the personal realm. Its focus is upon the human condition of men, women and young people caught into a situation where work has become a scarce resource and a variety of personal and social adjustments are having to be made. Amid all the perplexity and difficulties of the current situation it searches for the most promising responses. While recognising the crucial part that both economic and political contributions have to make in the debate about best responses to the dilemma over work, my intention has been to start a bit further back. For first, before harnessing the resources of both economics and politics, we have to ask some fundamental questions about human needs, social relationships and the kind of society that we are trying to secure. It is my hope that this survey of the present social scene and future possibilities will assist in delineating certain desired social goals. It will then be for economic and political policies to be so directed that we can achieve those particular goals.

The correct statement of the problem is the first stage towards its effective resolution. I do not in any way claim that in terms of analysis and evaluation what is set down in these pages is the truth, the whole truth and nothing but the truth. With respect to comprehending what is happening to work in our times, we all find ourselves echoing the words of St Paul, 'Our knowledge is imperfect and our prophecy is imperfect'. And at this confusing period of human history, strain the eyes as we may, we are permitted only to 'see through a glass darkly'. A certain intellectual humility and a willingness to hear what others say they see is perhaps the most productive stance if we would really grow in our corporate understanding and it is in such a spirit that I write this book. Not as the final statement in the debate about work and unemployment but as a working contribution which hopefully will lead the discussion on to some new ground and serve to sharpen perception within a broad cross-section of the public. What is laid out here for better or for worse is just one man's overview of the issues which lie embedded within the current employment debate. They are the distillation of some ten years spent wrestling with the issues and the practical problems posed by rising unemployment. Such insights as are contained here spring out of the ongoing dialogue with ordinary men and women in and out of work, with the trade unionists and employers, government officials and the multitude of specialists who people my working life and who have helped to shape my thinking. They are a very broad social and political grouping and I am sure that not all would share in my analysis. However, all that I can do is to set down some markings and to report on what I now see after a decade in the field. Through the medium of this book I would hope to share what insights I have gleaned with others. If these and other contributions can be pooled we can perhaps all gain a more adequate understanding of the issues that now confront the nation and be moved to respond appropriately.

As this book goes to press, I am very conscious that time is not on our side. Social ills, like a ticking time-bomb, lie in our midst waiting to explode. The street riots in Bristol, Brixton, Toxteth and Moss Side gave some indication of the severity of our problems. They are now of an order of magnitude to give rise to grave concern. For in community after community the social divisions are deepening, income disparities are widening and feelings of frustration and resentment are strongly in evidence particularly amongst the young. There is therefore a considerable urgency about the need for us to relieve the pains of those who are presently without work. For the most part those pains are borne silently and courageously. But we should not mistake the quiescence of the unemployed with a belief that they are apparently content with their lot. I deeply suspect that their acceptance of their unhappy lot stems not from the silence of contentment but is the ominous silence of a section of society trapped into powerlessness. There is a festering sore in the midst of the nation and we are all called upon to deal with it. For there is a sense in which we are all part of the problem and inevitably we shall all have to make some costly accommodations if we genuinely desire to see that problem resolved. In that regard the finer detail of the unemployment statistics as they appear month by month is really not all that significant. With the ending of the recession, or an accommodation in policy, the unemployment statistics may steady and even begin to drop down a bit. I sincerely hope they do. But be warned, that is the danger point. When unemployment statistics are escalating and redundancies are

being announced there is great public concern. But when these
things drop out of the news and a marginal improvement can be
demonstrated, the great mass of people still secure in employment
can be lulled into thinking that all is now well and a complacency
sets in with respect to those who still remain upon the register. Such
a situation must not be allowed to occur. The Many must not forsake the Few. Whether we have three million unemployed or two
million or even one million, the unresolved problems relating to the
distribution of work outlined in these pages will be there in our
midst. Until that large-scale social ill is dealt with I believe that the
issues raised in this book will continue to have some relevance.

Perhaps one other thing might be said at the outset about the
stance of this book. Essentially this book is about the social order.
That is, it concerns itself with certain characteristics of our life in
Britain today and with the kind of society in which we would want
to live. Its focus is upon work and the central place that it has in
our personal lives and in the life of society. But above all my book
is about people and the way we choose to work out our lives
together within the one community. How do we share what work
we have and what wealth we have within the one nation? That is a
question which is pertinent in both the good times and the bad.
What work deserves to be done? How do we organise that work
and how is that work to be distributed amongst the many potential
claimants? It is as we begin to ask these questions that we find ourselves moving beyond purely technical considerations and into the
area of having to make moral choices. At the heart of the work
debate lie the prevailing attitudes and value systems that give
character to our communal and national life. This book is written
in the belief that there are moral preferences to be made and that,
given the corporate will, it is possible to restructure society to make
more adequate provision for all its citizens in these testing and uncertain times.

Running through this work the reader will be conscious of
various recurring themes and issues. They are the great issues of
the outworking of justice and compassion within the social order,
the discovery of an appropriate lifestyle, of a wholesome participation in the riches of community life, and of social acceptance. These
themes are approached unashamedly from my own stance as an
Industrial Chaplain.

My work inevitably involves me in a lively dialogue with those
who work within and manage the paid economy and with those

men, women and young people who are without work. These two
groupings form the inhabitants of the two nations—those in and
out of work who, in statistical terms, constitute the Many and the
Few. In order to understand the problem of work in our times it is
necessary to portray the human condition of man both in and out
of work and to examine in some detail the relationship between the
Many and the Few. However, I hope that this book will be
something more than a piece of careful sociological documentation.
One cannot move within the ranks of the unemployed in my kind of
job and be content just to observe. One is impelled by what is seen
at first-hand to engage in the ferment of debate and to work for far-
reaching change. Thus, what follows, although it may have started
as documentation, emerges as polemic and challenges the persistence of social and economic arrangements which are currently
contributing to the re-creation of an under-class.

My concerns in this book are both for the principles and the consequences of policy. In wrestling with the great and disturbing
issues presented by mass unemployment in our times I have tried to
draw upon the insights that seem to me to emerge from the Christian tradition. The insights of men like R.H. Tawney and
Archbishop William Temple, who engaged their minds with similar
problems a generation ago, form a line of Christian social thought
which stretches back over the decades in relation to the problems of
poverty and unemployment, its causes and its social remedies. Today that same social concern emerges in the more secular guise of
the writings of men like Peter Townsend, Adrian Sinfield and Frank
Field and in the reports of the Supplementary Benefits Commission
and the poverty lobby. In them I hear the concern of those who, in
the words of the beatitudes, 'hunger and thirst to see right prevail'.
That sense of urgency about the need to make some profound
changes within the social order echoes what can now be heard
within a much larger global framework. The new consensus of
social understanding that has emerged of late within the ranks of
the World Council of Churches, so powerfully expressed in its
reports, has also greatly influenced me. The overall vision of the
need for people in all nations to construct a just, participatory and
sustainable society forms a useful framework when thinking about
many of the key issues in today's world and has been seminal to
my thinking. (1) Further, it enables the Christian to speak about
society in such a way that others not sharing his belief may yet
hopefully respect and understand. For in a pluralist society it is

vitally important that Christian and non-Christian find ways of sharing their primary concerns and discovering the common ground.

I am also deeply indebted to Bishop Ted Wickham, a pioneer in British Industrial Mission, who many years ago taught me that if we wish to change society in such a way that it will permit human beings to live a more abundant life, then we have not only to bring about a change of attitudes among individuals and groups. We must also seriously engage in the equally difficult task of bringing about change within the prevailing economic, social and political structures. It is these which form the 'principalities and powers' of this age. The way life is structured, the way our institutional arrangements operate, the way agreed policies and the social mechanisms function have the powerful combined effect of giving shape and character to the social order and do much to predetermine the life chances available to certain social groups. The combined effect of these social arrangements can result in either the enhancement of the dimensions of human life or they can so reduce realistic human options as to leave us stunted. 'Demonically, they may hold us trapped and frustrated; or in an angelic way, liberate and humanize us.' (2)

While recognising that in the final analysis men and women need to find their own sense of meaning, purpose and self-fulfilment within the realm of 'biographical experience' (which is beyond anything that can be structurally organised or created by the social planner), there is nevertheless in every age a profound need for the optimal 'enabling structures' that *allow* such lives to be lived in their God-intended fullness. If we are serious in our concern to grapple with the dilemmas that lie at the heart of the unemployment crisis, then, it seems to me, we are in all conscience impelled to engage in the search for what Tawney once called the form of social arrangements which ensure that men and women have 'the essentials of a civilised existence and show a proper respect for their dignity as human beings'. (3)

References and Notes

Please note London is the place of publication except where indicated.
  1. 'Christian Social Thought in a Future Perspective', *Anticipation* 26, World Council of Churches, Geneva, June 1979, pp. 25ff.
  2. Wickham, E.R., *Encounter with Modern Society,* Lutterworth Press, 1964, p. 17.
  3. Tawney, R.H., *The Attack and Other Papers,* Allen and Unwin, 1953, p. 91.

SECTION I

THE CREATION OF WORK

The Arena of Economics

Chapter 1

FULL EMPLOYMENT IN A FREE SOCIETY: THE LOSS OF AN IDEAL

Before looking in some detail at the dilemmas which presently confront the nation over employment it might be helpful to put our current situation in historical context. I want to take as my starting point the closing years of the Second World War when William Beveridge, the architect of our social security system and a great British reformer, published his classic report *Full Employment in a Free Society*. Given our present circumstances it is a book worth rereading, not for its economics, which have dated, but for its vision of a society set free from Idleness. By 'Idleness' Beveridge meant the social curse which had dogged Britain down through the years. The curse brought about by being saddled with an economic system which consistently failed to provide sufficient job opportunities for those genuinely seeking work. On past record, market forces alone had only rarely and briefly provided work for all. Escape from Idleness would only come, so Beveridge believed, through the state deliberately committing itself to a policy of full employment and so orchestrating the economic and social arrangements of the nation as to ensure that job opportunities were available for every member of the working population.

By the term 'Full Employment' Beveridge did not mean literally no unemployment. He recognised that some measure of unemployment was inevitable in a complex industrial society. With admirable clarity he sets out his case:

In every country with a variable climate there will be seasons when particular forms of work are impossible or difficult. In every progressive society there will be changes in the demand for labour, qualitatively if not quantitatively; that is to say, there will be periods during which particular individuals can no longer be advantageously employed in their former occupations and may be unemployed till they find and fit themselves for fresh occupations. Some frictional unemployment there will be in a progessive society however high the demand for labour. Full employment means that unemployment is reduced to short intervals of standing by, with the certainty that very soon one will be wanted in one's old job again or will be wanted in a new job that is within one's powers. (1)

Remembering the grave social ills that arose in the 1930s, Beveridge believed that unemployment both could and should be kept to 'an irreducible minimum'. His aim was to get the Government to implement a series of far-reaching policies that would have the effect of pulling unemployment down from the 10–22 per cent levels experienced in Britain between the wars and containing it in post-war Britain to no more than 3 per cent. It will be convenient to use Beveridge's definition of Full Employment in the discussion that follows as an unemployment level which does not exceed 3 per cent and where the structure of job opportunities within particular communities is sufficiently buoyant to offer reasonable choice. In practice this means always having slightly more vacant jobs than the number of persons registered as unemployed. It means that the jobs on offer are at fair wages, that they are so located as to be within reasonable travel distance and, in consequence, the time lag between losing one job and being able to secure another is kept short. These were Beveridge's aims. He believed that Full Employment, as he had defined it, was 'something that the British democracy should direct its Government to secure, at all costs save the surrender of the essential liberties'. (2) He had seen with his own eyes the growing despair, the bitterness and the loss of social purpose that follows in the wake of prolonged and widespread idleness. He recognised too that for the state just to provide some source of minimum income for the unemployed was not enough. The state had a greater responsibility to its citizens—that of engineering what Beveridge called freedom from idleness. 'Idleness is not the same as want, but a separate evil, which men do not escape by having an income. They must also have the chance of rendering useful service and of feeling that they are doing so.' (3)

The 1944 White Paper on employment policy did not go as far as Beveridge had hoped, but nevertheless the Government of the day did commit itself to 'the maintenance of a high and stable level of employment after the War' and for twenty very formative years the percentage of those out of work ranged between 1 and 2 per cent and only rarely and temporarily exceeded 2 per cent. For much of the period the number of long-term unemployed was negligible and politicians and the electorate grew accustomed to there being virtually work for all. By 1965 it looked as if this pattern was assuming a degree of permanency. Indeed, during these years the recurring problem tended to be that of an acute labour shortage in a number of sectors, particularly in the export industries. Repeated appeals were made to married women to rejoin the workforce. Large numbers of immigrants were encouraged to come to Great Britain from the Commonwealth nations and were readily absorbed into the work needing to be done in a number of essential services and industries. Women were actively recruited and day-care facilities were provided for mothers with young children. Meanwhile ramps were built and machines specially adapted in order to enable the disabled to go to work. A great variety of training schemes were set up. All were responses intended to reduce those obstacles which might have prevented others from playing their full part within the paid economy thereby allowing as many as possible to contribute their precious energies and skills to the reconstruction of Britain after the devastations and privations of the Second World War.

The Return of Mass Unemployment

Looking back, those were the twenty fat years of continuous full employment. 'It was an unprecedented period for Western Europe, a conjunction of all the most favourable of circumstances and as a result it appeared that work could be provided in all circumstances.' (4) During this period of growing economic confidence and personal affluence there was little talk of 'unemployables' or the 'inevitability of unemployment'. Memories of the dark days of the Depression began to fade and a new expectation was born in Britain. It was that mass unemployment was a thing of the past and that full employment was the assured social and economic norm within a welfare state. Without really thinking about it too much we came to take it for granted that each year personal living standards would rise, public squalor would diminish and that anyone between the ages of 16 and 65, provided they were fit and willing to work, would be able to find employment. Here and there the job seekers might be required to move from their original place of residence or undergo training, but there would be work for those who wanted it and indeed a choice of work. Today that assumption no longer holds. Bit by bit mass unemployment has returned and with it a collapse of life choices for a significant number of our people. The story of this change is both important and disturbing.

Perhaps the first signs that something was beginning to go wrong emerged after 1966. Between 1967 and 1974 registered unemployment never fell below the half million mark and during the severe recession of 1975–1978 it rose alarmingly to a peak of some 1.37 million (excluding school-leavers). But these figures now seem as nothing compared to what has happened to unemployment levels in the period 1979–82 when the Government's anti-inflationary policies have combined with other factors to bring unemployment levels up to over three million.

To begin with, the departure from the ideal of Full Employment was seen as some freak abnormality, attributable to economic mismanagement by whichever political party happened to be in power. Alternatively, it was put down to the poor productivity record of British industry or some cyclical difficulty. The ideal of Full Employment, however, was still thought of as politically attainable and its promise vital to the winning of the election. By now full employment had become so much a bench-mark in the public mind that it was inevitable that the early economic difficulties thwarting its achievement should have been presented to the electorate as short-term problems which a change of Government or some other easily identified simplistic measure would resolve. In fact some very major structural changes were taking place in the world of work and the problems of managing the economy were becoming more complex than those with which Keynes and Beveridge had had to deal. Further, the process of technological change was bringing in its wake a major demanning in many of the traditional industries. Overall employment levels, however, were not being much affected because the productivity shake-up in manufacturing was counterbalanced in the mid-1970s by the growth of jobs in other sectors (notably within banking, insurance, local government and the Civil Service, health and education services where a large number of female and part-time opportunities were emerging).

Even in the mid-1970s, however, many unskilled and labour-intensive tasks were fast disappearing and those people at the bottom of the skill hierarchy were finding work increasingly difficult to obtain. The young too were finding entry into work particularly difficult. The nature of work was changing and many of the simple tasks which might have provided employment for an inexperienced school-leaver were being erased by the introduction of more sophisticated work methods. Employers were increasingly looking for 'experienced employees' but without an opportunity to start work somewhere young people could not attain that needed experience.

From the mid-1970s onwards, among the young and the unskilled some serious mismatches were beginning to appear within the labour market leading to more and more people remaining on the unemployed register for worryingly long periods. But perhaps even more disturbing was the inability of the economy to cope with the steady increase in the size of the potential workforce. From 1972–79 over a million extra people came on to the labour market, many of them married women wishing to return to work, many of the rest were school-leavers searching for their first job. However, sluggish growth meant that the number of jobs available within the economy remained relatively static during the latter half of the 1970s and the numbers out of work consequently showed a steady increase. (See Charts 1 and 2.)

Meanwhile, not only was Britain sinking further and further into the slough of despond but our counterparts in the other advanced industrialised nations were also experiencing a similar set of problems. Some like Sweden, Germany and Japan were riding their difficulties a little better than others. Some like Switzerland were exporting their unemployment by returning very large numbers of their migrant workers back to their homelands. Some like Britain were trying to shovel back the tide of rising youth unemployment by adopting massive training schemes for their young people, others were propping up existing jobs by an extensive system of state subsidies. But still, despite these efforts, unemployment levels were rising. In Britain we were drifting further and further away from the ideal of Full Employment and there were disturbing signs all over Europe that we were not being particularly effective in our control over the economy. As one wag put it in the late 1970s, 'Work doesn't seem to be working.' The tragic consequences could be seen in virtually every community in the steadily lengthening dole queues. Less visible but equally disturbing was the length of time that certain individuals had been without the opportunity of securing any kind of employment. By 1981 this latter problem had become acute.

Here then is our first area of concern—the loss of full employment. For some twenty years the Keynesian system of economic management seemed to have put the ideal of Full Employment firmly in our grasp. But despite all the efforts of successive govern-

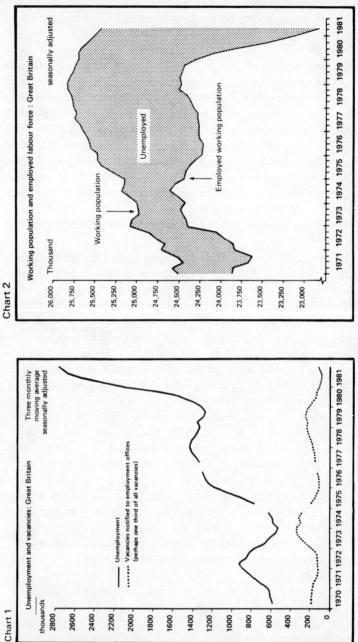

Chart 1

Unemployment and vacancies: Great Britain   Three monthly moving average seasonally adjusted

thousands

—— Unemployment
········· Vacancies notified to employment offices (perhaps one third of all vacancies)

2800 2600 2400 2200 2000 1800 1600 1400 1200 1000 800 600 400 200 0

1970 1971 1972 1973 1974 1975 1976 1977 1978 1979 1980 1981

Chart 2

Working population and employed labour force : Great Britain   seasonally adjusted

Thousand

Working population

Unemployed

Employed working population

26,000 25,750 25,500 25,250 25,000 24,750 24,500 24,250 24,000 23,750 23,500 23,250 23,000

1971 1972 1973 1974 1975 1976 1977 1978 1979 1980 1981

Reprinted from Employment Gazette, January 1982

ments and the varied economic advice of the Treasury, in Britain, as was the case in many other industrialised nations, we were not able to run the economy in such a way that it was capable of providing us with enough jobs for all the potential claimants.

The Prospect Now Before Us

The prospect with regard to unemployment levels during the remainder of the 1980s now looks exceedingly disturbing. By the late summer of 1981 nearly three million people had either been shaken out of the paid economy or else had failed ever to enter it. The question that must now be asked concerns their future and their well-being. How long might it take to get the bulk of these individuals back to work? 'How long?' is something more than a purely technical question which looks for a carefully balanced reply. We need to remind ourselves that in essence it is a question about human hope. Further, it is a question which quite properly is going to be asked more and more insistently by those who remain locked out of the paid economy. Those thus marginalised will be demanding, and to my mind quite rightly demanding, of those in work and those who manage the economy, the opportunity to participate to an equal degree in the benefits and satisfactions that come from engaging in paid employment. The time-scale within which that legitimate demand can be met may be all important with respect to the survival of human hope. The failure of a democratic society to achieve those goals speedily may put democracy itself at risk. For as we have seen with Poland, if a people feel strongly enough that a particular social system is intolerable they will take it into their hands to overthrow it in the hope that something better might take its place.

Britain in the post-war years, greatly assisted by massive injections of Marshall Aid payments from the USA, succeeded in rebuilding its economy and achieving Beveridge's great ideal—that of full employment in a free society. For a number of years, while we continued to enjoy particularly favourable growth rates, it was possible to keep high levels of unemployment at bay and work opportunities buoyant. But most commentators recognise that we are now into a completely different economic situation and Britain is having to operate in a greatly altered world scene which makes the attainment of similar rates of growth much harder to achieve. Apart from the internal technical constraints which hamper the economy being run at very high growth rates, there are also the moral constraints

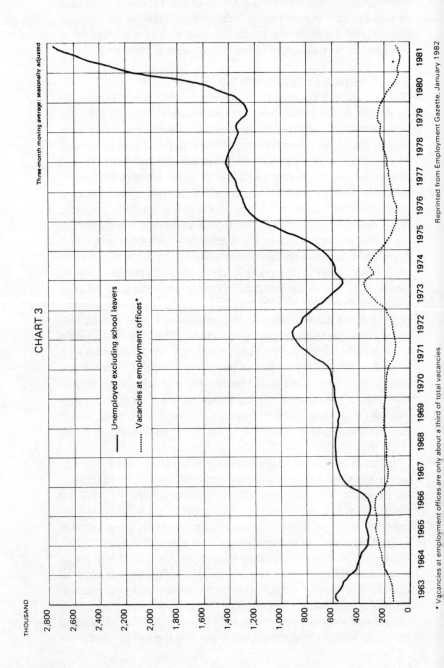

CHART 3

THOUSAND

Three-month moving average : seasonally adjusted

—— Unemployed excluding school leavers

······ Vacancies at employment offices*

* Vacancies at employment offices are only about a third of total vacancies

Reprinted from Employment Gazette, January 1982

which emerge from our recognition that many of the earth's resources are finite and must be stewarded responsibly. Growth patterns can no longer be set within the narrow confines of a particular nation state but must now have regard to the legitimate needs of other inhabitants of the global village as well as safeguarding both our and their future. How then within the framework of these broader responsibilities do we resolve our present unemployment problems? Operating in more difficult circumstances where responsible economic choice is more limited and starting from a base line of three million unemployed, is it possible for a free society to move back to full employment? Is it possible to regain Beveridge's ideal and once again be in a position of being able to offer the opportunities of work for all? That is the challenge to our nation, to the economic system which has brought us thus far and to the present social order. If we fail to meet the legitimate demands of our young people, of our ethnic minority groups and of many other ordinary people living in those communities where the structure of work opportunities has effectively collapsed, then it may not be too much to say that the social stress inherent in such a situation may threaten the very future of democracy itself. As R.H. Tawney reminds us in that passage which is quoted at the front of this book, men desire 'the essentials of a civilised existence' and social arrangements that 'show a proper respect for their dignity as human beings. If they do not get them in one way, they will try to get them in another.' (5) These are chilling words that cast a sombre shadow over the years that lie ahead.

References and Notes

1. Beveridge, William H., *Full Employment in a Free Society*, Allen and Unwin, 1944, p. 18.
2. *id.*, p. 258.
3. *id.*, p. 20.
4. Jenkins, Clive and Barrie Sherman, *The Collapse of Work*, Eyre Methuen, 1979, p. 27.
5. Tawney, R.H., *The Attack and Other Papers*, Allen and Unwin, 1953, p. 91.

Chapter 2

THE DILEMMA OF OUR TIMES

The problem which confronts the British nation is that if the anticipated demand for paid employment is to be fully satisfied during the 1980s then something in the order of three million extra jobs will need to be created.(1) That is certainly a very ambitious task and however high it may appear on the political agenda it will not be at all easy to achieve that target whichever party is in power. It is true that there have been periods in the past when the economy has expanded rapidly and with it the number employed. But the kind of conjunction of favourable circumstances which made for such a dramatic increase in jobs is probably no longer with us. The employment base within British manufacturing industry has been severely eroded during this prolonged recession. Many communities have witnessed the closure of the factories, offices and mills that formerly gave them employment and in many cases those are irrecoverable losses. The new jobs will need to come from elsewhere through the development of new products and services and that will take time. Even in the most favourable of economic circumstances and given the maximum of assistance and encouragement from national government, it will be a painfully slow business rebuilding in every community what has been lost.

It will be painful and slow for a number of reasons, principally to do with problems of competitiveness and the new technology. We will be operating in an increasingly competitive global market with a challenge to the sale of our goods coming not just from Europe, Japan and the United States. We need to remember that over and above these traditional competitors lie the new industrialising countries. Hong Kong, Taiwan, South Korea, Yugoslavia, Singapore and Brazil have all shown that they also have the capacity to capture large sections of our traditional export market. Their ability to harness a low-wage economy to newly acquired advanced production processes enables them to undercut quite substantially the price of the goods offered by the best of the EEC manufacturers. Britain can only hope to retain her competitive edge in a number of important world markets if she maximises the efficiency of her production processes. It is this which fuels the drive towards harnessing all the advantages of the new technology.

The application not only of microprocessors, but of all the other significant advances, to the way we design and make our products, the way we transact our business and handle a multitude of administrative tasks, could be vital in retaining our competitive edge. There are signs that we have already delayed too long in seizing the advantages that the new technology provides. Our innate conservatism and the financial difficulties of these past few years have slowed down the pace of manufacturing investment and product innovation. We have as yet failed to revolutionise our office procedures in both the private and public sectors by harnessing the full potential of the new office technology in routine paperwork tasks. The pressures are therefore already upon us to move with speed into these areas in order to keep pace with our competitors, let alone overtake them. We thus find ourselves caught into a tide race of change with respect to the introduction of the new technology as we enter the 1980s. It offers us significant competitive advantages and its introduction, by enabling us to keep unit costs down, will be essential if we wish to *retain* jobs. Whether in the short term it can be reasonably expected to *increase* substantially the cumulative stock of jobs is an open question. Indeed there are a number of commentators who believe that in the short term the introduction of the new technology will in fact have the reverse effect and actually substantially *erode* the sum of jobs available in the country through the displacement of labour, making our present unemployment situation considerably worse. (2)

The truth is that the business of trying to predict how many jobs will be gained and how many lost, not only on account of the new technology, but resulting from numerous other significant agents of change, is complex and highly hazardous. Predictions made about how the employment situation will stand at the end of this decade can be no more than informed 'guestimates'. No one at this point of time is really in a position to be able to predict the precise outcome of the microprocessor revolution and all kinds of constraints could still delay the adoption of its full potential. My own fears are that we will delay too long and in doing so will jeopardise our chances of securing a vigorous wealth-creating base in the rapidly advancing new markets. Should this happen it could lead to a yet greater erosion of jobs particularly in the manufacturing sector. There are very real anxieties with regard to the new technology and its impact on job security and we do a disservice by underestimating them. On the other hand, we should be on our guard against those who, on minimal evidence, extrapolate wildly into the future with their prophesies of massive unemployment. I would prefer to steer a more median course between the extremes of doom and euphoria and would expect to see an initial, but limited, erosion of jobs particularly in routine paperwork and assembly tasks. Later, given a healthy economy, I could anticipate some small measure of growth in employment towards the end of the decade. But these are no more than informed guesses based on the best evidence available to me. (3)

Certainly, with or without the aid of the new technology, at the end of the recession the drive will be on to execute our work as efficiently as possible and to keep labour costs to a minimum. Thus beyond the present unemployment crisis there lies another in that we are almost certainly going to be faced with a considerable reluctance to recruit labour in many sectors. Whether in manufacturing, the utilities or public administration, labour-intensive methods are going progressively to give way to a more capital-intensive approach. Word processors in the office, robotics in routine assembly tasks, automatic monitoring devices in the process industries, will ensure that additional work can be done without necessarily having to recruit more labour. The economic pressures are such that in deciding whether to purchase a machine or employ an unemployed individual, the decision may frequently come down in favour of the purchase of a machine. In this way we may move into a situation where the economy is back on course and where exports are booming, but where little is happening to recruit those currently unemployed back into the paid economy.

Because of these difficulties, which box us in on so many fronts, many responsible commentators now believe that it is no longer realistic to suggest that our high unemployment levels can be speedily resolved. Of course, it is well within the bounds of possibility that eventually we shall see the level of unemployment steady and then drop a little and that here and there, as has been occurring even in the midst of the recession, particular individuals will find their way back into the paid economy. In this regard it is important to bear in mind that the labour market is never static and even in the most grievous economic conditions there will always be a turnover of individuals joining and leaving the unemployed register. But such signs of hope for some may still do little for that worryingly large section of the community who now have been unemployed for a considerable period of time. During this lengthy recession the number of long-term unemployed has been steadily increasing so that there are now more long-term unemployed than there were unemployed in all categories in the 1960s. How many more years will it take to get this client group recruited back into the active labour force? How long will it take to resolve our massive youth unemployment problems and what policies will ensure that that happens? The problems have been allowed to accumulate and will now be all the more difficult to resolve.

Past experience shows that following on a major recession it has taken the nation a very long time to reabsorb substantial numbers back into the paid economy. In the Thirties some measure of economic recovery began to be felt as early as 1933. Unemployment began to fall in that year from its peak of almost three million but there were still over two million out of work in 1935 and it was not until the first year of the Second World War that unemployment fell below a million.(4)

Additional studies made during the Seventies show that even in smaller recessions those who have been unemployed for a considerable period of time experience major difficulties when trying to resecure a job even when the upturn comes.(5) In an employment situation where there is an excess of applicants over vacancies employers can afford to be highly selective and in the past the tendency has been for employers to recuit from the ranks of those who have been unemployed for the shortest possible time, leaving the recruitment of the residue of the long-term unemployed to last. This mechanism of the market works to the great disadvantage of those unemployed in excess of six months who, when they appear for interview, are frequently discounted from engagement solely on the basis of the length of time that they have been without work. Even by April 1980 the Department of Employment was reporting that some 41 per cent of those registered as unemployed had been without work for more than half a year and, as the recession continues, the chances of the reabsorption of these clients back into the active labour force can be expected to worsen.(6)

Where do these observations lead us in our attempt to grapple responsibly and creatively with the problem of unemployment in our times? They suggest that on the quantitative issue of generating the jobs needed, not only for those already on the unemployed register but also for those who can be expected to join the labour force during the remainder of the 1980s, we are faced with a strategic task of mammoth proportions.

The Distributive Problem

Even on the most optimistic projections, working with a sustained and buoyant economy and given every encouragement by central government it would now appear that it will take the bulk of this decade to create that number of additional jobs.(7) Should the economy fail to move back into sustained growth, or the labour-displacing effects of the new technology be larger than anticipated, even these hopes of closing the job gap by 1990 could be frustrated. We are thus faced with an immediate, pressing and essentially moral dilemma over not only the presence, but the long-term continuance of mass unemployment in the midst of the nation. During these years when there is not sufficient paid work for all, how do we distribute what paid employment there is amongst so many claimants? It is in essence a question about sharing. Sharing out such job opportunities as the nation has at any one moment of time in a way that is seen by all to be just and acceptable. Part of the unacceptable nature of unemployment at the present time is that work, its satisfactions and its rewards, is inequitably distributed throughout the nation. In Britain the choice has been to operate a mixed economy and to give market forces of supply and demand a fairly full rein in employment matters. For many years that has operated very successfully. We have been able to create both wealth and employment. We have been able to advance personal living standards and at the same time increase a wide range of welfare provision. These have been very significant achievements. But increasingly these same market forces which have achieved so much are coming under criticism because they have done little to reduce major disparities in income and they seem incapable of achieving a more equitable distribution of employment within our present situation of economic adversity. Both in terms of wealth distribution and employment distribution market forces on their own tend to strengthen the position of the strongest groups but do not necessarily provide sufficient protection for the weak. The market, which is run by those who want to hold on to what they have got, tends to establish mechanisms which broadly work to ensure the territorial rights of those already in employment.(8) Those who have been displaced from work and those who have never had a place within the paid economy find themselves in a much weaker position. The end result is that, in the absence of any mechanisms for job rotation or job sharing, the bulk of those in full-time paid employment retain their security and their rewards and the other claimants to work, particularly the young and the long-term unemployed, are kept waiting. When the numbers of such claimants is small the hope of their recruitment when an upturn comes remains good. But in modern Britain, as in many other industrialised countries of the world, structural changes and the severity of the recession have moved us far beyond that stage. The hopes of recruitment in the near future for many of these claimants is now tenuous in the extreme. How long will the unemployed be prepared to wait whilst others work and they do not? What feelings of envy, bitterness and alienation fester in such a social situation and where do such feelings of powerlessness and frustration lead? Do they lead to resignation and the collapse of all hope, or to the demand that society should no longer continue to treat one as a non-person and to visible revolt? What is happening within the ranks of our young whose entry to the world of work has become more and more problematic in recent years? Have we accommodated as much as we might to make room for them within the world of work? And again, there are the able-bodied adults perhaps with dependants to support. Is it right that they should be expected to continue to manage on just the basic state benefits whilst others in the same community have so much more to live on?

These are issues which we will need to pursue with some vigour in the ensuing pages and this can only be done by making a careful evaluation of the extent of the deprivations which come with loss of work. Despite the dramatic rise in unemployment in recent years it remains very much a minority experience. There are still a great many people who do not know what the loss of work for some prolonged period of time really entails. It is hoped that what is set down in the following pages will do something to remedy that gap.

Notes and References

1. *Employment Gazette*, April 1981, p. 167.
2. Jenkins, Clive and Barrie Sherman, *The Collapse of Work,* Eyre Methuen, 1979, *passim.*
3. Clarke, Roger, *The Microprocessor Revolution*, Church of Scotland Church and Industry Committee, Edinburgh, 1979.
4. Stevenson, John and Chris Cook, *The Slump: Society and Politics During the Depression*, Quartet Books, 1979, p.3.
5. Harrison, Richard, 'The Demoralising Experience of Prolonged Unemployment', *Department of Employment Gazette*, April 1976, pp. 344–345.
6. *Employment News*, June 1980, p.74.
7. Sherman, Barrie, *Tribune*, 29 August 1980.
8. For a more detailed examination of the way in which institutional practices within the labour market protect certain groups while erecting barriers against the entry of others see *The Workless State*, eds. Brian Showler and Adrian Sinfield, Martin Robertson, Oxford, 1981, pp. 122–147. In this respect, both employers and the employed wield considerable power over recruitment. Together they act as the 'gatekeepers' to the institution of paid employment. It largely rests in their hands whether or not others will be admitted to their world of work and precisely who those entrants will be.

SECTION II
THE LOSS OF WORK
The Arena of Personal Troubles

Chapter 3

THE SIGNIFICANCE OF WORK

In this section we move from the macro-economic world into the personal realm and in doing so we will need to speak about work in a different way. It is part of the complexity of work that it cannot be fully comprehended and analysed in its wholeness if we remain locked into one disciplinary approach and thereby ignore the equally vital insights of other commentators. In the previous section we were talking about the factors that influence the working of the economic system in which the chief aim of work is seen as the efficient production of goods and the provision of services. Viewed from this angle, labour costs, because they can endanger competitiveness and profitability, are a factor to be kept at an irreducible minimum. Having heard the voice of those who bear the responsibility of operating the economic system I now want to build in a bit of dynamic tension to the debate over work by hearing another voice. It is the voice of those who have fallen victim to the working of the economic system. It is the voice of those whose labour has been shed and whose services have been dispensed with in the drive for increased efficiency and profitability and who now stand idle.

From the subjective stance work is seen as important because it provides us with a social arena in which a number of basic human needs are met. Thus employment provides us with an income and gives us purchasing power. Work is important in our society because social honour attaches to those who earn their living and because work is closely associated with our image of adulthood. Further, having an occupation provides us with a life-script which gives a basic structure to our lives. Opportunities to work are also important because they enable people to do something for others and work also meets many of our sociability needs. Finally, work is important in power terms and in the processes of democracy

because territorial rights within the realm of work give the employed a say in decision-making. Because cumulatively these
aspects of work are so important to individuals and to our society I
want to look at these seven points in greater detail below. (1)

1. *Employment provides us with an income and gives us purchasing power*

One of the reasons why we value having a job is that it is 'the key
to the kingdom of consumption. It is the admission ticket by means
of which the individual gains entrance to the goods and services the
society produces.' (2) The state does, of course, provide a sub-
sistence income for its unemployed but, with the exception of very
low-paid workers, those in employment are substantially better off
than those out of work. In our consumer society, therefore, access
to regular earned income is of great social significance. As Harvey
Cox says: 'The indispensable link between production and distribution is the job, and he who has no job does not participate in the
economy. The system works comparatively well in a society where
the market requires enough, or nearly enough, jobs to go around.
But it fails catastrophically when the number of salable jobs is
fewer than the number of people who need to be linked to the distributive economy.' (3)

2. *Social honour attaches to those who earn their living*

The money that we receive through selling our skills on the labour
market is seen as important within our contemporary culture not
just because it gives us the purchasing power we need in order to
obtain our daily bread, secure housing and buy clothes, etc. The
wage we receive is more than instrumental. It is something more
than a certain quantum of purchasing power which we can use
within the market for the purchase of goods and services. The
money gained from employment and its transaction between one
party and another also has a deep symbolic significance. It is one of
the principal ways in which we indicate value and worth. Those
whose work we value highly we tend to pay highly; those whose
work we deem of less importance receive less. Where within this
hierarchy of values do we place the unemployed? They are made to
feel that they count for nothing. They have no opportunity of selling their skills and abilities within the paid economy. Nobody
wishes to buy what they have to offer. The signal that the unem-

ployed then receive from a money-based society is that their contribution is not wanted; their contribution has no money value. From this it is but a short step to feel that a person counts for nothing and has no personal worth. In contrast social honour attaches to those who earn their living and who provide for themselves and their dependants by virtue of their earnings.

3. *Work is closely associated with our image of adulthood*

In our society the business of earning a living is closely associated in our minds with our image of adulthood. During childhood we are financially dependent upon our parents and beyond retirement we again become financially dependent. However, this time it is upon a pension that we ourselves have earned by virtue of our contribution to society throughout our mid-life years. Yet during the mid-life years there is a strong social expectation that as adults we will be standing on our own feet financially, not living in monetary dependence upon other parties. It is this attainment of financial independence that is so important to the teenager. That first wage packet is seen by them and their parents as the symbol of their arrival into the ranks of adulthood and is viewed with a great sense of pride.

It is the loss of this ability to 'earn one's living', brought about by the decline in work opportunities, which disturbs and offends those squeezed out of the paid economy. The unemployed feel that they have lost their accustomed dignity as wage earners. With the loss of their financial independence they feel that they have lost something of their self-respect as an adult. For not having a job forces one to live again in child-like dependency upon others, this time upon the state. No longer is there a healthy dynamic in which the adult individual makes a valued contribution to society and in return receives appropriate recompense. Sylvia Shimmin comments: 'Most people nowadays are conditioned quite young to the idea of "earning one's living", that is they grow up expecting to have a job which will give them a recognised place in the community. This aspect of work is perhaps as important to the individual as any other, financial security included. For to have a job confers status and self-respect.' (4)

Whether it is possible to break out of that social conditioning, enabling men and women to discover a sense of value and dignity outwith the framework of the paid economy, is something which we will need to explore more fully in Section V.

4. *Having an occupation provides us with a life-script*

Having a job gives us a task to perform and a role to fulfil. It provides a structure to our day and gives shape and character to our mid-life years. It gives us something to do and somewhere to go each day of the week. Our place of work gives us a territory outside the home where we are known and which we can legitimately inhabit for part of each working day. It is the removal of all this that faces the unemployed individual with a major challenge. How does one build a new centre to one's life? In some ways it is similar to the challenge faced by the bereaved individual.

Paid employment is so much the social norm for a man between the ages of 16–65 that to know how to live without it presents the individual concerned with very great difficulty. For we live in a society where there appears to be no alternative model of dignity for a man in his mid-life years save that derived from having an accepted place within the paid economy. It is not surprising, as we shall see in what follows, that men in particular find themselves totally at a loss when attempting to live without work over an extended period in what is a work-orientated society. Their upbringing, education and previous experience have taught them what is expected of those who have membership of a wage-earning group. But terminate that membership, break the ties with the structure that work provides in the living of our lives, and the individual is confronted with the task of constructing a purposive and socially rich existence around quite different principles. That is an inordinately difficult task and one for which culturally we are all singularly ill-prepared. Nor is the unemployed individual greatly helped in this task by other outside agencies within the community. This is because the institutions of our society are all traditionally geared to operating within a situation of near full employment. As Marie Jahoda comments: 'Nobody prevents the unemployed from creating their own time structure and social contacts, from sharing goals and purposes with others, or from exercising their skills as best they can. But the psychological input required to do so on a regular basis, entirely on one's own steam, is colossal.' (5)

5. *Work enables people to do something for others*

'Part of the frustration, depression, anger of unemployment is the feeling of being shut out. Knowing that you are reasonably able and competent but being denied the opportunity of using your

talents. We need to put the unemployed back into an active situation, giving them scope to do something, to make a contribution.'
(6) That heartfelt cry from an unemployed school-teacher expresses
very well another human need that paid employment provides. It
gives us scope for the exercise of competence and skill. At its best
our work is experienced as a purposive activity which 'links an individual to goals and purposes which transcend his own'. (7) It is
then that work becomes particularly meaningful and rewarding.
Thus the bricklayer, in Fraser's book of twenty autobiographical
accounts of work, who had been engaged in building much needed
houses in an area that was being cleared of slum properties could
say with a full heart: 'I found the job itself pleasurable and I felt I
was performing a social service.' (8)

As the recent proposals emerging from the Lucas Shop
Stewards' Combine Committee have shown, there is a strong desire
still within the British workforce to be engaged in socially useful
tasks. Tasks that will lead to the enhancement of human life and
which contribute to the common good. This is an area which we
have perhaps neglected far too long in all our careful assessments
of what might motivate people to work with a will. There is a sense
in which we want to give the best of ourselves to some truly
worthwhile human endeavour. Man is made for community and
there is within that context an innate desire to give what we have to
give via our work and for that offering to be received,
acknowledged, accepted and used. Arnold Wesker, the playwright,
hints at this when one of his characters says: 'Being a carpenter
[stationed in Ceylon] I used to watch the local carpenters at work.
They used to make their own tools and sometimes they'd show me.
They'd sit out on the beach fashioning the boats or outside their
houses planing and chiselling away at their timber, and they let me
sit with them once they knew I was also building boats. And, you
know, one day, as I watched, I made a discovery—the kind of discovery you discover two or three times in a lifetime. I discovered an
old truth: that man is made to work and that when he works he's
giving away something of himself, something very precious.' (9)

6. *Work meets many of our sociability needs*
Work is essentially a social activity. It puts us alongside others and
in contact with others. It has the effect of binding us to the rest of
society. It is this experience which is so vital in the growth of our
young people to maturity. Throughout their years of schooling they

have remained largely within their peer grouping and have had only a restricted experience of living alongside adults. Beyond their contact with their parents and their teachers their relationship to older age groupings has been fleeting. It is at the point of entry into work that life changes for the young, and instead of living primarily alongside those of their own generation they have to learn the social skills of relating and working with those who are more distant from them in age and life experience. The present collapse of work opportunities for the young is particularly damaging in this regard. It has the effect of postponing the process of maturing and instead of the late teenage years being used to bind the generations together within the co-operative activities of work, the young unemployed become increasingly a culturally autonomous and potentially alienated, anarchic group.

The opportunities that work provides for interaction with others is important not just to the young, but in fact throughout our mid-life years meets a broad range of sociability needs. 'The workplace has always been, for some, a place to meet people, converse and perhaps form friendships as, for example, when married women previously tied down to home and children welcome the chance to move into a wider world.' (10) These regularly shared experiences and contacts with people outside the nuclear family serve to gear us into society and often provide much needed support and warmth of human contact. As sociability within one's place of residence declines, so the support of the intimate work group becomes increasingly important and it is often the severing of these ties that makes the lives of many unemployed individuals so socially isolated.

7. Territorial rights within the realm of work give the employed a say in decision-making

Within the world of work opportunities are given to influence decision-making. The degree to which they are taken up and utilised may be very variable. The mechanisms for participation may be only poorly developed, the processes of representation may have to pass through several layers and appear to be remote. Nevertheless, however embryonic and inadequate they may be it is possible through trade unions, staff associations, professional bodies and trade organisations for the views of collective groups to be expressed and power exercised in such a way that it can influence vital areas of decision-making. The unemployed have no such voice in our society. They are not represented around the bargaining table when issues like overtime, which clearly affect their interests, are being discussed. Their group interests are not formally represented on any statutory bodies. They have no say in the kind of training which they might value or the level of benefit which might reasonably be deemed adequate. They have no corporate voice within the corridors of power. They are therefore left in the role of spectators, looking on while other groupings make the decisions which may have a determining influence over their future. Because they are voiceless in any corporate sense their interests are often ignored and little heed is given to their needs. Instead it is the interests of those in employment that are advanced, leaving the weak and the powerless to go to the wall.

Concluding remarks

In this chapter we have examined various aspects of paid employment from the standpoint of the individual. We see that being in employment carries with it many advantages in our society and that the loss of work is likely to lead to multiple deprivation. It is not surprising therefore that in our society to have work is a much desired thing. To be threatened with the loss of work is something that is feared and fiercely resisted in many quarters. However much benefit might accrue to the employing organisations or to the nation through the reduction in manning levels, the individual sees such moves not as gain but as a major private loss. From the subjective standpoint to lose one's job and to have no immediate replacement is a serious business. For in losing paid employment so many of the props which normally sustain us are knocked away and it is as though a very large section of our life, as we have known it, is threatened with collapse. It leaves us bereft of a well-defined place in the social order. It takes away our life-script and an earned income. It severs us territorially from our place of work and socially from sustaining contacts with our former work group. It strips us of our former purposive tasks and the identity which came through our occupational role. Cumulatively, in social and psychic terms, these can be very substantial losses.

The outline of the contrasting states of employment and unemployment has begun to appear. It still requires some elaboration and substantiation and this will be done in Chapters 5 to 8. However, at this point the principal features which generally characterise the inhabitants of the world of work can be set out below and at the same time contrasted with their polar opposites.

Power	Powerlessness
Access to goods and services	Relative poverty
Dignity and social honour	Stigma and social unease
Structure to life	Structureless lives
Purpose in life	Purposeless lives
Satisfaction of being a contributor to society	Enforced dependency on the state
Sharing life with others	Socially isolated lives
Having a voice	Voiceless position in society

As we shall see, it is these antithetical features which tend to give character to the lives of those denied access to work.

Notes and References

1. Readers might like to compare this list with that suggested by John Hayes and Peter Nutman in their book *Understanding the Unemployed: The Psychological Effects of Unemployment,* Tavistock Publications, 1981, pp. 38–43. Hayes and Nutman list six functions of work:
   Work is a source of income
   Work is a form of activity
   Work structures time
   Work is a source of creativity and mastery
   Work is a source of identity
   Work gives to a person a sense of purpose.
2. Cox, Harvey, *The Secular City*, SCM Press, 1966, p. 182.
3. *id.*
4. Shimmin, Sylvia, 'Concepts of Work', *Occupational Psychology*, 40, 1966, p. 197.
5. Jahoda, Marie, 'The Psychological Meanings of Unemployment', *New Society*, 6 September 1979, p. 495.
6. Unemployed school teacher, Glasgow, 1980.
7. Jahoda, Marie, 1979, *op. cit.*, p. 494.
8. Fraser, Ronald, ed., *Work 2: Twenty Personal Accounts*, Penguin Books, 1969, p. 141.
9. Wesker, Arnold, *I'm Talking about Jerusalem*, Penguin Books, 1960, pp. 19–20.
10. Fox, Alan, 'The Meaning of Work', quoted in *Work, Urbanism and Inequality: UK Society Today*, ed. Philip Abram, Weidenfeld and Nicolson, 1978, p. 58.

Chapter 4

THE CRUCIFIXION OF HOPE: THE SEARCH FOR THE JOB THAT ISN'T THERE

What happens to the inner morale of those who, try as they may, cannot secure employment? This is the life situation which confronts many of our young people at the present time who are desperately trying to enter the world of work either direct from school or having completed their term on a Youth Opportunities Programme project. Because of the collapse of suitable opportunities for the young and the unqualified in our society many are now spending extended periods of time without the offer of work. These young people find the maintenance of morale during this phase of their lives exceedingly difficult to sustain. Leaving school should be a high point in adolescence, marking as it does the rites of passage in the transition from dependency to independency. But all the hopes which have previously attached to this change rapidly start to turn sour if there is no job to go to and many young people become deeply depressed, some even suicidal. Society seems to be saying that it does not need them, that it has no place for them. They are left to live out their lives in a sort of adolescent limbo on the fringe of the adult world: no longer a school child and part of the school community; not yet an adult with a recognised place within the adult world of work; but instead caught into a featureless No Man's Land, lacking a defined social role and with no useful function to perform. Such a negative life-existence is very far from the sort of stretching, learning, growing, joyful experience that we would want for our young people at this stage of their lives.

The young bear a particularly heavy burden at the present time and their lives are severely diminished by our failure to provide them all with adequate opportunities to enter the world of work.

But increasingly the lack of recruitment reflected in the chronic shortage of vacancies also afflicts the older worker. Shaken out of their previous employment by the recession or changing manpower needs, the fear that grips the mind of many of today's unemployed is the fear that they will not be able to find another job and will never work again. That is an unpalatable accommodation which is hard enough to make even in the years that would normally directly precede retirement. Increasingly I hear this fear of not being able to work again being expressed by very much younger men. From men aged 50 and even amongst those still in their mid-40s. For the totally unskilled, despair sets in at an even earlier stage of life. Almost universally the desire for work is initially very strong. But something happens to those whose hopes for alternative employment are repeatedly dashed. If, within the community in which you live, the requisite job vacancies are just not there then hope and motivation are exceedingly hard to maintain. It is difficult enough to sustain one's morale through the first six months of unemployment. Beyond the year it is the exceptional individual who can still keep their hopes buoyant. From that stage on more and more will fall victim to that inner collapse of morale that is characterised by resignation, passivity and despair.

A personal account of collapsing hope

In trying to understand the slow crucifixion of hope that takes place within the individual when alternative employment is unavailable it might be helpful to set down E.W. Bakke's account of the fruitless search for work as experienced in the life of a 28-year-old mechanic and lorry driver from Greenwich. Although now somewhat dated it still remains a fine piece of descriptive writing. Indeed when speaking with an unemployed works study engineer during the preparation of this book I found almost exactly the same experiences were being recounted. In this passage Bakke sensitively and succinctly portrays the progressive collapse of morale that takes place when no job can be found.

I met 'A' one evening after we had been listening to a political speech on the street corner. He had just come out of work three days before. He was confident of getting another job soon. There weren't any vacancies at the labour exchange, but, 'You don't need to expect much there, anyway. There's plenty of jobs for a man with my experience. I've never been out more than a week or so before, I'll soon be back. . . .'

Three weeks later

'I'm beginning to wonder how plentiful jobs are. It's a funny thing. It's never been like this before. It's most discouraging, Mr Bakke, most discouraging. You feel like you're no good, if you get what I mean.' During these three weeks he had written in response to every 'ad' for drivers, in the London district, which appeared in *The Times* and the *Daily Telegraph*. . . .

Eight weeks later

He had just come in from a long tramp in search of work. 'I'm beginning to wonder what is wrong with me. I've tried every way. I've had to walk in the back way in order to get at the governor. Then he said, "How do you get in here?" And then he tells me he don't need me. Then I have to dodge the company police to get into another place. It makes you cunning, you know. Then they say, "How long you been out?" And you don't like to, but you lie. I never thought I'd lie even to get a job. But I know if I tell them two months they'll say, "What's wrong?" And even if I prove my character is right, I'm started on the wrong foot with him. I don't like it. "We'll take your name and address", they say. How many times I have heard that! But those words don't give you work to do.'

Eleven weeks later

During the intervening period, I had kept in touch with 'A'. The diligence with which he explored every possibility of work aroused my admiration. He worked far harder and far longer hours at this task than at his regular job. . . . Here is his comment at the end of eleven weeks. 'There's one of two things, either I'm no good, or there's something wrong with business around here. Of course, I know that things are slack. But I've always said that a good man could get a job even in slack time. That's not so. And the man who says so is a liar . . . I feel when I walk down the streets here that all my old mates are looking at me and saying, "Wonder what's wrong with A. He never used to keep away from work so long." Even my family is beginning to think I'm not trying. So I can't talk much with them any more. I get in some nights as late as 10, eat a bite and then go to bed. Some nights we never say a word. Then I lay and try to plan like I used to when one job came to an end. But somehow the plans don't come like they used to. I reckon I've tried them all. And it's up at 5.30 or 6 in the morning to start out again. But you don't wake up feeling like going again. For you don't know which way to go. But you do. . . .'

Seventeen weeks later

'A' didn't say much the last time I saw him, he was sullen and despondent. He wasn't completely discouraged yet. The search for a job had lost all zest for him, and had settled down to a drab search for what experience told him he could not find. It was during this last interview that he expressed what lies at the root of a long period of unemployment: 'It isn't the hard work of tramping about so much, although that is bad enough. It's the hopelessness of every step you take when you go in search of a job you know isn't there.'(1)

As the trade recession worsens, as public expenditure cuts bite deeper, as new technology reduces manning levels, so the number of vacancies available in any given community decreases and more and more people find themselves in a situation where the demand for jobs dramatically outstrips the supply. In his 1944 Report, Beveridge had aimed at running the economy in such a way that there would always be slightly more vacant jobs than those registered as unemployed. In this way the time-lag between losing one job and being able to secure another would be kept short. How far we have fallen away from Beveridge's ideal can be seen by studying Chart 2. Even taking into account the Department of Employment's important caveat that their employment offices only receive about one-third of the total vacancies, the present discrepancy between the registered number of unemployed and the registered number of vacancies gives us something of the measure of the huge problem which now confronts us. The position of particular groups and particular communities is even more extreme than the global figures would suggest.

Thus for example within my own community of Dundee in the month of August 1981 there were some 1688 young people registered as being unemployed chasing only five notified vacancies. In the Cleveland area the prospects for 1981 summer school-leavers were even worse. In this north-east English community by August 1981 there were 6800 registered unemployed 16-18-year-olds, there were a further 5000 temporarily placed on the Youth Opportunities Programme and only seven job vacancies known to be available. Thus for every known vacancy in that particular community there were close on 1700 potential young applicants in search of a permanent job. Meanwhile in the north-west region of England in June 1981 there were 128,112 general labourers on the register. They found themselves as an occupational group in competition for the 297 labouring jobs that were on offer. A ratio of applicants to vacancies of 431:1.(2) These figures give some indication of the gravity of the mismatch particularly amongst the ranks of the inexperienced and the unskilled.

The decline in the number of unskilled jobs is not new. It has been going on for some time and is not just a consequence of the recession. The Manpower Services Commission reported that in the period 1973–80 600,000 unskilled jobs disappeared and anticipated that another 900,000 would go by 1985.(3) The hopes of regaining a job as a general labourer by those displaced from such work in recent years would therefore appear slim in the extreme and this will be true despite what might happen to the general economy. What, then, are the life prospects of those who have been the 'hewers of wood and the drawers of water', whose energies and brawn are only minimally required in an increasingly mechanised and capital-intensive employment scene?

However, the problems of finding work are not just confined to the unskilled and the young. Many other occupational groupings are also facing acute difficulties. Thus in the north of England, government job centres reported having 18,834 clerical and related workers on their register in June 1981 and only 705 appropriate vacancies—a ratio of nearly 27 applicants to every notified vacancy, the vast majority of those applicants being female.(4)

In community situations like those quoted above there is now no hope in the foreseeable future that the expectation of a job, nurtured in our young by the educational system and deeply ingrained in their elders, is capable of universal fulfilment. The competition for the available jobs is too great. Perhaps those who find it hardest to accommodate to this harsh reality are the following:

(a) The young for whom securing their first job is closely associated with their bid for adulthood. To be denied entry into work is a major rebuff to their inner confidence and to their assessment of personal worth and acceptability. They see the adult world as not wanting them and they are forced to prolong their childhood—continuing to live in complete economic dependence upon their families and the state, rather than being enabled to make the transition to wage-earner.

(b) Those who have previously enjoyed good job security and for whom job loss is a completely new experience. This group may well find that the search for a job in such a hostile economic climate is a particularly humbling experience and one which they are psychologically ill-equipped to handle. They may be in considerable need of support and counsel as they try to come to terms with a quite foreign life-situation.

(c) Those who believe that if only they will try hard enough a commensurate job will be rapidly secured and life can continue as· before. This group are to be commended for their persistence and high motivation in their search for a new job, but if vacan-

cies really are at a very low ebb their dynamism is likely to lead
to hopeful application after application being rejected.

As Bakke himself comments, 'This added agressiveness in looking for work is just the factor which throws a man, if unsuccessful,
against rebuff after rebuff.'(5) The accommodation to the employment realities and the knowledge that the prospects of recruitment
diminish the longer you remain out of work, can be a crucifying
personal experience. How many rejections, how many unsuccessful
interviews, how many unanswered applications can the individual
take without the hurt of that experience penetrating to the deep
psychic centre of a man's soul?

Prolonged unemployment is for most people, a profoundly corrosive experience, undermining personality and atrophying work capacities. And it
is an experience to which some of the worst disadvantaged groups in our
society—the over 55s, the unskilled, disabled people, the mentally ill, and,
in particular areas, immigrants—are particularly vulnerable, and all are
more vulnerable in areas of high unemployment. Many others are also at
risk.(6)

Richard Harrison wrote that in 1976 when unemployment stood
at 1,234,600, or 5.4 per cent. Unemployment has risen
dramatically since then, with job vacancies at the lowest level since
the war. However, what is a much more worrying figure, far less
commonly quoted, is the dramatic increase in the number of long-
term unemployed as opposed to those who are only transitorily unemployed. The 1980 study of the Manpower Services Commission
opens with this highly significant statement:

One disturbing feature of the rise in unemployment since 1974 has been
the massive increase in the number of those out of work for long periods.
By October 1979, the number of those registered as unemployed for more
than one year (our definition of long-term unemployment) stood at
337,000, or just over a quarter of all registered unemployed. Long-term
unemployment in 1979 was higher than at any time since the Second
World War and in the last decade alone had nearly quadrupled.(7)

The MSC study of the long-term unemployed goes on to say:

On present employment forecasts the number of long-term unemployed is
expected to grow in line with total unemployment up to 1982, and thereafter is more likely to rise faster than total unemployment if unemployment continues to rise then.(8)

By the beginning of 1981 the Chairman of the Manpower Services Commission was reporting that in the Commission's view the
number unemployed in excess of a year would reach 500,000 or
more by early 1982.(9)

Temporary job loss is one thing, but long-term unemployment is far more spiritually corrosive. It eats away at hope. It undermines morale and destroys self-respect. Eventually the sense of hopelessness and pain become too much and the unemployed person is driven to the point of capitulation. He gives up really trying. As the MSC study says: 'There comes a point where people can no longer sustain their motivation in face of continued rejection, heightened awareness of their own shortcomings, disillusion with job-finding services, belief that all available options have been covered, and a knowledge that jobs are scarce anyway.'(10)

For the long-term unemployed the loss of the opportunity to work is not the only loss which they have to bear. As the next chapters illustrate, financial constraints which begin to bite deeply beyond the first year of unemployment serve to increase the distress and place considerable curbs even on those trying to find alternative creative lifestyles.

Notes and References

1. Bakke, E.W., *The Unemployed Man*, Nisbet, 1933, pp. 64–67. An in-depth study of unemployed men in Greenwich in 1932.
2. *Employment Gazette*, August 1981, Labour Market Supplement. p. 536.
3. *Network*, 18, March 1981, Reported comments of MSC Chairman.
4. *Employment Gazette*, August 1981, op. cit., p. 536.
5. Bakke, E.W., *op. cit.*, p. 71.
6. Harrison, Richard, 'The Demoralising Experience of Prolonged Unemployment', *Department of Employment Gazette*, April 1976, p. 347.
7. *A Study of the Long-term Unemployed*, Manpower Services Commission Report, February 1980, 1.1.
8. *id.*, 1.3.
9. *Network*, 18, March 1981.
10. Manpower Services Commission, February 1980, *op. cit.*, 5.1.

Chapter 5

LIVING ON THE DOLE

In their book, *The Collapse of Work*, Clive Jenkins and Barrie Sherman paint a vivid picture of the way in which the work ethic pulls people out of their homes and into their places of work every morning.

[People] feel they *have* to work—and not only for the money. The work ethic is so deeply ingrained in British and other industrialized societies that work has acquired a value in itself, even though it is widely regarded as unpleasant.

Each ordinary weekday morning roughly 18 million people leave their beds and then their homes to go to work. At the same time $11\frac{1}{2}$ million children and students of varying ages go through the same routine to learn and acquire the necessary knowledge and skills to *enable* them to go to work. . . . This movement to the place of work results in the rush-hour. Roads are jammed by vehicles designed for four passengers but carrying only one driver. Buses, trains and the underground system are full; queues develop and lengthen, tempers fray and few kindly words, indeed few words are spoken. That same evening the process will be repeated. Whatever the weather, whatever the counter-attractions and however much people dislike the work itself, this process repeats itself—it has its own dynamic. (1)

Few of us enjoy getting out of the bed in the morning. Few enjoy facing the snarl-up of the traffic that the journey to work entails and there must be many occasions when we secretly wish we could opt out, escape from the race against the clock and instead lounge around at home. For many a harassed worker there is a sneaking envy of the unemployed living in dependence on the state who can continue to sleep in the warmth of their beds while the rest of the world has to be engaged in the hassle of earning one's living.

The man who does not have to work is regarded with envy, resentment. . . . Men may long to have leisure without having to work for it; to hand over responsibility for the support of self and family without having to give up one's freedom to the weekday work routine. This is the picture, composed from men's dreams, their frustrations and their desires . . . unemployment is valued for its negative worth—no work and no drudgery and the supposedly attendant benefits of no responsibilities and no worries. It is a state both desirable, because it seems so pleasant, and contemptible because it means "shirking" and "cheating"—for some, even dangerous because it threatens the present way of life. (2)

But what is the reality? What is life really like for those who have no work and who, when the rush hour has departed, are left behind in their communities of residence with the whole day to fill in and beyond that another day and another and another? In the next chapters I draw upon the careful work of a variety of researchers whose interviews with the unemployed build up a pastiche of what life is really like on the dole. We begin by taking a look at the financial realities.

Tightening Your Belt: The Progressive Drop in Income

The average chap that's faced with unemployment, he's cushioned for six months—and this is the danger of the Earnings Related benefit: the majority are unemployed for a short period, under six months, and they leave the unemployed queue with the impression that it's not so bad after all. But once you've been on the dole for a year and your dole has stopped completely, you're drawing supplementary benefits, then the harsh reality of unemployment hits you smack in the bloody face. Clothes are beginning to wear out; things need replacing in the house; and then your income is drastically reduced. (3)

The above comment succinctly describes an important feature of our present state benefits system which is arranged in such a way as to reduce step by step the level of income received by claimants the longer they remain out of work. In a situation where alternative job opportunities are available such a system acts as a deterrent to the idler and makes reasonably adequate provision for the bulk of the unemployed. But where the opportunities of resecuring employment in a particular community are very slender and, as a result, unemployment continues on over an extended period, such a system of decreasing payments is punitive in its impact. For those who are made to suffer by having less and less to live on are not 'idlers' but those who genuinely desire work and who cannot obtain it.

How then, are the unemployed paid? At the time of writing there are three benefits for the unemployed: the flat-rate unemployment benefit, the earnings related supplement and the supplementary benefit. In addition a worker may qualify under the redundancy payment scheme and if the individual concerned has a young family to support they will continue to receive child benefit. In order that we might have a firm grasp of the circumstances of the unemployed in our midst I want to say a word about each of these sources of income and to dispel some of the popular myths that surround them. The fine detail of provision depends on the particular circumstances of the individual concerned but broadly speaking, earnings related benefit is paid for the first six months, flat-rate unemployment benefit throughout the first year and supplementary benefit, which can be paid alongside the first two, on its own thereafter. Eventually after a year the unemployed drop down to the lowest level of welfare provision and will be in receipt of supplementary benefit alone and that paid at the basic rate.

Redundancy payments

Under the Redundancy Payments Scheme those who have worked for an employer for at least two years continuously and who are below retirement age are eligible for a lump sum—normally tax free. Twenty years' service is the most that can count and the highest weekly pay on which the lump sum can be worked out is currently £130. Thus the most that you can get under the scheme is 30 weeks pay, or £3900.

Over and above the statutory provision there is, of course, the opportunity for any particular employing organisation to negotiate with its employees a more generous scale of lump sum payment. Many companies now do this and in some cases they may choose to add on an additional 50 per cent. Where there are major closures, severance pay can also sometimes be paid in order to obtain the consent of the trade unions. It is these severance payments which often catch the headlines in the media but it needs to be pointed out that such provision is far from universal practice.

The recent DHSS Cohort Study of the Unemployed—a nationally representative sample of men who became unemployed at the end of 1978—revealed how small a lump sum most people receive on leaving their place of employment. (4) Three-fifths of the group surveyed got under £100. One-fifth got between £100 and £300 and only the remaining fifth got over £300. These survey results in themselves do much to dispel the popular myth that everyone made redundant is likely to be well cushioned for the first period of their unemployment by being in receipt of large redundancy payments. But Moylan and Davies' research goes on to reveal that less than 10 per cent of the total sample receive either redundancy pay or pay in lieu of notice.

The reason why so few obtained any redundancy payment was because of their age (19 per cent were 16–19-year-olds and so ineligible), and others lost out because of the effect of broken service. Forty-nine per cent of the sample had already experienced at least one spell of unemployment earlier in the year. Thus not surprisingly in view of this pattern of intermittent employment and low wages even when in employment, 56 per cent of the men interviewed were found to have no personal savings by the time they had been unemployed for a month. (5)

Earnings Related Supplement

At the time of writing the Government have declared their intention to bring the earnings related supplement to an end in January 1982. For those unemployed for only a short period of time the ERS payments cushioned the financial impact of job loss and gave recipients time to make the necessary budgeting adjustments. With the loss of ERS the financial realities will be more sharply felt at a much earlier stage of unemployment and savings are liable to be eroded more rapidly.

Unemployment Benefit

Provided one has been in regular employment and paying into the national insurance scheme at the full rate one will probably be entitled to unemployment benefit during the first year. Those who have not been paying in sufficient contributions in the preceding qualifying period may either receive benefit for a shorter period or else may not be entitled to receive unemployment benefit at all.

Until quite recently most people went through their working lives and never experienced unemployment at all, except perhaps for a brief spell of frictional unemployment, while changing jobs. The Manpower Services Commission have recently made a study of the financial impact of job-loss and this is what their researches reveal:

The typical unemployed person will have previously been working in a low income occupation earning only about three-quarters of the national wage. On becoming unemployed individuals are therefore often moving from low earnings to even lower benefit incomes, with the size of this reduction in weekly income depending on the number of family dependants and, over time, on unemployment duration, as well as on previous earnings.

On average unemployed people currently receive in social security benefits about 65 per cent of their former net weekly earnings. . . . The percentage loss will be larger for those previously on higher wages and smaller for a short duration group receiving earnings related supplement. The drop in net disposable income is inversely related to family size: for example, a married man with a dependent wife and four children might receive about 90 per cent of his former net weekly income when unemployed.

In a typical household with an unemployed man, working wife and one child, net disposable income would drop from £112 to £67 per week, leaving the household with 60 per cent of its previous income. (6)

Supplementary Benefit

Supplementary benefit is generally available to people 16 and over who are not working full time and who do not have enough money to live on. As already indicated, it can be paid on top of other benefits in the early months of unemployment. But as the Child Poverty Action Group points out, there are many unemployed people who do not have sufficient national insurance contributions for them to be entitled to claim unemployment benefit. Further, because people at the present time are unemployed more often and for much longer than they used to be, many have exhausted their 12 month entitlement to unemployment benefit. By the end of 1978, 1 in 6 of the unemployed were not receiving any benefit at all (280,000 people); over 42 per cent were receiving only supplementary benefit (537,000) and fewer than 2 in 5 (513,000) were receiving any unemployment benefit (and nearly 95,000 of these were having to claim some supplementary benefit as well to bring them up to the poverty level). (7) Beyond the first twelve months of unemployment, supplementary benefit is the sole source of income for the unemployed. These different sources of income for the unemployed are indicated in the diagram below.

Benefits received by the unemployed

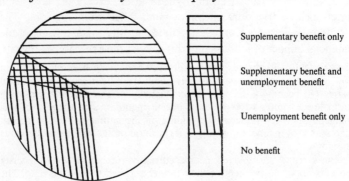

Supplementary benefit only

Supplementary benefit and unemployment benefit

Unemployment benefit only

No benefit

Living on the Dole

How adequate are the various benefit schemes to sustain the lives
of the unemployed and their families in Britain today? In trying to
frame a balanced reply let us begin by listening to the comments of
the unemployed themselves.

> I scratch along. I just make it. I can't afford cinemas or anything like
> that. This enforced idleness has been a bit of a let-down, I can tell you.
> Somehow, I've got so that I accept it, but it's not living.

Sixty-year-old bachelor, interviewed by Peter Townsend. He had
been obliged to return his television set to a rental firm because he
could not afford the rental. (8)

> We've just got to scrimp and save. Like we get our family allowance to-
> day and that just pays your debts that you owe out. . . . You've got to try
> to save for three or four weeks to get a pair of shoes for the bairn and
> that's just for one of them. . . . All you can do for clothes is just to hand
> down from one to the other.

Young woman whose husband has been out of work for almost
three years. (9)

> The worst thing, the thing that really gets you down, is the uncertainty;
> that you've got no future. The future is the next electricity bill and whether
> you can pay that.

This speaker had recently finished a government retraining scheme
to become a carpenter, but nobody wants to take him on when
there are skilled and experienced carpenters on the dole. He has the
skill and the time to improve his home, but:

> If you want to put up some shelves, even if you've got the wood left over
> from something else, you find you can't afford to go out and buy brackets.
> I could have repainted the whole damn house but I can't afford to go out
> and buy paint. (10)

> I'm a one-parent family and anything's better than being on social
> security. I get £35.57 a week and have to pay £18 rent. It's ridiculous. The
> kids say: I want this, I want that. And you can't do it. They notice the
> difference. You're that few shillings better off if you're working and you
> feel better in yourself as well. (11)

Pervasive Complaints of Financial Hardship

The Manpower Services Commission study of the long-term
unemployed published in February 1980 reported on the previous
year:

> For those still unemployed at the time of the interview the average amount
> of benefit received was approximately £25 per week and the total of

income received on average was £31 per week. Amounts of benefit naturally varied with family circumstances, so that married people got significantly more than single people. For example, the average received in benefit by married men in the sample was £34.50. Overall though, only 12 per cent were receiving benefits of £40 or more a week and a quarter said their *total* income was £40 or more. In contrast to these people 28 per cent of those still unemployed had a total income of less than £20 a week. (12)

The *Department of Employment Gazette* indicates that in the same period in Britain average weekly gross income per household was £120.45, which gave a disposable income (after deduction of income tax and national insurance contributions) of almost £100 per week. (13) These comparative figures begin to help us see something of the gap in living standards that exists between those in employment and the long-term unemployed. This pattern of relative poverty comes through strongly in all the reports of the last few years. It is the picture of a largely forgotten community of poor people living at the lowest levels of state benefit who constitute a 'Fourth World' in the midst of comparative urban affluence.

The 1980 Manpower Services Commission study, for example, revealed pervasive complaints of financial hardship.

Most respondents found money extremely tight—enough for 'existence rather than living'. Sacrifices were not unusual: a number of people spoke of selling possessions. There were several complaints that poverty greatly restricted the travel necessary for job-hunting. Observation confirmed that many respondents—especially those in households completely dependent on social security—led greatly impoverished lives. (14)

In their annual report for 1978 the Supplementary Benefits Commission commented on the inadequacy of the benefit rates, particularly for the unemployed and for those with children. The SBC expressed its concern at: 'The prospect of so many children being raised in an atmosphere of social and material deprivation which unemployment so often brings.' (15)

The 1980 joint report of the Family Service Unit and Child Poverty Action Group added yet more evidence in its survey of sixty-five families living on supplementary benefit. It found that many of the families were borrowing money to make ends meet, many were missing out on meals and living on a nutritionally inadequate diet and that there were insufficient finances to meet fuel and clothing bills. 'The problems the families faced were made worse by the sheer drudgery and monotony of such restricted standards of living; they were compounded by the misery of being hungry, or

being cold, of continually worrying about stretching the money
through the week and about the health and well-being of their
children. More than anything else, it was for their children that the
parents were anxious.' (16)

By November 1979 the SBC had estimated that there were
nearly half a million children with fathers out of work and in receipt
of benefits. Since then, the figures have risen dramatically. Concerned at the possible impact of unemployment upon the families of
those who were without work the SBC conducted its own survey as
to the adequacy of the benefits provided. They concluded, 'For claimants with children—particularly those who have been unemployed for a long time—benefits are generally too low. . . . The supplementary benefit scheme provides, particularly for families with
children, incomes that are barely adequate to meet their needs.' (17)

Since that report the Government has made various adjustments
to the level of benefits to be received by the long-term unemployed
resulting, as we shall see in the next chapter, in opening up a yet
bigger divide between those in and out of work.

Notes and References

1. Jenkins, Clive, and Barrie Sherman, *The Collapse of Work*, Eyre Methuen,
   1979, p. 2.
2. Sinfield, Adrian, *The Long-term Unemployed—A Comparative Study*, OECD
   Report, 1967, p. 60.
3. Gould, Tony, and Joe Kenyon, *Stories from the Dole Queue*, Temple Smith,
   1972, p. 174.
4. Moylan, Sue, and Bob Davies, DHSS, 'The Disadvantages of the Unemployed', *Employment Gazette*, August 1980, p. 832.
5. *Supplementary Benefits Commission 1979 Report*, HMSO, September 1980,
   5.5.
6. *MSC Review of Services for the Unemployed*, Manpower Services Commission, March 1981, 2.23–2.25.
7. Child Poverty Action Group, 'So who's "better off" on the Dole?: Myths and
   Facts about Unemployment'. *Poverty Fact Sheet*, February 1980, p. 6.
8. Townsend, Peter, *Poverty in the United Kingdom*, Penguin Books, 1979, p.
   607.
9. *On the Stones*, Report by Newcastle-upon-Tyne Centre for the Unemployed,
   September 1980.
10. Cox, Sarah, and Robert Golden, *Down the Road*, Writers and Readers
    Publishing Co-operative, 1977, p. 79.

11. *A Study of the Long-term Unemployed*, Manpower Services Commission, February 1980, 7.6.
12. *id.*, 7.3.
13. *Employment Gazette*, November 1980, 'Pattern of Household Spending in 1979'.
14. Manpower Services Commission, February 1980, *op. cit.*, 7.6.
15. *Supplementary Benefits Commission 1978 Report*, HMSO, 1979.
16. Burghes, Louie, *Living from Hand to Mouth: A Study of 65 Families Living on Supplementary Benefit*, Poverty Pamphlet 50, A Joint Family Service Unit and Child Poverty Action Group Publication, December 1980, p. 72.
17. *Supplementary Benefits Commission 1978 Report*, op. cit.

Chapter 6

THE FRACTURE OF FELLOWSHIP AND THE MAKING OF AN UNDERCLASS

'Bread for myself is a material problem,' wrote Nicolas Berdyaev, the Russian Orthodox philosopher. 'Bread for other people is a spiritual problem.' In this chapter I want to begin the task of making a moral critique of our society in respect to the distribution of work and income at a time when labour supply far outstrips labour demand. The financial deprivations that long-term job loss entails is only one aspect of a broader cycle of deprivation which increasing numbers are coming to experience and these other important aspects are explored more fully in later sections. But any serious attempt to grapple with the realities of unemployment today quickly leads us to a discussion of the way in which income levels are currently distributed between those in and out of work. Income levels are vitally important because they have a determining influence on possible lifestyles within our society, and the way incomes are distributed throughout what we like to think is a 'caring society' has much to say about the moral credibility of that claim. Professor David Jenkins put it very well.

The oppression and neglect of the poor throws into relief those features of society which are contrary to the will of God for his covenant people. . . . It is by paying attention to those whom society leaves poor or makes poor that we can be alerted to those features of our social and political life which are under the judgment of God. That is to say that it is the condition and treatment of the poor which point most sharply to those practices of ours which contradict the gospel of love, according to which all human beings are as human as all others, so that no human being can be fully human without all being fully human . . . hence the poor and the marginals are not primarily objects of charity and compassion, but rather subjects and agents of the judgement of God and pointing to the ways of the kingdom. (1)

A Picture of Relative Deprivation

For the unemployed there is no withdrawal from the money economy, they have to live in it as best they can. They have to shop for their food and the other necessities of life in the same stores as their neighbours, many of whom are benefiting from having two incomes to swell the family budget and to increase purchasing power. If they have children they will need to be clothed and provided with regular changes of shoes. But their children will also have their social needs. Their needs to share in the same kind of recreational and leisure pursuits as others of their own age grouping. But to engage in such normal social activities in association with their own peer group requires money and without that money they have to opt out. It is here that the restrictions on family income imposed by long-term job-loss begin to bite home. Similarly, for the adults within the home, loss of job does not mean starvation, but almost inevitably it will lead to a growing loss of mobility and reduced access to social interaction. A recent survey by the Department of Health and Social Security gave an indication of what tends to go first when you are unemployed and living on supplementary benefit. Nearly a third of the men interviewed said that they had given up going out for a drink or a meal and almost half said they had cut down on this type of social activity. A third said they had stopped taking the family on outings and nearly a quarter said they had stopped going to football or other sports. (2) These reports tally closely with the picture painted by Daniel and Stilgoe in the PEP study of the unemployed in 1973 and 1976.

For the unemployed generally life was a constant battle to find money for food, clothing and essential bills like gas and electricity. Entertainments and holidays belonged to the past. Even activities like going out for a drink with friends had been heavily curtailed. On top of these financial hardships there were the added deprivations of inactivity: boredom, social isolation and feelings of inadequacy and shame. Things were not so bad for the young, the single, women who had husbands in work, or older men for whom unemployment was a short transitional stage into retirement. But for men between the ages of 25 and 55, with wives and children to support, the picture was very black. (3)

What emerges from these reports is that the levels of state benefit have been so low as to act as a major deterrent to the unemployed and their families remaining as active participants in the rest of society. They have become marginalised by virtue of their low income. Or to use the Quaker phrase, those squeezed out of work are liable to become the 'economically disenfranchised' members of an otherwise affluent society. (4) The fact that the very activities which encourage contact with other people go first, would appear to be in direct conflict with the aim of the Supplementary Benefits Commission in setting the level of benefits. The Commission defines poverty in Britain as 'a standard of living so low that it excludes and isolates people from the rest of the community'. Their level of benefits, the Commission states, should enable them to be treated 'with the courtesy due to every member of the community. To achieve living standards that make that possible, supplementary benefit must not fall too far behind the incomes of the working population.' (5)

Financially, unemployment and the past level of benefits paid have had the long-term effect of creating a group apart. However, since those reports were written the financial circumstances of the long-term unemployed have been allowed to deteriorate yet further in relation to other groupings in society. And to those deliberate policy decisions we must now turn.

The Widening Gap

While most major Western countries have experienced record levels of unemployment in recent years, few have had such high rates of long-term unemployment as Britain. (6) In January 1980 the number of long-term registered unemployed stood at one third of a million, the highest level since the Second World War and with every indication, in a deteriorating economic climate, of climbing steadily towards the half a million mark. Faced by this major quantitative increase in claimants and in the light of the burden of evidence emerging from a number of carefully conducted surveys, the poverty lobby conducted a vigorous campaign during the spring of 1980 in order to persuade the Government to improve benefit levels for the long-term unemployed and their dependants. However, when the budget changes in social security were announced in the House the following policy decisions emerged:

> Earnings related supplement to be *withdrawn* from 1982.
> Unemployment benefit to be *taxed* from 1982.
> Unemployment benefit to be uprated by 5 per cent *less* than forecast price movements.
> Child benefit increased by 75p—a *cut* of between 8 and 9 per cent in real incomes for families with children.

Pensioners and all other claimants who have been living on supplementary benefit for one year to move on to the long-term rate, which is 25 per cent higher than the ordinary scale rate. *No such provision for the long-term unemployed.*

Commenting on the 1980 budget changes, the Supplementary Benefits Commission wrote:

It may be that the Government will have to tell the nation that we must pass through a time of tribulation during which there will be general reductions of living standards. If these are to be borne by everyone – the well-off as well as the poor – then it may be acceptable that social security beneficiaries, protected by some assured minimum safety net, should bear their share of the trouble too. If our constantly repeated argument that poverty has to be measured in relation to average living standards is accepted, benefits should rise when earnings rise, and they might have to fall when earnings fall. But to say that the rich must receive generous tax reductions and that pay and pensions must be index-linked, while the poorest and politically weakest members of the community should bear cuts in living standards which richer people are to be spared—that is morally indefensible. A social security system can be designed to unite a nation or to divide it. In the past it was usually at times of greatest national danger and hardship, during and immediately after world wars, that Britain took her boldest steps forward. The creation of family allowances, the National Health Service, the major social insurance schemes, the Assistance Board and then the National Assistance Board—these were not simply administrative inventions, they were deliberate attempts to rally and unite what might easily have become a divided and demoralised nation. They were practical expressions of the aspiration to create a caring society which helps each of us when we most need it.

Bodies like the SBC . . . play their part in a tradition which goes back through the Poor Law Commission of 1834 to the Elizabethan poor law and the justices of the peace of that time. Despite its limitations and failures, that tradition expresses a continuing public concern for the most vulnerable people and the duty of Government to care for them. All have a great deal to lose if that tradition is allowed to wither away. As a Minister in the present Government has said: 'A free state will not survive unless its people feel loyalty to it. . . . If the state is not interested in them, why should they be interested in the state?' (7) Can this country meet new challenges as courageously as the best of our predecessors did? We have shown how present trends are tending to impoverish the working poor, and warned that this may provoke hostility between those in the more secure core of the labour market and those on its precarious periphery, thus making scapegoats of the unemployed and many of the most vulnerable members of society. But those trends could also be reversed. We should work for a national unity based on public policies which express equal concern for all citizens. (8)

I have quoted the Supplementary Benefits Commission report at some length because it is a powerful piece of writing standing very much in the best Judaeo-Christian social tradition of concern for the poor and the underprivileged. What is being reflected here is not simply a concern for the individual but also for society. As John Atherton has pointed out, the moral adequacy of our social order is constantly being tested by the quality of our treatment of the poor. (9) Thus we are led into a discussion, which we will need to develop at greater length later on, regarding the kind of society we would wish for ourselves and our children, our neighbours and our neighbours' children. There is 'no touchstone, except the treatment of childhood, which reveals the true character of a social philosophy more clearly than the spirit in which it regards the misfortunes of those of its members who fall by the way'. (10) How do we handle the distribution of the nation's wealth at a time when the economic system is so dislocated that whichever political party happens to be in power it seems incapable of providing employment for all who have come to expect and desire it?

For what is now becoming increasingly clear is that even if we were to begin to pull out of the present deep recession we will still have massive unemployment among certain sections of the community for many years to come. As we have seen, those sections who face the bleakest prospect of long-term unemployment are likely to remain the young, the unskilled, the disabled and members of our ethnic minority groups. For the most part these are groups who have no great power base, no strong voice in the management of the nation's affairs. Unless someone speaks up for them their interests will be very easily forgotten in the scramble to retain the remaining jobs and anticipated incomes. Unless a determined effort is made to pull these groups back into the future employment pool we face the prospect of perpetuating a major and quite disastrous cleavage in our society. That division will be between two nations. (11) On the one hand, there will be a majority group composed of the most able and skilled holding down jobs and benefiting from relatively high rates of pay and the social satisfactions that work brings; and on the other hand, there will be a minority group 'born to fail', handicapped by poor educational attainment or physical disability, unable to obtain a footing in the world of work and therefore relegated to a life of enforced dependency on inadequate state benefits—a life characterised by frustration, social isolation and low income. It is because such a scenario is not morally acceptable to me that I feel impelled to explore in the later sections of this book other alternatives which might more adequately embody the ideals of a just, participatory and sustainable society.

Notes and References

1. Jenkins, David E., *The Contradiction of Christianity*, SCM Press, 1976, p. 49.
2. *Guardian*, 18 November 1980. Article by Aileen Ballantyne.
3. Daniel, W.W. and Elizabeth Stilgoe, *Where are they now?: A follow-up Study of the Unemployed*, PEP, XLIII, 572, October 1977, p. 95.
4. *Quaker Social Responsibility and Educational Journal*, 1.3, November 1979, Religious Society of Friends Publication, p. 12.
5. Aileen Ballantyne, *Guardian*, 18 November 1980, op. cit.
6. *Supplementary Benefits Commission 1979 Report*, HMSO, September 1980, Table 5.1, p. 33.
7. Sir Ian Gilmour, 'Conservatism' lecture at the Cambridge Union, 7 February 1980.
8. *Supplementary Benefits Commission 1979 Report, op. cit.*, 1.47–1.50.
9. Atherton, John, *Religion and the Persistence of Poverty: A Challenge to British Social Democracy and the Churches*, William Temple Foundation, March 1980, p. 2.
10. Tawney, R.H., *Religion and the Rise of Capitalism*, Penguin Books, 1948 ed., p. 265.
11. Disraeli, Benjamin, *Sybil or The Two Nations*, Oxford University Press, 1981.

Chapter 7

ORGANISING DAILY LIFE

A major problem faced by those who are without work in a work-orientated society is that of organising their daily lives. As the Pilgrim Trust's study in the 1930s pointed out:

Work provides for most people the pattern within which their lives are lived, and when this pattern is lost they have thrown on them a responsibility which, in the case of most unemployed men, their working lives have in no way qualified them to bear, the responsibility for organising their own existence.(1)

Employment imposes a time structure on the waking day and this is an aspect of work which is perhaps more important for many people than it may at first seem. As Marie Jahoda comments on the research studies she did into the lives of the unemployed in an Austrian village:

Our study (published in 1933) showed that being unemployed is something very different from having leisure time. The unemployed decreased their attendance of clubs and voluntary organisations, their use of the free library, their reading habits. Their sense of time disintegrated.(2)

Both those studies were done during the 1930s. Since then, we have seen the advent of shorter working hours, flexitime, longer holidays and a boom in recreational activities. Do the unemployed still have difficulty in organising unstructured time? One of the most recent comprehensive surveys of the unemployed, that done by the Manpower Services Commission in 1979, seems to suggest that for the long-term unemployed at least very little has changed.

Very few respondents seemed to be able to fill their time in a satisfying way. Boredom, idleness and listless depression were frequent complaints and many respondents did little but sit around, take walks, read, and watch television. In the words of one respondent:

'It does bother me. But if you ponder on it, you'd go loony. You can't plan ahead, so you just live day to day. . . . It's not just the money. Work gives you something to do. I'm just wasting away.'
Although a minority insisted on maintaining a workaday type of schedule, others, notably some of the younger men, drifted into lethargy.(3)

For those who have only recently been made redundant there is a more buoyant attitude towards the opportunities that non-work brings. In those early days what is uppermost in the mind is the liberation that comes in *escaping from* the relentless round that work imposes on our lives:

At first it feels marvellous. It's as though you've left the rat race, you're not in it any more and you can look at it and wonder why people bother. You look at them setting out in the morning at 7.30 and coming back at night at half past five, and you think, 'Why bother?' The first few days you sit at home and relax, and it's like a holiday.(4)

The same holiday freedom was noted by Dr Halliday in the Pilgrim Trust studies(5) and much more recently by Dr Leonard Fagin, a consultant psychiatrist for the London Claybury Hospital, in his DHSS studies.(6) But, as Erich Fromm has pointed out, there is a critical break between 'freedom from' and the existential dilemma of 'freedom for what?'(7) Without cultural guidelines, the freedom to choose is a burden, not an opportunity, and at the core of the unemployed community's dilemma is the absence of such guidelines. Instead of a broadly socially acceptable way of using unemployed time there is a great gaping void. There is no accustomed role or set of tasks that the unemployed individual can with the consent of society properly assume. This kind of cultural ambiguity helps to explain why being without a job cannot be viewed merely in terms of its consequent economic, social or psychological problems, or even a combination of these. The dilemma that we are touching upon here has also to be understood as an existential problem for the unemployed person and as a critical social problem for society as a whole.

Leisure takes on a different quality when you are unemployed. It involves staying longer in bed, watching more television or just lazing about but lacks the sense of restoration this brings when you have a "meaningful" job. It is one thing to come home after a day's work and flop down in front of the television screen, but quite another to watch television during the day because you simply have nothing else to do.(8)

The Handyman about the House Syndrome

Unable to engage in purposive activities within the paid economy, in this age of do-it-yourself, many of the unemployed try to direct their creative energies into a variety of home-based maintenance and improvement tasks:

One of the problems is that the working class has never experienced having leisure time; we just don't know what to do with our leisure time. I'm quite fortunate with having a garden, but that can't last for long—you can only spend so much time in a garden. One really gets bored stiff. This is the main thing about being out of work: absolute boredom. . . . Financially it's terrifically hard . . . but the boredom affects you more than anything. You have to really try hard to stop yourself going downhill: you have to go to libraries; you have to go for walks in the parks; you have to do the garden, decorating—even when you can't afford to decorate. I've stripped the landing but we don't know how we're going to pay for it! It didn't really want stripping, but it's just something to do. You have to try to keep your mind occupied and it's a full-time job trying to do this; because I know the end result—with thinking quite a lot about it and having the time—the end result would be a mental breakdown.(9)

The 'handyman about the house' syndrome may sustain the unemployed for a limited period, but there comes a time when there's nothing to do, unless you make the absurd decision to undo what you've just done. How does one use one's mid-life years and what kind of prospect faces the young unemployed who have failed to obtain even their first foothold within the adult world of work? What is life about if, within the time-scale of 16 to 55, there seems no prospect of working again and one has already invested the trivial round of filling-in tasks with more meaning and significance than they can adequately bear? When unemployment is no longer transitory but continuing, what is the point of planning when there is nothing solid to plan for? That is the existential dilemma of many ordinary people in our society at this time.

The Importance of having a Time Structure

The time structure imposed by work as a social institution is important, so Marie Jahoda believes, because it ties us to the here-and-now. 'It prevents us being swamped by the past, or by dreams of the future. We often resent the imposed time structure. But remove it totally, and you get the time experience of the unemployed.'(10)

'I'd do anything just to get my mind occupied. I get depressed. . . . It's not the money, I want something to occupy my mind.'(11)

The crie de coeur that these surveys record and which I have found echoed poignantly again and again in my own conversations with the unemployed, links in closely with the experiences of a number of other groups studied by Stanley Cohen and Laurie Taylor. Cohen and Taylor were particularly interested in analysing the experience of long-term prisoners detained in Durham Prison's maximum security block. They noted that there are occasions when 'the daily planning and allocation of intervals, the according of hours, days and weekends to specific activities, breaks down'.(12) In the normal scheduling of life the pressure of events and our own innate activism keeps speculation about meaning and purpose in life and the deeper questions regarding our own identity at bay. But given the life situation of an unemployed person faced with negligible prospects of resecuring a place in work, or a long-term prisoner in a maximum security wing who can only anticipate a 20 to 25 year span of continued imprisonment within the same surroundings lying before him, you have a landscape of future time which has no features upon it.

The unreality of time is palpable. Each second falls slowly. What a measureless gap from one hour to the next. When you tell yourself in advance that six months—or six years—are to pass like this, you feel the terror of facing an abyss. At the bottom, mists in the darkness.(13)

In prison, time accumulates a new dimension. You try to eat it away rather than enjoy it.(14)

You do your time in little daily jerks, living from one microscopic pleasure to the next.(15)

It is all very well for the unemployed person engaging in relatively 'meaningless' activities in order to keep their spirits up so long as it can be seen as part of a finite period. That is to say, inner morale can be sustained for a certain period by these 'substitute' work activities provided they can be seen as interim devices which give a structure to daily life during the period between jobs. Morale is sustained during this period because it is still assumed that at the end of this period of enforced idleness one's contribution within the paid economy will be needed again and one can move from a roleless role back into a recognised occupation. But what if that is an unrealisable dream? What if all the politicians' promises of a return to full employment and the golden lands of work for all who want it are unachieved or unattainable? What then? That is almost an unendurable thought and so painful that most of us in an at-

tempt to escape it will throw ourselves into any kind of meaningless
life-project, rather than allow the mind to play with such an un-
thinkable future.

> Not a single landmark is visible. Months have passed like so many
> days; entire days pass like minutes. Future time is terrifying.(16)

'If I really thought that I had to do another seventeen years, I'd
do myself in,' remarks Roy, one of Durham's long-term prisoners.
And I imagine that many of those who are currently out of work
would feel the same.

'What is man's true life?' This question, remarks Zehrer, 'is the most
natural, but also the most radical question man can ask. For which reason
he seldom asks it, preferring to assume that the answer is known. When as
an individual he asks this question, one can infer that something which
gave him security has come to an end. When the question emerges in the
historic course of a given culture, it is a sign that the foundations of the
culture have become faulty and that people are no longer un-
selfconsciously at home in it. . . . That is precisely what is happening on
the continent of Europe in the twentieth century. Traditions and institutions which long gave security to life have been largely swept away. Man
is stripped and isolated, confronted with the question he formerly concealed from himself: "What is my true life?" '(17)

To these profound questions about meaning and purpose and
personal identity which are posed to individuals and to our society
by the prospect of what Jenkins and Sherman have called 'The
Collapse of Work' we must return later on.

Notes and References

1. *Men without Work*, A report made by the Pilgrim Trust, Cambridge University Press, 1938, p. 149. The biggest study of unemployment made in the
   1930s. Under the Chairmanship of Archbishop William Temple a study was
   set up in which 900 men and women spread throughout six towns—Deptford,
   Leicester, Liverpool, Blackburn, Crook and Rhondda—were interviewed. In
   November 1936 these respondents had been unemployed for virtually all the
   previous year.
2. Jahoda, Marie, 'The Psychological Meaning of Unemployment', *New Society*,
   6 September 1979, p. 492. The study that Jahoda refers to was by Jahoda,
   M., P.F. Lazarsfeld and H. Zeisel, *Marienthal: The Sociography of an
   Unemployed Community*. Tavistock Publications, reprinted 1972. The study
   was of 478 families—the total population of Marienthal, a small industrialised
   community in Austria—carried out in January 1932 after the town's
   factory—the sole local employment—had closed.

3. *A Study of the Long-term Unemployed,* Manpower Services Commission, February 1980, 5.23(b). This report brings together two pieces of recent research. A large-scale structured survey of 1698 long-term unemployed people randomly selected from those registered at job centres and employment offices and fifty depth interviews with long-term unemployed people, including ten who were registered with the Professional and Executive Register. Both samples were selected in March 1979 and interviewing took place during May, June and early July 1979.

4. Marsden, D., and E. Duff, *Workless – some unemployed men and their families,* Penguin Books, 1975, p. 190.

5. Pilgrim Trust, 1938, *op. cit.,* p. 136.

6. *Guardian,* 18 November 1980, Article by Aileen Ballantyne referring to DHSS study by Dr L.H. Fagin of the Claybury Hospital and Mr M. Little, Lambeth Social Services, on *Families and the Effect of Unemployment.* A descriptive study of the psychological effects in twenty families, focusing on changes in relationships, the emotional reactions to financial restriction and attitudes to social security benefits.

7. Fromm, Erich, *Escape from Freedom,* Farrar and Rinehart, New York, 1941, passim.

8. Hill, John, 'The Psychological Impact of Unemployment', *New Society,* 19 January 1978, p. 118.

9. Gould, T., and J. Kenyon, *Stories from the Dole Queue,* Temple Smith, 1972, pp. 40–41.

10. Jahoda, M., op. cit., p. 494.

11. Manpower Services Commission, February 1980, *op. cit.,* 4.32.

12. Cohen, Stanley, and Laurie Taylor, *Psychological Survival: The Experience of Long-term Imprisonment,* Penguin Books, Second ed., 1981, p. 97.

13. Serge, Victor, *Men in Prison,* Gollancz, 1970, p. 56.

14. Rosevear, John, 'The Fourth Mad Wall' in Ross Firestone (ed.), *Getting Busted,* Douglas Books, New York, 1970, p. 234.

15. Godwin, J., *Alcatraz: 1938–1963,* Doubleday and Co., New York, 1963.

16. Serge, Victor, 1970, *op. cit.,* pp. 56–57.

17. MacQuarrie, John, *An Existentialist Theology,* SCM Press, 1955, p. 135, quoting H. Zehrer, *Man in this World,* Hodder, p. 28. There are resonances here between Zehrer's comments and what R.D. Laing has called 'ontological insecurity'. (R.D. Laing, *The Divided Self,* Penguin Books, 1965, p. 46.) This term describes the state in which one doubts the integrity of self.

Chapter 8

THE SOCIAL ISOLATION
OF THE UNEMPLOYED

There is one additional area which we have not yet explored in our analysis of the broad common experiences of the unemployed and to this we must now turn our attention. It relates to the subtle changes that take place in the pattern of family and community relationships when one is no longer a member of the working community. Being in employment not only gears us into membership of a particular working community, it also regularly takes us out of the house and into contact with the outside world. In our society work serves many of our sociability needs, providing us with a range of opportunities for healthy interaction with others. When we lose our jobs the bridge to those social contacts is destroyed and we are driven back into the home and the immediate residential community in our search for human support. But because having a job confers status and self-respect in our work-orientated society, the loss of employment is something that we and others often find difficult to handle. Sylvia Shimmin catches this well when she writes: 'To have a job . . . provides a standard by which to judge and be judged by others. Thus, "What is his job?" or "What do you do?" are regarded as normal questions surrounding introductions, to which the expected reply is a specific occupation. The person with no job, whether he lives on private means or on National Assistance, arouses ambivalent attitudes, unless he is retired and can be accorded the social status of his former occupation.' (1)

The unemployed in Britain today feel uneasy about their social status and this lack of certainty as to whether they have an accepted place in our society, coupled with decreased spending power, drives them into increasingly home-based isolation.

Thus John Hill, senior consultant at the Tavistock Institute of Human Relations, writes:

A major effect of unemployment is that it tends to be socially isolating. At the psychological level there is the shock, shame, loss of confidence and loss of occupational identity. This results in a tendency to withdraw from contact with others. There is also the direct loss of the work place as a source of conversation and social contact. The whole effect is exacerbated by the fact that the economic effects of unemployment enforce curtailing leisure pursuits and social life. (2)

The unemployed who were interviewed for the 1980 MSC study complained that unemployment diminished their social activities and led to a loss of friends. Young people in particular showed their concern over this tendency: 'When I was at school, I used to have loads of friends. Now a lot of them . . . have got jobs and you tend to lose contact. I've become lonely . . . I do get terribly depressed at times. I think I'll end it all, but I haven't got the nerve.'

Others noticed with a measure of distaste that any social life they did have tended to revolve around other people in similar circumstances and that this formed a separate structure divorced from the mainstream of social activity. Unemployment also led to a loss of social status. Several respondents noted that other people tended to view them as scroungers and ne'er-do-wells. (3)

An unemployed miner from Dunfermline, aged 23 when interviewed, articulates how it felt to be without work when he was younger:

Then being on the dole was just emptiness. A feeling of being outside everything, you know? Things happening, like society going on outside you. You did na' feel complete, did na' feel a real man. I didn't have any real dignity and I got hurt when people said to me, "Oh, you're on the dole", you know? And it made me feel workshy, things like this. And then immediately you get a job, people's attitude changes towards you, and immediately you're a responsible member of society, but you know inside yourself that you're no different. You're just the same as you were on the dole. (4)

One of the railwaymen Dorothy Wedderburn spoke to said this about his feelings:

I feel ashamed. I go round the back streets, and I don't want to meet people. They say, "Aren't you in a job yet?", and I feel ashamed. I don't like going out any more. (5)

Another unemployed man has expressed the experience like this:

What happens is, after they've been on the dole for a long time they lose their spirit, they've got no fight in them, they crawl into their bloody holes, they sit round the fire, they get used to doing nothing, they stand at the bloody window watching the world pass them by, sort of, and then the begin to feel resentful, they get depressed and they lose all their will to do anything again.

When I'm working I can go on my holidays, I can go away to the coast several weekends in the year, I had a car which I used to replace every three years—that's gone. There's a tremendous loss straightaway. I'm used to going out to clubs, I'm used to going to a nightclub now and again, lots of chaps are—that's gone. I'm used to buying clothes and getting dressed up and going out, and so is the wife—that's gone. Now the fellow that's working has still got these things. If I'd got a car now, say for some reason I'd been able to keep my car, and I drove down the road for a pint to the pub—instead of people saying, "I'm glad to see that he's keepin' his pecker up, he's going out", their reaction would be, "Oh that bastard, he's havin' it good on t'dole". You know, born of ignorance and prejudice, fed by subtle propaganda and this mythology that a man's having it good on the dole. The attitude now to a man on the dole is that his place is in the house: "If you're not working then you sit at home, boy, and be thankful that we're feeding you." (6)

Family Tensions and Expressions of Inner Stress

Faced by the loss of their former work community, lacking the spending power to frequent many of their former social haunts and unsure of the degree of understanding and acceptance they will receive in their encounter with the outside world, the unemployed are driven back into the home and into a shadowy half-existence lived on the margins of society. Unsupported by a society whose structures and social expectations are still geared to an ideology that believes that full employment is the norm and the phenomenon of unemployment a temporary economic aberration, the unemployed are forced to work out all their hurts within the home. Treated as a non-person by a society in which he previously enjoyed full participative membership, the last sanctuary remaining to the unemployed is the family.

For the family man . . . the family becomes the main source of social contact and therefore the major social setting within which the stresses of unemployment are experienced and dealt with. (7)

This channelling of all the frustration, resentment, hurts and anxiety of unemployment into the home, fuelled by over-proximity and continuing financial worries, can make for a potentially explosive situation in human relationships.

One is subject to intense pressures by virtue of one's imprisonment and one tends to regress to childhood, to the stage where little things mean a great deal. As our feelings are linked directly to external influences over which we have no control, people tend to be hypersensitive and, as with children, take it out on those closest to them. (8)

That passage was in fact written by a long-term prisoner of his experience within the confines of a maximum security block, but it echoes what many unemployed people find happening as they try to resolve the turmoil of their emotions within the confines of the domestic setting. In such circumstances it is not surprising to find the Manpower Services Commission reporting that when they interviewed fifty long-term unemployed people, 'Several said that budget reductions and over-proximity caused frequent tensions between family members, sometimes explosively. In one case this had led to divorce, in another to violence, and in many cases to numerous arguments.' (9)

You feel confined—you're in the house all on your own—the kids come in and get on your nerves—they don't realise it. They don't realise what I have to go through sitting in the house on my own. (10)

It got worse. My Mum started shouting at me to get a job. She threatened to throw me out and in the end I just walked out of the house and walked the streets till four o'clock in the morning. (11)

The result of unemployment is so often such a friction between husband and wife, between parents and their children, and between unemployed teenagers and their parents, who resent their lying around the house all day. These are all manifestations of what Archbishop William Temple called the 'corrosive poison' of long-term unemployment. (12)

Notes and References

1. Shimmin, Sylvia, 'Concepts of Work', *Occupational Psychology*, 1966, 40, p. 197.
2. Hill, John, 'The Psychological Impact of Unemployment', *New Society*, 19 January 1978, p. 120.
3. *A study of the Long-term Unemployed*, Manpower Services Commission, February 1980, 5.28(d).

4. Cox, Sarah, and Robert Golden, *Down the Road*, Writers and Readers Publishing Co-operative, 1977, p. 68.
5. Wedderburn, Dorothy, *Redundancy and Railwaymen*, Cambridge University Press, 1965, p. 90.
6. Gould, T., and J. Kenyon, *Stories from the Dole Queue*, Temple Smith, 1972, p. 175.
7. Hill, J., op. cit., p. 120.
8. Cohen, S., and L. Taylor, *Psychological Survival: The Experience of Long-term Imprisonment*, Penguin Books, Second ed., 1981, p. 87.
9. Manpower Services Commission, February 1980, *op. cit.*, 5.28(c).
10. Hill, J., op. cit., p. 120.
11. *The Shock of No Work*, South Manchester Churches' Working Party, March 1980, quoting from the experience of Stephen Lord.
12. Temple, William, *Christianity and the Social Order*, Penguin Books, 1956, p. 20.

SECTION III

THE DISTRIBUTION
OF WORK

The Arena of Social Issues

Chapter 9

OF WANT, FEAR
AND CIVIL STRIFE

In the preceding chapters my analysis of the problems created by
unemployment has been focused on subjective experiences within
the biographical realm. I have illustrated the multiple nature of the
troubles experienced by those who are without work using the best
available research evidence and supplementing it with anecdotal
quotations gleaned from the unemployed themselves. These latter
statements couched in the language of ordinary folk are particularly precious and need to be heard. They sometimes have a
quality of human poignancy about them which leads us into the
heart of the matter better than all the careful statistical weightings
that the social scientist can supply. In a balanced assessment,
however, we need to hear both from the 'participants' and from the
'experts'. The participant, in the form of the unemployed individual,
is able to express what a particular human situation feels like from
the inside. It is important that such authentic comments should be
carefully recorded in order that they might be shared and heard by
others within the community for they have their own inner power
and validity. They will, however, be particularised and variable in
nature because the response of individuals to their life circumstances is not by any means identical. The limitations of the
anecdotal approach are to some extent countered by recourse to
careful statistical research gathered together by the 'experts' whose
disciplined observations enable us to make a sociological map of
what happens to particular groups at a time of diminished employment opportunities. However, there is perhaps yet another dimension which needs to be introduced in any Christian evaluation of
social issues. St Paul in his Letter to the Philippians prays that
God's people should have both 'knowledge' (*epignosis*) and 'sensitive perception' (*aisthesis*), for it is out of these that 'love' (*agape*)

springs. (Philippians 1.9) Thus in this survey I have tried to give knowledge of the facts, but I hope also that out of this material something reaches the heart. For '*aisthesis*', which is the Greek word Paul chooses to use in that passage, is that added quality of the heart and mind which is sensitive to that within the contemporary social order which is wrong.

There are many disturbing features within the contemporary order brought about by the recent drastic reduction of job opportunities. In this chapter I want to elaborate on just three of them. They are the triple social evils of Want, Fear and Civil Strife.

On Want within the Social Order

Broadly speaking, we have failed in our collective responsibility to make adequate provision for those who find themselves the victims of a changed economic order and in consequence the experience of losing one's place within the paid economy for any extended period of time is almost universally a wretched business. Our national insurance scheme was constructed on the assumption that unemployment was some kind of socio-economic accident which might on rare occasions be fleetingly encountered during one's full working span. It was assumed that those becoming unemployed would have been in regular employment for a number of years and therefore would have had the opportunity to accrue sufficient contributions to the fund to tide them through the hiatus of temporary job loss without having to experience too great a drop in income. It was further assumed that there would be sufficient work opportunities within each community for any able-bodied individual to return to full-time working within a matter of weeks. The economic situation, however, has now deteriorated so much in particular communities and for particular social groups that those working asumptions have nothing like their previous validity. In consequence the arrangements for the provision of an adequate income for the unemployed is now in need of urgent review. As the Supplementary Benefits Commission itself comments:

The national insurance scheme is constructed on the assumption that unemployment is an occasional, short-term, social accident for people with regular earnings. The assumption has always fitted some of the unemployed, but for the last five years it has not applied to the major group of the jobless. (1)

The 1979 Supplementary Benefits Commission Report continues:

In the great inter-war Depression the major studies that revealed the personal and social deprivation of unemployment did not, in general, appear until the late 1930s when unemployment had been extremely high for five or six years. There is something of a similar lag in the publication of evidence on the personal, social and economic costs of the current level of unemployment. However, the findings that are beginning to appear are worryingly reminiscent of the 1930s. (2)

The Government's decision to up-rate unemployment benefit in November 1980 by 5 per cent less than the rate of inflation, the withdrawal of the earnings-related supplement early in 1982 and the rapid increase in the number of unemployed individuals who have still not found work when their unemployment benefit allowances eventually run out are all factors which will combine to bring the number of unemployed supplementary benefit claimants up to about 1.5 million by the summer of 1982. (3) The implications of this are disturbing in the extreme. The Supplementary Benefits Commission itself has been consistent in calling for increased benefit levels for claimants in general, but they have also stressed 'that all the available evidence shows that it is claimants with children who have the hardest time and who most need extra help'. (4) Further, the unemployed now find themselves in the anomalous and unenviable position of receiving a lower rate of supplementary benefit than all other long-term claimants. They remain entitled only to the basic rate however long they may remain in need of state support. As a result of a recent Government decision, 'The unemployed, alone among claimants, are still not to receive the long-term rate, in spite of the general recognition that there are no grounds, other than cost, for continuing to discriminate against them in this way. All the emerging evidence shows that the unemployed, especially those with children, are the hardest pressed group of all those who have to rely on supplementary benefit.' (5)

The reluctance of our society to make a more adequate level of financial provision for the unemployed and their dependants, who are the victims of major structural changes within the global economy, is a symbol of the failure of collective responsibility on the part of the strong towards the weaker members of the community. Instead of the burdens of the present time being borne by the broadest backs they have been allowed to rest upon those with the least resources. The consequences of failing to review the benefits system for the unemployed can only serve to perpetuate

misery and privation within a growing sector of the one nation
state, leaving social scars and bitter memories which it will be
difficult to erase. In a progressive society there will always be some
measure of unemployment and as we accommodate to a new
economic order we may see the amount of paid employment within
the manufacturing and other sectors continue to decrease as
machines replace the work of men. These are economic realities
which we may have to learn to accept. What is not acceptable in a
civilised society is that the victims of change should have to live
lives of wretchedness because of acute financial privation.

On Fear within the Social Order

The evil inherent within such a situation of privation is not confined
to the ranks of the unemployed. At a time of diminished job opportunities the poison of fear spreads out to infect those who are as yet
still in jobs but who in uncertain economic times feel themselves to
be at risk. People should not have to live their lives in fear any more
than they should have to live their lives in material deprivation. Yet
at this moment of time fear of future job-loss is pervasive in many
sectors of the world of work.

The fear that grips those in work is the fear of the financial consequences of job-loss coupled to the fear that having once lost one's
foothold within the paid economy in these times it may prove exceedingly difficult to regain employment. For men in their later
years, those near the bottom of the hierarchy of occupational skills
and those living in communities where the structure of opportunities has suffered severe erosion the anxieties will be particularly
great. Those still in the prime age-range, those who have skills and
abilities which if need be can be traded down and those with the
resources to move to other communities where job opportunities
may be more plentiful may feel a little easier about job-loss and job
transfer. But for increasing numbers the retention of the work that
one has remains a lively area of concern in Britain today. Such a
high level of anxiety is not conducive to the advancement of
progressive policies. If the individual members of a workforce are
in a state of fearfulness over their future job security they will be
suspicious of technological innovation and organisational change.
That will not help our economic recovery. In an attempt to preserve
their own interests they will retard delivery dates, baulk at the introduction of labour-saving devices, or resist greater skill flexibility
and increased productivity arrangements. To the outsider the

response may appear self-defeating, irrational and myopic, but fear when it takes a grip is not always responsive to reason and the longer term view. A pervasive climate of fear makes it exceedingly difficult to get enlightened collective decisions. It breeds in those thus affected inflexibility and the preservation of narrow self-interest. Instead of the spirit of corporate solidarity which encompasses the need of one's neighbour and one's neighbour's child there is a retrenchment of generosity and openness. 'What I have I will share' is replaced by 'What I have I hold'. For fear fractures fellowship. It is essentially antisocial, privatising concern so that it focuses on self rather than on self in relation to others. As such, it is a considerable social evil and corrosive of the body politic.

As Adrian Sinfield points out, a major failure in the current debate about high unemployment has been the inadequate attention given to some of these broader issues. In particular he directs us to the way in which job insecurity inhibits the achievement of a number of desired social goals.

Full employment enables society to pursue many societal goals with much greater success than in a recession. At best, high unemployment slows down the progress towards these objectives; more commonly it may stop their achievement and even put them into reverse. It turns the publicly avowed pursuit of such objectives into a hypocrisy and a sham; it allows us to utter many worthy sentiments of concern but denies us the means of putting them into effect. (6)

Speaking on the radio early in 1981 Sinfield added this:

We tend to forget that during long periods of high unemployment it is not just the unemployed who lose out. Many other people whose chances of a better career are disappointed. Many people stay in dead-end jobs making the best of a bad job during unemployment. Policies that we would support for other reasons, for example Equal Opportunities for Women or Equal Opportunities for Blacks, or in Northern Ireland, Equal Opportunities for Roman Catholics, cannot be achieved when you have got increasing unemployment because those people who are in work now use their experience, their muscle and their trade union power to hold on to those jobs which are available. (7)

Running the economy with a high level of unemployment has the effect of curbing occupational choice and eroding the dimensions of life for a great number of people and not just for those on the unemployed register. To these social ills must be added others. The intense competition for work which high unemployment induces has the social consequence of setting man against his neighbour and group against group. In particular it puts in jeopardy the well-being of those who do not operate from a strong power base, yet who have an important contribution to make. The New Testament speaks to us of being 'members one of another' (Ephesians 4.25) and St Paul in his vision of God's people sees them as constituting the 'Body of Christ' in which 'The eye cannot say to the hand, "I do not need you"; or the head to the feet, "I do not need you" ' (I Corinthians 12.21). Instead, the vision of the good society is of mutuality and interdependence among all its constituent parts. The social outworking of this 'other-regard' which lies at the root of Christian love is that 'there should be no schism in the body; but that the members should have the same care one for another. And if one member suffers all the members suffer with it' (I Corinthians 12.25–26). This vision of the solidarity that binds people together in the good times and the bad to form a caring, sharing community I find to be a fruitful one to lay alongside the present troubled social scene.

Two Nations or One?

Despite the recession, for the majority of those remaining in employment living standards continue to rise. It is not true that in a time of national economic difficulty, 'When one member suffers, all suffer together.' Instead job-loss is seen largely as a private misfortune rather than as a public responsibility to be collectively shared. Thus, as yet, Britain has failed to formulate sufficiently adequate socio-economic mechanisms to cope with the moral problems of justice in a time of reduced job opportunities. Britain, therefore, increasingly emerges as a two-nation society as the recession deepens in contrast to the ideal of the fraternal society of which Professor A.H. Halsey spoke in his 1978 Reith Lecture. Speaking of our still markedly unequal society Halsey said this:

Our experiences of industrial, nationalist and racial conflict continually demonstrate the need for a new sense of equality to replace old class-restrictive liberties and status-crippled fraternities. We still have to provide a common experience of citizenship in childhood and old age, in work and play, and in health and sickness. We have still, in short, to develop a common culture to replace the divided cultures of class and status.
Our society cannot stand on such shifting foundations. To strengthen them, we need principles and practices of social distribution which are acknowledged to be just by the great majority. And in a world of growing visibility of reference groups, these principles will be seen as just only if they actually are just. The implication is that in a political democracy

which secures our liberties, the paramount principle of distribution must be equality. Equality of opportunity is not enough . . . we need full equality of the basic material conditions of social life. If poverty remains in Britain this is not because the technical means to its abolition are missing: it is because of an inadequate sense of moral implication in the lives of compatriots. It is a failure not of economic production but of fraternal distribution. (8)

This failure of fraternity expresses itself in many ways in the present recessionary situation. It manifests itself amongst hourly paid workers and management in the remarkable resilience of overtime working even in the midst of the slump. As Robert Taylor reports: 'Britain's manual workers are still clocking on for more hours of work than any other workers in the Western industrialised world, and the deepening slump has made surprisingly little impact on the amount of overtime being worked by those lucky enough to have it.' (9) These facts which emerged in 1981 in a TUC Working Paper show that average overtime worked by male manual workers has fallen from 10.6 hours on top of the basic working week only to 10.3 in the past six years. Overall the number of overtime hours worked in November, 1980 were an enormous 9,187,600, the equivalent of 229,700 full-time jobs in sectors where there were 592,536 registered unemployed. Receiving these figures, Mr Len Murray, the TUC General Secretary, is reported as having commented that the existence of so much overtime per overtime worker in areas of high unemployment was an affront to unemployed people. (10)

But whereas the failure of the hourly paid worker to share what work is available more extensively with other potential claimants in the community is a readily identified failure of fraternity, it should not serve to divert our attention away from the other employment sectors where job security tends to be far greater than that of the hourly paid man and where earnings have moved ahead in real terms even in spite of the slump.

It is among these occupational groupings who, in earning power, constitute the broadest backs where perhaps more of the fiscal sacrifice might have been borne had the ideal of the fraternal society been more of a reality. Instead, the preliminary findings of the Policy Studies Institute in a survey of the unemployed made for the Manpower Services Commission in May and June 1980 'suggest that the slump is being borne by a relatively small, disadvantaged portion of the workforce'. (11) That survey showed that at that point of time the vast majority of jobless were manual workers from small firms earning relatively low pay and not in trade unions. In comparison those who had lost their jobs from within the public sector were relatively few. 'Slightly more than a third of the jobless worked in manufacturing industry and 23.2 per cent in construction. But only 4.6 per cent had been in jobs in public administration; 8.5 per cent in personal services and 1.3 per cent in financial services. Only 1.4 per cent of the unemployed came from the Civil Service; 3.8 per cent from a local authority and 7.2 per cent from the nationalised industries.' (12)

The 1980 PSI study also revealed two other important things. First, that only 39 per cent of the unemployed had received any payments on leaving their last job and only 14 per cent mentioned an actual redundancy payment. Only 5 per cent of those receiving such compensation got more than £2000. As Robert Taylor commented on these findings, 'The golden handshake is an inaccurate tabloid cliché for all but a lucky few.' (13) Second, the PSI study shows that the young dominate the unemployment figures with 63 per cent of the male jobless aged between 18 and 34.

The Unequal Burden of Unemployment

These findings confirm what has emerged in a number of previous studies of the sociological distribution of unemployment. They indicate that the experience of unemployment is unevenly spread across the workforce. As Elliot Liebow puts it: 'Unemployment does not, like air pollution or God's gentle rain, fall uniformly upon everyone . . . it strikes from underneath and it strikes particularly at those at the bottom of our society.' (14) Thus, for example, the ethnic minority working population many of whom have been situated in low-paid jobs within the manufacturing sector have been particularly hard hit during the slump. In the 12-month period between February 1980 and February 1981, whereas overall unemployment rose by 40 per cent, among the ethnic minority groups it rose by 82 per cent nationally and by 104 per cent in the north-west of England. (15)

It is the way unemployment can concentrate its devastating impact upon particular sociological groups and within particular communities that deserves far closer attention because it is here that the problems it creates can be so much greater than the national averages suggest. Thus within particular housing schemes unemployment may be running at 50 per cent while elsewhere on other residential estates virtually all are in steady employment. As the recession proceeds, certain sectors of employment, certain occupational groupings, certain regions of the United Kingdom and certain age groups continue to bear a markedly disproportionate share of the jobs that are lost, while other more favoured social groupings get by relatively unscathed. We know for example that during the 1930s a similar uneven regional and sociological pattern tended to emerge. 'The picture of depression was not evenly spread, but was concentrated in the old industrial areas. Unemployment rates in 1932 varied for the different regions of the country between 36 per cent in Wales and only 13 per cent in London and the South-East. By the mid-1930s the disparity was even more striking, with unemployment rates in some towns in the depressed areas revealing tragic stories of the decay and impoverishment of whole communities; places such as Brynmawr, Dowlais, Jarrow, Gateshead, Greenock and Motherwell had almost three-quarters of the insured population out of work in 1934, while other parts of the country were experiencing almost boom conditions. (16) As Cook and Stevenson who have studied that period in some depth comment:

It would, of course, be fatuous to suggest that the 1930s were not for many thousands of people a time of great hardship and personal suffering. But beside the picture of the unemployed must be put the other side of the case. There were never less than three-quarters of the population in work during the 1930s and for most of the period considerably more. Alongside the pictures of the dole queues and hunger marches must also be placed those of another Britain, of new industries, prosperous suburbs and a rising standard of living. . . . For those in work, the 1930s were a period of rising living standards and new levels of consumption, upon which a considerable degree of industrial growth was based. This was the paradox which lay at the heart of Britain in the Thirties, where new levels of prosperity contrasted with the intractable problems of mass unemployment and the depressed areas. (17)

The disparity in circumstances which Cook and Stevenson so vividly describe has strong resonances with the contemporary scene. For the majority of the 23.5 million still in employment at this point of the recession material conditions have not markedly altered and life continues on much as before. Elsewhere, as we have seen, job-loss is experienced as a personal catastrophe and income levels for a family can sustain a sharp drop. These major disparities between the circumstances of the two nations, between the secure and the insecure, the working and the non-working, are important on two counts. First, these differences impose their strains upon the social fabric. Second, they lead to significant differences in perception and this, as we will see, has important implications for the formulation of public policy.

On Civil Strife in the Social Order

Feelings of enmity, bitterness, resentment and envy breed where there are deep social divides within a nation. Where many of those who have been dispossessed from work are young, where a quite disproportionate number of them thus affected are drawn from the ethnic minority groups or live in deprived inner-city regions of the United Kingdom, these feelings of antipathy and alienation over unemployment fuel other grievances. It is in these circumstances that the seeds of violence can be sown and pent-up feeling explode upon the streets, as has already occurred in Bristol, Brixton, Toxteth and Moss Side. Alternatively, frustration can take a variant form in resort to political extremism.

Large-scale unemployment, especially amongst the young, is a fertile ground for political agitation and reaction: extremist policies of the Right and Left have the attraction of radicalism and advantage that as the policies are unlikely to be implemented there is no need to be constrained by responsibility or practicability. (18)

Edward Heath MP, equally concerned about the political impact of unemployment among the young, added this comment in the House of Commons:

The consequences of that unemployment will be that young people will start to challenge the system. They will say, "Frankly whatever system is chosen, whether it be private enterprise, state sector or the parliamentary system, it is not meeting our needs. Our basic need is to have a job." We shall then have the kind of situation that was thrown up by the Tavistock inquiry in the 1930s, which showed that in Europe a large number of young people supported those who sought to overthrow the system. It is no coincidence that the National Front is now giving just as much publicity to unemployment as it is to immigration. It is no coincidence, because that is where the National Front is obtaining support among young people who have no jobs. This is part of the political consequences in the period in which we have been living. (19)

If the major political parties and society as a whole cannot give to unemployed young people some hope with regard to their future, then we must expect an increasing measure of disenchantment with 'the system'. Whether that disenchantment will lead to revolution or resignation only time will tell. But in either case, 'The conclusion seems inescapable that without urgent and large-scale action on this problem, society will have created an embittered, cynical and negative generation—a generation with no faith in the ability of democratic processes to produce a worthwhile society for them.' (20)

However difficult it may be for white jobless youngsters it is that much more difficult for second generation black young people, many of whom live in our deprived inner-city zones. A large number of our ethnic minority young people have suffered various forms of disadvantage throughout most of their conscious lives, but as they pass through the lonely years of adolescence their perception of discrimination and disadvantage grows. It is when they have left school and have failed to find work that disillusion and hardcore alienation sets in. As the 1976 PEP Report on Racial Disadvantage was to put it:

The first signs of a more profound disillusionment . . . are to be found among the West Indian teenagers, an alarming proportion of whom are unemployed and homeless. The seriousness of these feelings, and the acuteness of the conditions from which they spring, should not be underestimated. . . . At present, this frustration does not amount to a cohesive political force . . . [but] if present injustices are allowed to continue, political organisation by the minorities, when it comes, is likely to be extremist and destructive.' (21)

It is important to recognise that what is being described here is one extreme of the total response to the problems that arise in the wake of unfulfilled aspirations. Within certain cultural groupings there may be a greater propensity to 'act out' one's deep feelings of hurt and disillusion. Elsewhere other groupings may be equally pained but the problems become internalised. Just as in a classroom situation indications that a particular child may have problems will come to the attention of the alert school teacher both from the behaviour pattern of the very passive, unassertive and uncommunicative child as well as from the child who is 'acting out' in attention-seeking ways, so too indicators of the existence of major social problems may be expressed both overtly and covertly within the community. Thus the alert social observer should not allow the drama of the street riot to detract attention from other possible indicators of a serious malaise within the social order. Elsewhere the unemployed may not be 'acting out' their problems by taking to the streets. Instead they may be strangely passive and undemonstrative and in their house-bound isolation just quietly wasting away.

It was George Orwell who noted that the overriding characteristic of the unemployed in Wigan during the years of the Depression was 'the frightful feeling of impotence and despair'. (22) The unemployed were demoralised by their circumstances and demoralised armies do not fight. During the 1930s 'fatalism, depression and apathy were far commoner among the unemployed than participation in politics'. (23) Allegiance to extremist parties or participation in violent demonstrations gained only minimal support. Instead 'the talk of revolution was conspicuous by its absence' and a great mood of passivity prevailed. (24) Again when we observe the contemporary scene there are strong resonances with the behavioural patterns of the 1930s. It is to the psychodynamic root of this social behaviour pattern that I now wish to turn.

Notes and References

1. *Supplementary Benefits Commission 1979 Report*, HMSO, September 1980, 5.12.
2. *id.*, 5.16.
3. *id.*, 5.15.
4. *id.*, 2.9.
5. *id.*, 2.10.
6. Sinfield, Adrian, *What Unemployment Means*, Martin Robertson, Oxford, 1981, pp. 119–120.
7. Sinfield, Adrian, speaking on BBC Radio 4, 'Focus on Unemployment', January 1981.
8. Halsey, A.H., *Change in British Society*, based on the Reith Lectures, Oxford University Press, Oxford, 1978, p. 164.
9. *Observer*, 11 April 1981, article by Robert Taylor, commenting on *TUC Working Paper on Working Time*.
10. id.
11. *Observer*, 26 April 1981, Article by Robert Taylor.
12. *id.*
13. *New Society*, 23 April 1981, p. 143.
14. Liebow, Elliot, 'No man can live with the terrible knowledge that he is not needed', *New York Times Magazine*, 5 April 1970.
15. *Guardian*, 6 April 1981, Report based on Department of Employment records.
16. Stevenson, John, and Chris Cook, *The Slump: Society and Politics during the Depression*, Quartet Books, 1979, p. 5.

17. *id.*, pp. 4–5.
18. Jenkins, Clive, and Barrie Sherman, *The Collapse of Work*, Eyre Methuen, 1979, p. 162.
19. Heath, Edward, speaking in the House of Commons debate on 30 January 1978, reported in Hansard p. 82.
20. Scottish Trades Union Congress, *Scottish Convention on Unemployment Base Paper*, November 1980.
21. Smith, David J., *The Facts of Racial Disadvantage: A National Survey*, PEP, 1976, quoted in *The Fire Next Time: Youth in a Multi-Racial Society*, produced by the Commission for Racial Equality, March 1980, 4.12.
22. Orwell, George, *The Road to Wigan Pier*, Penguin Books, 1981, p. 77.
23. Stevenson, J., and C. Cook, *op. cit.*, pp. 269–270.
24. Bakke, E.W., *The Unemployed Man*, Nisbet, 1933, pp. 60–61.

Chapter 10

MOURNING THE LOSS OF WORK

The severe street riots in the Toxteth district of Liverpool on 3 July 1981, which were then echoed in a number of other major cities later that week, served to rivet public attention on to a number of major social problems which had been disregarded for too long. Principal among them were the feelings of hopelessness, frustration, antagonism, fatalism and despair which colour the way so many of our young people now look out on the world. At the present time the prospects of work for them are clearly minimal. The collapse of job opportunities leaves them bereft of constructive direction at a crucial stage of their lives. They find themselves in the limbo situation of being neither schoolchildren, nor beginning to earn a living within the adult community of work. Without acceptable social role or status they are the 'no marks' kids who aimlessly wander the streets with little money in their pockets and all the time in the world to kill. Having no work has not ushered in the marvellous world of leisure. Unlike many of the retired, who have found genuine satisfaction from engaging in a whole range of leisure pursuits and for whom the termination of work is often a liberating personal experience, the vast majority of the unemployed, whether young or old, show themselves unable to adapt constructively to their new social situation. Instead, the lives that they lead outside the bounds of the paid economy tend to be coloured by a grey drabness. When one talks with those who are now entering the category of the long-term unemployed all the zest seems somehow to have been drained out of them. All the initiative has gone. Indeed whole communities can be afflicted by this dulling of the spirit and the term 'one of the depressed areas' aptly describes the prevailing atmosphere which hangs over these work-bereft localities. It is as though the people in their unemployment are caught up into a continuing grief. They are engaged in mourning the loss of work.

As one who, in my professional role as a pastor, has frequently had to minister to both the bereaved and the workless I have been particularly struck by the close similarity in behavioural response between those who are mourning the loss of a loved one and those who in mid-life find themselves bereft of a job. Both are major loss situations.

In normal economic circumstances, of course, those who suffer job loss are usually only without work for a brief period of time and their redundancy is seen merely as a temporary hiatus. (1) The time between jobs is usually taken up with the task of finding a replacement occupation and in emotional terms morale remains relatively buoyant. But in the present economic circumstances active job search is often experienced as a distressing reality-testing encounter which serves only to persuade the unemployed that, try as they might, the desired jobs are just not there. In such circumstances work loss closely parallels our behavioural response to intense and irretrievable personal loss. It is felt in the deep centres of our being and leads to deep distress, to moods of anger and depression and to a disorganisation of normal, healthy, purposeful living. These are the classic symptoms of the mourning process. (2)

Job Loss as a Bereavement Process

Very little research work has as yet been done in this field, but prima facie there does seem to be a close correlation in the responses of the bereaved and those unable to resecure work. Both face the predicament of having to accommodate, in terms of lifestyle and the emotions, to a situation of irretrievable loss. Both groups experience a great gap or feeling of void at the centre of their lives. As one unemployed man expressed it to me recently: 'In the jigsaw of our lives there is a work-sized hole for which only a work-shaped piece will fit.' His phrase catches the sense of inconsolable loss, the feeling of emptiness and the strong sense of yearning which characterises the early stages of grief. This is a particularly painful and distressing phase in the mourning process. But whereas the widow or the widower hopefully will receive a fair measure of understanding and social support as they accommodate to their personal loss, our society has been much slower to recognise the emotional pains which are in the main privately, silently, yet courageously borne by the long-term unemployed. For them very little social and emotional support is offered as they painfully accommodate to their loss. Specialised counselling facilities are minimal and the grief remains privatised, rather than being talked out. In view of the very large numbers now experiencing long-term job loss this is perhaps an area where greater supportive provision requires to be made and a closer study undertaken of what happens in psychological terms when in a work-orientated society we find ourselves bereft of any form of paid employment.

The research work that so far has been undertaken with respect to the psychological responses to long-term job loss is still of a somewhat tentative nature. Certain frequently encountered behavioural responses are now beginning to emerge and I have tried to chart these in Chart 4 opposite. The experience of job loss would appear to be a complex process with various psychological adjustments having to take place at successive staging posts. (3) However, in trying to chart those various staging posts two important cautionary points need to be introduced. The first is that progression through the various stages of Initial shock ⟶ Early optimism ⟶ Active job search ⟶ Diminution of hope ⟶ Pessimism and anxiety ⟶ Active distress ⟶ Fatalistic adaptation is not strictly linear. Rather the individual tends to swing backwards and forwards in mood along this general line over the course of time. Thus at times unemployed individuals may briefly recapture their early optimism temporarily escaping from their pessimism and anxiety, but despite the repeated pattern of progressions and regressions the direction of movement over time is generally towards the diminution of hope and the collapse of self-esteem. As one 43-year-old man put it: 'The longer you're off the worse it gets, it eats into you.' (4)

The second cautionary word has to do with the extent of the felt loss. As in bereavement situations certain personal losses are more deeply felt than others, depending upon the degree of bonding that has taken place in earlier stages of life; so also with job-loss. Its effects upon different individuals varies. The loss of their job may have an extreme impact on those for whom their work has been everything. For others who find that they are able to obtain their sense of identity, value and purpose from other quarters of life the psychological losses may not be quite so keenly felt. As Richard Harrison quite properly reminds us: 'It is crucial to remember that it is *individuals*—with their own distinctive personalities, expectations, previous experiences and networks of relationships—who become unemployed. Their reactions both to the fact, and to the ensuing process, will obviously vary.' (5)

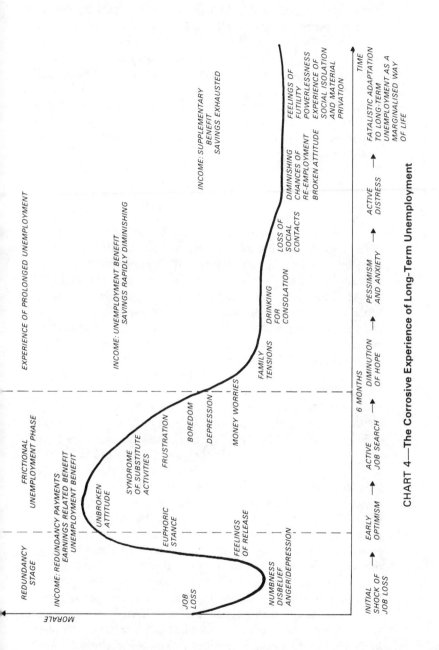

CHART 4—The Corrosive Experience of Long-Term Unemployment

My own observations would lead me to believe that the accommodation processes closely follow our response to other forms of major loss. That is to say, there is initially a strong urge to regain that which is lost. For the unemployed this is the active, sometimes almost frenetic, job search stage. As Marsden and Duff discovered in their researches, the motivation to find another job and to recover their place within the paid economy is exceedingly strong in most workers. 'So strong are the pressures and informal sanctions supporting work in our society that some of the workless cling to the desire to work to a much greater degree than our society has the right to expect in view of what they had experienced through work and unemployment.' (6) But if, day after day, week after week, month after month, all one's attempts to resecure work prove fruitless, then eventually, the early hopes of working again become diminished to the point of virtual extinction. The reality-testing procedures, of applying for vacancies and never getting anywhere, attending the Job Centres, scanning the newspapers and talking with friends caught in a similar predicament, ultimately push the long-term unemployed to the point where hope collapses and the battle against the odds is abandoned. 'Eventually, you know, you come to lose the appetite for work.' (7) For some months despair, anxiety and depression have advanced and receded like a tide against the sea-wall of residual hope. At times washing right over the inner psyche; at other times being pushed back when the chance of another job perhaps seemed to be in the offing. But in the end many individuals give up the fight. A colossal weariness and inertia takes over. They have lost their motivational drive.

In such a state it is not I believe true to say that they have as yet *accepted* their condition of worklessness. Rather they are in that stage of mourning which Bowlby identifies as the second stage. (8) It is the stage of *disorganisation* which occurs when the response systems have now ceased to be focused on the lost object and the efforts to recover a job have ceased too. Bowlby describes this phase as being accompanied by pain and despair. In employment terms it is reached when the individual concerned comes to believe that he or she will never work again. This is a phase of psychic withdrawal, of apathy and of disorganisation. The previous behavioural pattern which was intended to recover the lost object (viz. a job), has been abandoned. But as yet there is no new centre to group one's life around. An individual in this psychic state is not likely to respond to the impassioned pleas of the Unemployment

Rally organiser to join him on the march or to be greatly stirred by
the speeches of those who would advocate radical political alternatives. He is caught at the mid-point of the mourning process. His
life has no sense of direction, no meaning, no strong sense of working towards desired goals, and those caught up in this condition are
not the stuff of which rebellions and determined protest are made.
This is not a stage of great personal initiative or of great social
response. It is a period of disorientation in which the emotions have
not yet regrouped their drive. It is a phase in which a new centre to
life requires to be found. A new and satisfying model of living has
to be discovered—that of a life without the prospect of work.

Finding a New Basis for Living

For retired individuals the transition from employment into the
workless state may constitute quite a major and difficult change-
point in their lives. But at least they will probably have been prepar-
ing mentally for this eventuality for quite some time and the provision of pre-retirement courses may well help ease the transition.
Further, the retired are able to terminate their working life with
some degree of social honour. Society's stance towards them is
positive and that makes all the difference. They are liberated from
feelings of guilt by virtue of their official retirement and they are set
free to enjoy non-work to the full. They have already played their
part in the maintenance of the fabric of society. They have earned
their rest and the words 'Well done thou good and faithful servant'
still seem to ring in their ears from the rites of passage of the retirement ceremony. (9) There are social clubs geared to the pensioner's
post-retirement needs and a range of concessionary travel arrangements assisting access to civic provision and aiding general
mobility. All around the freshly fledged pensioner sees a rich
variety of ways in which, provided one has the necessary finance, it
is possible to attain to a full and satisfying lifestyle in one's post-
work years. But for the unemployed individual unable, for reasons
beyond his or her control, to resecure paid employment the overall
scene is very different. What alternative models of dignity are
available in our society for the workless who find themselves
through no fault of their own forever outside the social framework
provided by the paid economy? If life is not about working and earning and being free to spend what you have earned (i.e. all that is
associated with the vast complex sphere of production and consumption), what is it all about? If I am no longer to obtain my prin-

cipal reference points for living from this world of work, then where do I turn for a cultural alternative? This is the personal dilemma of those who believe that they will not work again.

There is no one to assist the unemployed in the discovery of some new lifestyle, some new centre for being, a new model of a civilised and dignified social existence. The loneliness of that situation is therefore both overwhelming and terrifying. Their previous life-centre has gone and in consequence unemployed individuals find themselves out of congruence with their cultural surroundings. They are called to live without work in a work-orientated society for an indeterminable period of time and no cultural guidelines have been provided. No role is expected of them save that of job search which has proved fruitless. What best option then lies open to them? What activities are legally permissible, financially possible, socially acceptable and inwardly satisfying?

As our life is presently constituted, the unemployed in fact find great difficulties confronting them as they try to come to terms with their predicament. The conditions under which payment is made to the unemployed through our social security system places great curbs on the initiative of the unemployed in trying to improve their financial situation through obtaining even a modicum of casual or part-time work. In previous periods of history many a worker could not obtain regular full-time employment. But they could use their initiative and bring in a little income by offering their services, engaging in whatsoever casual employment might be available. Or they could use their skill of hand within the home and hawk what goods they might manage to produce around the neighbourhood. But in our age of formal contracts of employment, complex income tax and national insurance levies and above all the tight bar on earnings built into our present system of state benefits, such entrepreneurial activities run into all kinds of institutional problems. Instead of allowing the unemployed to do something for themselves to supplement incomes and maintain morale we have tended to adopt Draconian measures to prevent this. (10) We expect our unemployed either to find sufficient employment to become wholly self-supporting (which hundreds of thousands are currently unable to do) or else we expect them to adopt an economically wholly passive pose. There appears to be no acceptable halfway position. It is important to realise, however, that this has not always been so in our country nor is it so in other countries at the moment. The situation in Australia is, I gather, a good deal more liberal and the

unemployed are given far greater discretionary areas in which they
can supplement state incomes to a modest degree.

Financial Constraints

Attempts by the unemployed to restructure their lives around some
other principle than that provided by the institution of work are
made all the more difficult by reason of financial constraint and unhelpful public attitudes. The low level of income received by the
vast majority of long-term unemployed individuals and a general
lack of capital severely curb what it might be possible to do in the
absence of a full-time occupation. As we have seen in Section II,
the reality of having to budget all one's expenditure out of what is
received on the dole severely restricts access to civic provisions and
travel. Further, it curbs hobbies, do-it-yourself activities, leisure
pursuits and social interaction generally. Whether in mid-life on the
dole, or in retirement on an inadequate pension, the quality of life
and the realm of the possible are severely affected by the harsh
economic realities of minimal income. For those used to having
money in their pockets, which could be used in a variety of ways to
fill one's leisure hours, the gift of much greater tracts of unstructured time but with minimal financial resources constitutes a major
organisational problem.

   Finally, the search for a new lifestyle, an acceptable alternative
mode of living and a social identity not in any way based on occupation, income levels and consumer possessions, is made all the
more difficult because the unemployed are called upon to construct
that mode of existence in a society whose attitudes are still largely
coloured by the Work Ethic. As we shall see when we explore this
issue in greater depth in Section V the cultural climate is such that
there remains a suspicion of those who do not work for their living.
Whereas retired individuals now have a recognised place in society
and because of their past contribution social honour still attaches
to them, no such cultural accommodation has as yet taken place
with respect to those still in their mid-life span whom no one will
employ. Our attitudes towards them are at best uneasy and at
worst punitive. The unemployed cannot but sense this and it makes
the processes of inner reorganisation all the more difficult. Having
lost the self-image that comes from a place within the hierarchy of
work they desperately need to find a new model of social dignity
which will endow them with feelings of inner worth and well-being.
But our work-centred society has as yet no adequate social niche

for those who, through no fault of their own, stand idle. That there is no well-defined and generally acceptable pattern of living that they can attain to as workless individuals makes the emotional accommodation to job loss both bewildering and distressing. Whereas in other loss situations the processes of mourning enable us in the course of time to abandon our close attachment to one life-centre and to so reorganise our inner psychic resources as to find an alternative *modus vivendi*, the workless in our society have great difficulty in achieving a satisfactory completion to their particular mourning process. So strongly have we affirmed the values of the Work Ethic that we find ourselves at a loss to know what to affirm in the lives of the workless. To this topic we must return in Chapter 17 for the cultural dilemmas posed by the collapse of Full Employment are no less acute than the distributive ones. I am, however, increasingly persuaded that at least a partial resolution of the distributive problems is an essential precursor to achieving some advance on the cultural issues.

Sharing in the Cultural Accommodations

At the moment it seems to me that in the face of adverse national circumstances we are asking the unemployed, a minority grouping, to do *all* the accommodating. They are the scapegoat group upon whom all the economic ills of the nation have been placed. They carry the burden for us and we have allowed them to be driven into social isolation and a marginalised existence. Meanwhile the rest of us, secure in our employment, enjoy the fruits of our labour and with lifestyles unaffected continue on with life very much as before. It is these deep divisions now so evident within the nation and the very unequal sharing of economic adjustments across the community which so deeply disturbs me. As inhabitants of the same community and as children of the same God I believe that in moral terms we are inescapably yoked together. What serves to diminish the life of my brother man diminishes the overall life of the community of which I also am part. I cannot therefore in moral terms be unaffected by my brother's misfortune, for fullness of life is only attained when all members of that community have the opportunity to enjoy that abundance together. Only when all are complete do I find my full completeness and until those social goals are attained I remain flawed. Thus in adverse economic circumstances I cannot turn my back on my unemployed brother's misfortune. I have responsibilities towards him. Those responsibilities involve not just some marginal easement of his sufferings but also an assault against the root cause of those sufferings and this in turn may involve me in some major readjustments of my previous lifestyle.

Why should those who have been squeezed out of the paid economy be expected to do all the accommodating? If the economic determinants of life are changing, would it not be better if all within the community shared in that process of occupational, financial and cultural accommodation? In that way the accommodations and adjustments experienced in individual lives would be more gradual and far less severe. The nation would come through the transitions together as one people and there would be a higher level of sensitivity, understanding and mutual support because all would be sharing in a common social experience. At the present time those who find themselves wholly unemployed are overwhelmed by the psychic task of having to rebuild a whole new life for themselves and then, from all the weakness of a minority social position, sustain that life model in the midst of a majority culture still dominated by the old Work Ethic. I believe with all my heart that if there are accommodations that have to be made at this point in time then it is far better, for the sake of the health and wholeness of the nation, that we should go through that process of change and cultural discovery together. It is to this end that I would argue the case for a redistribution of both work and freedom from work.

Notes and References

1. Daniel, W.W., 'Why is high unemployment still somehow acceptable?' *New Society*, 19 March 1980, p. 497.
2. Bowlby, John, 'Processes of Mourning', *International Journal of Psycho-Analysis*, XLII, Parts 4–5, 1961, passim.
3. See in particular John Hayes and Peter Nutman, *Understanding the Unemployed*, Tavistock Publications, 1981. Hayes and Nutman provide some very helpful interpretations of the various psychological adjustments commonly found in the long-term unemployed.
4. Hayes, John, and Peter Nutman, op. cit., p. 30.
5. Harrison, Richard, 'The Demoralising Experience of Prolonged Unemployment', *Department of Employment Gazette*, April 1976, p. 340.
6. Marsden, D. and E. Duff, *Workless—some unemployed men and their families*, Penguin Books, 1975, p. 264.

7. Unemployed man, Dundee, 1980. He had been unemployed for a year.
8. Bowlby, John, op. cit., p. 334.
9. Atchley, Robert C., *The Sociology of Retirement*, Schenkman Publishing Company, Cambridge, Massachusetts, 1976, pp. 53 ff.
10. *Guardian*, 18 February 1980, 'Campaign against "benefit fraud" under fire'. Article by Melanie Phillips. See also Deacon, Alan, 'Spivs, drones and other scroungers', *New Society*, 28 February 1980, and *Guardian*, 5 December 1980, 'Stop working, and get yourself into the dole queue'. Article by Jean McKenzie.

Chapter 11

THE INGREDIENTS OF SOCIAL INERTIA

Having outlined some of the personal and social pains, problems and dilemmas which lie inherent in the present crisis over work I now want in the remaining chapters of this book to look at the possibilities of creative change. That creative change will need to address itself both to the easement of acute personal pains and to the construction of a more acceptable and sustainable social order. It will be particularly difficult because it is occurring during a phase of human history when the number still desiring a place within the paid economy considerably exceeds the requirements of the market. How long we shall continue to be in that position no one knows. According to the manpower forecast used by the Department of Employment for the period 1981–86: 'It is possible only to speculate on activity rates and especially on what the demand for labour will be over this period. A working assumption has had to be made; that is that unemployment will rise from its present level of some $2\frac{1}{2}$ million to reach a peak sometime in 1982 and that thereafter it will decline to about 2 million in 1986.'(1) Within the parameters of this forecast the Manpower Services Commission envisage that by the summer of 1982 as many as 63 per cent of those under 18 might be jobless, while the number of people out of work for more than a year may well double from the present 500,000 to more than a million by 1984. It is important to remember that there is nothing predetermined in these figures but they do give us a sober estimate of the persistence of our present structural problems which are unlikely to melt away like the morning mist when the recession begins to lift. Should Britain's competitiveness in the global markets continue to worsen, or the impact of the new technology prove greater than we now anticipate, these estimates could be underestimates. On the other hand, if we had the will to

initiate a range of job-sharing schemes, if we funded targeted training and specific programmes of public works and if in general we
adopted more flexible work patterns, it might be possible to bring
far more into the active labour force, thereby reducing the numbers
wholly unemployed very considerably by 1986. To that extent the
future still lies in our hands and is not predetermined. However, the
latter course although bringing a number of major social and personal benefits at the end of the day could not be achieved without
cost. These costs, which are inescapably involved if the ends of a
just, participatory and sustainable society are to be achieved,
would need to be collectively borne by all those presently in employment in the form of some reduction of real or anticipated incomes and by certain accommodations in working practice.

At the heart of the crisis over work lies the cost of sharing and
there is no magical way in which those hard economic realities can
be side-stepped. The act of sharing always costs somebody
something either in money terms or in the relinquishing of past
practices and privileges. Thus we should be on our guard against
those who would apparently offer us 'costless' solutions to the present dilemmas over unemployment. Over against the apprehensions
about the cost of change, however, need to be set the burdensome
costs of running the economy as we are with approximately three
million unemployed. According to the latest Manpower Services
Commission estimates the total cost of unemployment to the nation
during 1981/82 will be in the order of £12.45 billion. This figure
which works out at about £4,380 per unemployed person per year
includes both the direct cost of benefits (about 32 per cent) and lost
tax which would have been received by the Exchequer had the unemployed stayed in jobs.(2)

MSC ESTIMATE OF COSTS OF UNEMPLOYMENT
1981/82
(Assuming average 2.84m unemployed)

	£bn
Unemployment benefit	2.004
Supplementary benefit	2.000
Loss of income tax	4.257
Loss of National Insurance contributions	3.280
Loss of indirect taxes including VAT	0.906
TOTAL	12.447

On economic grounds alone there is a very strong case for a major change of direction in employment policies. But in addition to the Exchequer costs there are profound human costs within a situation of high unemployment. As the earlier chapters of this book have demonstrated these hardships are having to be borne by those unfortunate enough to have been squeezed out of the paid economy and by our children who are unable to enter it. These costs in financial, social and psychological terms, because they are all focused upon the lives of the Few and are not borne collectively, make for circumstances of human wretchedness. Acute financial deprivation coupled to social isolation and loss of a purposive centre to life arise as a consequence of the present allocation of costs. These costs borne by the Few enable the Many to continue to live life in the manner to which they have grown accustomed despite the major structural changes taking place within the economy. Thus what we are talking about with regard to the future is not whether Britain should choose social and employment policies which involve some measure of cost over against a status quo position which is painless. That is not the reality of the choice. The key issue is how those costs which are inherent in the present dilemma over work are to be distributed. Do we continue to place all the ills of this age upon a particular 'scapegoat' grouping and drive them into marginalisation so that the rest of us might maintain our prosperity, or are the ills of this age something that should be borne collectively? These are the moral and political issues of the 1980s with regard to our handling of the unemployment problem and they are issues which test the corporate solidarity of the nation. As Professor Ralf Dahrendorf, Director of the London School of Economics, put it in a radio interview: 'I do write off the idea that a modern society, highly industrialised, can give people job employment in the traditional sense to the point of full employment. I think what we shall see in the future is an organisation of human lives which mixes employment with other activities, satisfying activities, in a totally different way. And unless we have the imagination to create such a society we will have the misery of unemployment as we see it today.'(3) Before moving on to sketch in some of the areas where that creative change might begin to take place, it is necessary first of all to make a review of some of the social constraints.

The Challenge to Vested Interests

Clearly the policy line being advocated in this book runs counter to
certain vested interests. Brian Showler and Adrian Sinfield identify
that particular problem in the concluding chapter of *The Workless
State:*

The immediate issues for public debate and policy-making can, we believe,
be stated simply. If unemployment is not going to decline in the near
future (and the main questions are where, how much and how fast will it
increase), the debate needs to be about how the work that is available
should be distributed, and how those excluded from any meaningful
economic activity should be treated. We need to discuss the principles of
justice and equity that should apply in the allocation. The present ways of
sharing out what work there is, and the changes people will allow to alter
that allocation, largely reflect the dominant values and choices tolerated
by those holding significant power in society. Any proposals to distribute
economic opportunities more evenly, let alone to provide work for all, are
bound to challenge established assumptions and the prevailing patterns of
the distribution of work if they are to be of any real help to those now unemployed and the many others likely to lose their jobs in the future. Even
a fairer distribution of the jobs there are will threaten the vested interests
of those who have managed to achieve greater security and privilege.(4)

The economic system is a power system with certain occupational groupings having aggregated over a period of time varying degrees of job security and financial reward and these tend to
be fiercely defended should there be any suspicion of encroachment
by other parties. Sectional interests are preserved through a complex variety of differentials, traditional practices and institutional
rules. As R.H. Tawney put it, within this occupational hierarchy
'those who can manipulate the more important levers are, directly
or indirectly, consciously or unconsciously, the real rulers of their
fellows'.(5) These realities of power are exceedingly important with
respect to the plight of the unemployed for it is only as a result
of those within the paid economy making certain accommodations
that the position of the workless can be improved.

Power Relationships between the Working and Non-Working Populations

In his book on power and powerlessness, John Gaventa speaks of
the patterns of power and powerlessness which can develop within
the social order over a period of time which are such that they 'can
keep issues from arising, grievances from being voiced, and interests being recognised'.(6) Those who are the inhabitants of certain occupational groupings continue to enjoy such powers, advantages and opportunities as past history and social arrangements

have conferred upon them, while other parties remain trapped into a very much weaker social position. These power relationships once established tend to be self-sustaining and a certain inertia sets in. We can see such power relationships clearly established within the global scene in the unequal trading relationships of what the Brandt Report calls the North and the South. The developing nations of the southern hemisphere find themselves trapped into persistent poverty because of the continuing economic dominance of the more powerful North. Such patterns of dominance are perpetuated at the global level and within particular societies because 'whoever decides what the game is about also decides who gets into the game'.(7)

That is, the advantage always remains with the established power groupings. Thus in any collective discussions about whether a particular employing organisation should recruit labour or go for additional overtime, the unemployed, as a social group have no place at the bargaining table. The discussion on such matters is between the two power blocks of the management and the representatives of the shop floor. Or again, in the discussion over the allocation of finances for training, those party to such discussions are far more likely to be drawn from the professional and skilled occupational categories than from those who might represent the training needs of the unskilled and the semi-skilled in society. Decision making in this country is so structured that for the most part the unskilled, the young, the long-term unemployed and the registered disabled are not party to the formulation of policy, the allocation of funds and the deployment of resources. Theirs are the unheard voices and their particular interests can generally only be introduced into the agenda by proxy. That makes for a very much weaker position and thus it is that generalised discontent can be present within certain quarters of society but it remains hidden, contained and in consequence is largely forgotten. An oppression of cruel innocence by those with greater powers can thereby be perpetuated, whilst amongst the powerless 'participation denied over time may lead to acceptance of the role of non-participation'.(8) Speaking of the position of those trapped into powerlessness, John Gaventa says this: 'Continual defeat gives rise not only to the conscious deferral of action but also to a sense of defeat, or a sense of powerlessness, that may affect the consciousness of potential challengers about grievances, strategies, or possibilities for change.'(9) In this way the status quo, even though inequitable, becomes 'accepted' by virtually all parties and power relationships may develop routines of non-challenge.

Differences of Perception

In Chapter 9 we noted the way in which the impact of unemployment is very unevenly distributed both geographically and occupationally. This has important implications with regard to the way unemployment is perceived by certain key groups and this, in turn, will have an influence upon the allocation of resources of help and the framing of social and political policies. In this regard it again might be helpful to turn back to the example of the 1930s to see how the uneven distribution of unemployment affected perception levels between those living in different parts of the United Kingdom. In a fascinating chapter entitled 'The Revolution that Never Was' Stevenson and Cook have analysed the reasons for the phenomenon of political inertia in the face of rising unemployment. Amongst a number of reasons suggested for the lack of national concern were the regional disparities to which we have already drawn attention. Stevenson and Cook speak of the geographical isolation of the unemployed 'hidden away in the closed communities of the Welsh valleys or the pit villages of County Durham. Once the trough of the depression was past, after 1933, the problem of the long-term heavy unemployment was concentrated, as it had been before 1929, in the regions of the first industrial revolution, the home of Britain's staple industries far from the prosperous suburbs and growing industrial estates of the South-East and the Midlands. As J.B. Priestley had found in his *English Journey* in 1934, there were several nations, of which the England of depressed industries and mass unemployment was only one. There were whole communities which had been left virtually untouched by the depression and many for which the years 1930–32 had been only a temporary interruption to steadily rising prosperity. Thus a social survey of Oxford in the late 1930s could dismiss the problem of unemployment as being 'almost negligible'. The unemployed were effectively cut off from the mainstream of public opinion for most of the Thirties. The hunger marches were an attempt to break out of this isolation and bring the plight of the depressed areas to the attention of a wider public and of Parliament. . . . This was one reason why the hunger marches had such an impact upon popular consciousness, representing for the inhabitants of more prosperous parts of Britain almost the sole evidence of conditions in the depressed areas. In spite of this, however, the unemployed became a new kind of 'submerged tenth', obvious enough if they were sought out, but more often than not ignored. The depressed English regions were alien enough for many writers, still more so the depressed areas of South Wales, Scotland and Northern Ireland.'(10)

People are concerned most about what touches them most closely. This was true of the 1930s and it is true of Britain today. We know from Clive Smee's research for the Economic Adviser's Office of the DHSS that the costs of the present economic recession have not been shared widely by the whole community, as they might have. Instead, in Peter Townsend's words, they 'have been borne disproportionately by the working and non-working poor'.(11) We know from the 1980 PSI study that the recession has been hitting manual workers in manufacturing and construction far more than it has affected professional, executive and technical groups and those employed in the public sector. We know that the young and the disabled and the ethnic minority groups are all disproportionately affected and that the peripheral regions of the United Kingdom have again had unemployment rates well above the national average, whereas the South-East and East Anglia have enjoyed a much more favoured position.(12) Further, we know from a study of flows on and off the unemployed register that in October 1980 over 40 per cent of those unemployed had been without work for less than three months.(13) As we have seen, whilst earnings related supplements were still being paid this earlier phase of unemployment, whilst traumatic in itself, did not bring the short-term unemployed face to face with the acute financial problems of living on supplementary benefit. Nor will they have yet experienced the full corrosive impact on the family circle and the psyche of the total loss of hope.

When we put all this information together we begin to see the contours of a sociological map of unemployment which is not all that dissimilar to that which emerged in the 1930s. The profile which emerges shows considerable experiential descrepancies between the various sections of our society. The lives of certain groups and particular communities have been devastated by the impact of the recession whilst elsewhere the impact until the autumn of 1980 could be said to be only marginal. When we then look at who governs Britain, which sectors have representation in decision-making circles, who have access to the corridors of power, we see that it is not for the most part those who have been most personally and directly touched by the impact of job loss, but those who stand occupationally and geographically distant from its harshest manifestations. It is these realities of perception and power which I believe in large measure have lain at the root of past *laissez-faire* policies and of our failure to date to frame the appropriate social mechanisms that would enable us to make a better adaption to the new economic circumstances.

However, as the recession continues and deepens, spreading its tentacles down from the peripheral regions of the United Kingdom to encompass the industrial heartlands of the Midlands and even the South-East and as redundancies work upwards through the hierarchy of the occupations to affect those groups previously immune, so real public concern over the issues grows. By the late autumn of 1980 unemployment had become the number one public issue and the swings recorded in the local authority elections in May 1981, showed something of the political potency of that concern. Further, as public expenditure cuts work their way through the system so the harsh realities of restricted job choice and even job loss begin to be felt in certain previously secure employment sectors. For more and more families an awareness of the acute curb on recruitment is coming home in the problems now being faced by adolescent sons and daughters struggling to obtain their first foothold in the world of work. Parental concern is growing about the employment prospects for their offspring and this perhaps may be one of the most powerful levers in the move from social inertia to initiating the momentum that could bring about creative change.

Other factors may also play their part. The decision to phase out the earnings related supplement in early 1982 will bring the harsh financial realities to the fore very much earlier in the unemployment process. The increasing numbers staying on the register for longer periods of time will bring more and more people into the supplementary benefit net and to the experience of an even further drop in income. Savings, hoarded in the early days of unemployment, are likely to become depleted and the plight of these families cannot but become more apparent as the number thus affected steadily increases. Just as in the Thirties it was some time before a full documentation of the privations of the workless emerged, so too it has taken some time for the latest social researches to be completed, analysed and published. It may be a matter of water

dripping on stone but these researches are slowly dismantling some
of the popular myths about unemployment, thereby contributing to
a change in public perceptions.

Little by little the mood is changing. The seriousness and the per-
manence of the underlying structural difficulties is coming home to
ordinary men and women. Less and less will they be duped by the
political rhetoric of either the Left or the Right that our unemployment difficulties are a mere economic hiccup which market forces,
a change in government, or a little more time will quickly resolve.
Increasingly it is bearing in on people that the times have changed
and that we are into a new economic era where the link between investment and new jobs is more tenuous, where global transitions
and energy constraints reduce our room for manoeuvre and where
great changes are having to take place in skill and employment patterns. Thus it is that as Britain enters the closing decades of the
twentieth century she finds herself in the midst of major economic
and social transitions. Britain is no longer the great workshop of
the world that she once was, yet her people are still gifted and talen-
ted. Despite all our troubles we are still rich in material terms in
comparison with many of our global neighbours. Yet somehow we
seen to have lost the way. As a people we are uncertain as to
our future. For so many of the previous landmarks by which the
nation steered seem to have disappeared. Nearly all the past co-
ordinates have gone and we are in that state which the Greeks
called *aporia*—a state of lostness, or perplexity, where we do not
have a clear common perception of the way ahead. And
qualitatively, in terms of the making of the fraternal society, we
also seem to have lost our way. That corporate solidarity which
some 40 years ago took us through the troubles and tribulations of
the Second World War has somehow seeped away. Instead of being one people and facing our difficulties together, making generous
provision for the victims of change, sharing one another's burdens
and, in collective terms, fashioning something imperishable and in-
domitable out of the ashes of a shared national hardship, we have
become a divided and increasingly self-concerned society.
Everyone has done what seemed right in their own eyes, but in
looking only to our own interests we have lost something of our
soul and it is this which now weakens the springs of the requisite
social action. The challenge both economically and spiritually to
Britain is to right herself, to find again the consensus needed to
bring about the necessary changes and accommodations within our

present creaking social structures and to regain that mutual concern which alone can make a nation great.

Notes and References

1. *Employment Gazette*, April 1981, p. 167.
2. *Financial Times*, 9 November 1981, and *Hansard*, vol. 10, No. 163, col. 379, HMSO.
3. Professor Ralf Dahrendorf speaking on BBC Radio 4 January 1981, 'Focus on Unemployment'.
4. Showler, Brian, and Adrian Sinfield, *The Workless State*, Martin Robertson, Oxford, 1981, p. 225.
5. Tawney, R.H., *The Attack and Other Papers*, Allen and Unwin, pp. 89–90.
6. Gaventa, John, *Power and Powerlessness: Quiescence and Rebellion in an Appalachian Valley,* Clarendon Press, Oxford, 1980, p. vii.
7. Schattschneider, E.E., *The Semi-Sovereign People: A Realist's View of Democracy in America*, Holt, Rinehart and Winston, New York, 1960, p. 105.
8. Gaventa, John, *op. cit.*, p. 255.
9. *id.*, p. 255.
10. Stevenson, John, and Chris Cook, *The Slump: Society and Politics During the Depression*, Quartet Books, 1979, p. 274.
11. Showler, B. and A. Sinfield, *op. cit.*, Foreword by Peter Townsend p. xiii.
12. *Review of Services for the Unemployed*, Manpower Services Commission Publication, March 1981, 3.10–3.24.
13. *id.*, 3.5.

THE FUTURE SHAPE OF WORK

The Arena of Employment Policies

Chapter 12

WHAT KIND OF SOCIETY DO WE WANT?

It might be helpful before taking the case for a redistribution of work any further to recapitulate on the ground already covered. We began by looking at work through the eyes of the 'operators'. That is, from the standpoint of those who hold the responsibility for running an efficient economic system. From this perspective labour is viewed as a cost—a cost which has to be incurred if goods and services are to be produced, but a cost which requires constant surveillance and which must be kept as close as is practicable to the irreducible minimum. No manager enjoys shedding labour but in a highly competitive home and international market such a course of action frequently has to be taken if the economic viability of his concern is to be preserved. As one Director of ICI has remarked: 'No matter what the growth rate is in this country there is no way we are going to employ more people. The difference between a successful and unsuccessful business strategy in the modern world is the rate at which numbers of people come down.' (1) It is these inexorable demands of the economic system upon those who work within it that drive us down the road of increased productivity, the replacement of men with machines and towards a reduced workforce size. Such a trend brings in its wake both financial benefits and social costs. It maintains the economic viability of the organisation, it preserves a certain core of employment in each profitable concern and it creates national wealth. On the other hand the tendency to shed labour at the margins and to place curbs on previous recruitment patterns creates the kind of deep personal and social problems which I have documented in Sections II and III.

As long as there is some kind of equilibrium between the erosion of job opportunities in one sector and the creation or growth of jobs elsewhere within the employment scene there may be dislocation as individuals are forced to move from job to job, or from one sector to another, but the overall stock of jobs will remain constant. In such a situation a progressive society will have to cope with the problem of job change and its primary need will be to provide adequate retraining and relocation facilities. Within such a social scene the role of the benefits system will be to provide short-term financial support to the victims of change. In other words, merely having the function of providing a temporary income's bridge between one job and another. In a situation of transition a nation's labour force will need to be adaptable, relinquishing previous skills and learning new ones; abandoning one way of earning our living and discovering new ways. In such a progressive society there may be a considerable element of job change. Many may experience short-term unemployment. There would be upheaval, but there would be hope. People would still have faith in the future because as one door closed another would be seen to be opening.

However, the present crisis over unemployment is not just a crisis over a quickening pace of job change. We are faced also with a major problem in the realm of job generation. When we look at the stock of jobs within the economy as indicated by the size of the employed working population in Chart 2 (page 8) we see that, although something of a rough equilibrium between gains and losses was maintained through much of the 1970s, a marked decline in the overall stock of jobs has occurred since we turned into the 1980s. The problems that this has caused are further exacerbated by the expectation that the number eligible and wishing to work will increase by yet another 700,000 by 1986. (2) It is these structural factors coupled to a disbelief in the ability of our sluggish economy to be able to generate so many new jobs in so short a time which causes the technocrat to shake his head sadly and pronounce that the continuance of mass unemployment at around the 2.5 to 3 million mark, for the mid-term at least, is inevitable.

As I write, virtually every independent economic survey supports this view. (3) At the most optimistic, Liverpool University would predict that unemployment levels might drop to 1.5 million by 1984. At the most pessimistic, Cambridge Economic Policy Group forecasts a rise in unemployment to about 4.35 million by the end of 1985. However, the main cluster of forecasts see unemployment staying at about the 2.5 to 3 million mark through until 1985. Such surveys, however well researched, do not predetermine the future, but there is now sufficient consensus to lead us to believe that labour demand will remain curtailed throughout the early 1980s, frustrating demands for a speedy drop in unemployment rates even though the economy may be considerably more buoyant by then. Thus it is that most responsible economists working on traditional models of supply and demand would assert that Full Employment, in the sense of everyone wanting a full-time job getting one, is now unlikely to be attained in the period 1981/86 irrespective of who holds the political reins of power. Indeed, there are a number of respected observers who would go even further and who would suggest that full employment as we have known it in the past will be very unlikely ever to come back. Professor Ralf Dahrendorf, for example, expresses this viewpoint when he says: 'It seems to me that we have run into a period in all industrial societies in which, to use a phrase used by others, "The Work Society is running out of work". That is, a society which is built around employment suddenly doesn't have enough employment opportunities for all its citizens.' (4) If Dahrendorf is right, and there are a growing number who would now support him in this thesis, then the challenge of the 1980s is not just to ride out some temporary economic difficulties but rather to engage in the task of restructuring our employment patterns. If our present adversities are the first symptoms of having moved into a new economic order then the personal troubles and the societal stresses which I documented in Sections II and III will not be likely to diminish in the next decade. If we make no creative response, those problems both personal and societal will become aggravated by years of neglect. The divisions between the employed and the unemployed will increase and the resolution of those problems will be all the harder to secure. We have already taken cognizance of the kind of ills which breed in a situation of high unemployment. These studies reveal the unacceptable face of the current situation. The destruction of hope in a people, the diminution of opportunities, the gross disparities in income within the nation, the creation and maintenance of an élite of those with work and an underclass of long-term unemployed individuals—these should not be acceptable features in a civilised society. Just as the maintenance of an élite through the enforced activities of an underclass of slaves had to be challenged at an earlier stage of human history, so too the maintenance of another élite through the enforced idleness of an underclass of the long-term unemployed requires to be challenged in the 1980s. It is so far

removed from the great principles of fraternity, equality and liberty
as to be a social order that is morally indefensible.

The Search for Alternatives

The purpose of the remainder of this book must be to lead the discussion on towards the charting of a more satisfactory alternative.
I want to begin that task in this chapter by asking some questions
about desired social ends and then in the concluding chapters to
focus on the means that might enable us to move towards those
ends. In this chapter and the next I want, quite deliberately, to
remain in the realm of dreams and visions, exercising in a disciplined way the creative outworkings of social imagination. In the
closing pages of this section I want to tread the pilgrim path: I want
to assess the costs and to feel the sharp flints of earth's hard
realities beneath my feet.

One of the sad things about the present situation is that our
social imagination seems to have atrophied. Our approach to the
problems posed by work and unemployment have tended to
become dry and mechanistic. They have centred around the dictates of the existing economic arrangements rather than concerning
themselves with the human condition and the dimensions of a
wholesome and defensible social order of which the economic
system is not master, but servant. Increasingly, like Erich Fromm, I
am disturbed that the development of the economic system appears
no longer to be determined by the question: What is good for man?
but by the question: What is good for the growth of the system? (5)
Somehow we need to bring our social imagination to bear upon the
present economic stalemate and this will perhaps involve us in having to ask subversive questions about the way that work and our
economic system are currently organised. For it ought not to be
taken as axiomatic that the interests of the economic system as it is
presently established in all cases coincides with an evolution
towards a more just, a more participatory and more sustainable
society where the full dimensions of the abundant life can be experienced by all parties. There are areas of conflict in work between
going for maximum profit and providing for people in the fullness
of their needs. For too long perhaps we have tried to mask the
sharpness of this conflict by making the bland assumption that
what was good for the growth of the system was also good for all
within the nation. But if the present economic arrangements, not
only in this country but throughout the one global village, are fail-

ing to produce the dimensions of life that we desire then the challenge to us is to change the system.

We need therefore to introduce a radical dimension into our forward planning. We need to use the precious gift of social and political vision which enables people to break out of the imprisoning bonds of a now arid conventional wisdom to see that things need not always be as they are. We need, of course, to take the present factual world very seriously, and I have tried to do this with some care in the earlier sections. But we also need the wings of imagination that encourage men and women to reach out for the 'not yet' and which envisage radically alternative life situations which are not only desirable, but possible. As Harvey Cox reminds us in his stimulating book *The Feast of Fools*: ' "Reality" is not a fixed or changeless category. It is what a particular culture decides it will be.' (6)

The Processes of Change

The task of shaping out a more acceptable economic and social future is, I believe, essentially a collective task. That is to say, it is the proper business of all ordinary citizens and is not something that should be left to an élitist few. The formulation of desired social ends is something which properly belongs to the people in a free and democratic society and is not something which can be left merely to government or to the captains of industry. Thus part of the challenge posed by the present crisis is a challenge to the effectiveness of our democratic processes to initiate a vigorous and informed debate amongst all sections of society. For it is out of the aspirations of ordinary men and women regarding the kind of society they would want for themselves and their children, their neighbours and their neighbours' children, that the guidelines for appropriate government and corporate action must be drawn. At the moment a sense of powerlessness pervades the land. We feel ourselves to be in the grip of economic and technological forces over which we have no control. Individually we do not see how we can gain any purchase upon the economic determinism which serves to perpetuate the present unsatisfactory state of affairs and in this condition of helplessness we feel unmanned. For part of our humanity consists in being creatively involved in the shaping of life's events, contributing to a desired future and not being the passive victim of the dictates of the principalities and powers of this world.

How do we bring about change? How do we engage in the vital task of bringing into being a condition that does not as yet exist in actuality, for our own sake and for the sake of our neighbour? It seems to me that the change process has a number of elements within it. It perhaps begins with a sober evaluation of the present realities. It uses the discipline of looking out on our world not just from our own accustomed stance but also finds its perceptions enriched by the insights of others. In particular we need to incorporate into our own understanding of 'reality' the experiences in the lives of those who are poor and marginalised. For it is as we view life through the eyes of those who have been pushed to the periphery of our society that we come to discern the working of its power systems and are permitted to understand why some sections of society live in comparative wretchedness whilst others seem to be able to live a life of comparative comfort and splendour.

It is the challenge which comes of knowing how things really are in God's world which again and again has acted as the spark which has fired the requisite social action. A second component in the change process is the contribution that comes from the ranks of the social visionaries. It is not enough just to document the unacceptable state of the present situation. If we are to move forward creatively and constructively we need to catch a glimpse of a better social alternative. We need to be drawn forward out of the present unsatisfactory impasse by the prospect of a more hopeful and wholesome social condition the other side of change. That is to say, it is more profitable that mankind should be drawn by hope rather than being driven by fear when setting out in a new social direction and engaging in the task of reorganising working time and working opportunities. Fear is a poor instrument for social advance. Hope on the other hand liberates the best that lies latent within the human potential. It unites a people through a common desired objective and is capable of sustaining a nation through the adversities which attend the pilgrim way. I therefore want to use the remainder of this book to flesh out the vision of a more wholesome social alternative. It can be no more than an outline sketch of the kind of direction in which I am now persuaded we should be attempting to move. In many ways it is a composite of a number of ideas canvassed by others and in some cases developed more fully by our Common Market counterparts. In some respects the social model which I envisage merely accentuates and develops certain features of the existing contemporary scene. In this regard I believe that many of the essential features of the future social order lie like dormant seeds within the present order. Their most promising features need to be carefully identified and given every encouragement to grow and develop. For it is out of these spontaneous social mutations that useful models for future living may begin to emerge. At the moment most of these inventive responses receive little public recognition because they do not form a substantial part of our formal economic system. But increasingly they are coming to merit far more serious attention by employment experts as providing us with potential models for bringing about some measure of real easement within the present all-pervasive work crisis.

In all that is set down in the next pages there is the need to do a great deal more detailed work. In some cases it may be found that promising lines of action in fact create too many negative side-effects to prove worth pursuing and these will have to be discarded or refashioned in favour of more effective social instruments. In many cases we will find that existing vested interests are being challenged and the cry will go up that traditional liberties and long established arrangements are being threatened by what is proposed. Such claims will need to be carefully examined and a balanced assessment made as to what is in the national interest. For as R.H. Tawney shrewdly commented: 'Classes already at the top of the ladder may fall, but cannot rise. The construction which they put upon liberty is the result of that position. Whether consciously or not, it is, in large measure, a defence mechanism. Put in a nutshell, it is a doctrine of liberty which regards it as involving, not action to extend opportunities and raise individual faculty to the highest possible level, but the continued enjoyment by individuals and groups of such powers, advantages and opportunities as past history and present social arrangements may happen to have conferred upon them.' (7) The existing and inequitable social order will inevitably be challenged by what is proposed and in the allocation of costs and opportunities there will be many areas of conflict. That should not deter us from attempts at trying to secure a more just, a more participatory and a more sustainable society. We will need to work for promising compromises amid the conflict of interests and bit by bit slowly edge things in the desired direction. In that task the building of informed majorities and arguing out the case for needed change will be all important, for the desired ends can only be achieved if there is sufficient consensus. The shaping of opinions at the base level is of crucial importance, for the greater the number desiring the change the faster will we be able to advance. As Simon Phipps puts it, 'Politics may be the art of the possible, but what is possible greatly depends upon what people really want. Small minorities with conviction and a good understanding of the way power operates, can create a new public opinion. When a new public opinion comes to want a change, the range of what is "possible" changes too.' (8)

Notes and References

1. *Sunday Telegraph*, 20 March 1979.
2. *Employment Gazette*, April 1981, 'Labour Force Outlook to 1986', p. 167.
3. Manpower Services Commission, *Manpower Review 1981*, Diagram 8, 'Comparison of Forecasts of Total Unemployment', p. 18.
4. Professor Ralf Dahrendorf speaking on BBC Radio 4, January 1981, 'Focus on Unemployment'.
5. Fromm, Erich, *To Have or To Be*, Abacus ed., Sphere Books, 1979, pp 16–17.
6. Cox, Harvey, *The Feast of Fools*, Harper and Row, New York, 1969, p. 70.
7. Tawney, R.H., *The Attack and Other Papers*, Allen and Unwin, 1953, pp. 85–86.
8. Phipps, Simon, *God on Monday*, Hodder and Stoughton, 1966, p. 104.

Chapter 13

TOWARDS A BETTER ALTERNATIVE

Is there any way out of the present economic impasse? Is there a more humane and constructive alternative to our present set of un-employment problems? I am convinced that there is and that broadly it lies in the hitherto largely unexplored domain of Work-Sharing. For under the broad umbrella of the present discussions over work-sharing a number of initiatives are beginning to emerge, a number of working models are being tested out at home and abroad and a catalogue of good ideas is being compiled. I do not naively believe that what is now emerging from this quarter can alone resolve all our structural unemployment problems. But I am now persuaded that it has a major contribution to make alongside the more traditional responses. I believe that there are a number of promising ideas which need to be more fully explored and given ac-tive encouragement. I am also convinced that we in Britain have much to learn from our European counterparts who are placing work-sharing stratagems far higher on their list of constructive national policy than we are here at home. I therefore propose to devote the whole of this and the next chapter to a discussion of the work-sharing option. We shall look at various suggestions for reallocating working time, laying out for the reader some of the costs and benefits of this more flexible approach to work patterns. Finally, I will assess its potential as a viable social instrument in relation to other more traditional yet promising employment policy measures.

The general aim of work-sharing as a social instrument is to so organise the volume of work available within the entire economy that all those wishing to work can at least find partial employment. At the present time we are looking for something in order of an 8 per cent adjustment in the present distribution patterns if those social aims are to be achieved. (1) Work-sharing can be achieved either through some of those currently employed giving up their jobs to other groups of individuals who up to then have not had a job (e.g. the Job Release Scheme), or through a new arrangement of working-time which allows the existing work to be shared by more workers (e.g. twinning and trebling arrangements). The advantages of work-sharing measures are both quantitative and qualitative. They enable us to bring more into the paid economy thereby increasing participation and allowing for a fairer distribution of the satisfactions and rewards that accrue from being in employment. But they can also bring an important added richness to human existence by increasing our range of choice as to when we work and how long we work at different phases of our life. For just as there is a problem in our society for those who want work but who cannot obtain it, so too there is the mirror image problem of those who find their time commitment to work burdensome and who desire increased freedom and leisure. The strength of the work-sharing option is that it offers the possibility of so adjusting working-time patterns that the unemployed obtain work and the overworked are give more time to do humanly significant things in their leisure.

Work Patterns in Historical Perspective

Because the work-sharing instrument in fact works with the grain of human aspirations, increasing personal choice, widening the range of opportunities to work only those hours that one wants and giving a greater flexibility during the working span, it has many attractions over against the present rigidities of our inherited work patterns. Those work patterns were fashioned to meet the needs of the old factory system when manufacturing was the principal employer of labour and man's working life was regimented by the dictates of the machine. The hours of work were long, the breaks for rest were minimal and the pattern of work's demands was unremitting over the length of the employee's active life span. Engels captures for us the conditions of working life as they existed amongst the textile workers of the early nineteenth century when youngsters were set to work in the mill from their eighth year and continued on into their old age. Speaking of the relentless pace and of the inflexible discipline of the production processes he writes of the hapless operator:

He must not take a moment's rest; The engine moves unceasingly; the wheels, the straps, the spindles hum and rattle in his ears without a pause,

and if he tried to snatch one instant, there is the overlooker at his back
with the book of fines. This condemnation to be buried alive in the mill, to
give constant attention to the tireless machine is felt as the keenest torture
by the operatives, and its action upon mind and body is in the long run
stunting in the highest degree. (2)

During the last 100 years we have moved away from the
debilitating grind of the 70-hour week that Engels so poignantly
described. Both working hours and the length of the working span
have been reduced in their duration. We have also seen an increase
in holiday entitlement which has broken up the pattern of the working year and brought us closer to the previous rhythm of the Middle Ages when official holidays numbered 141 days in each working year and life was a more balanced mix of occupational tasks
and convivial community activities. But still our organisation of
work leaves much to be desired when viewed by those with a concern for human health and wholeness. As John Newton in his
Presidential Address to the Trades Union Congress put it:

Where work gives little or no satisfaction to the worker, where there is no
freedom to exercise talent or skill, where men and women do not deter-
mine how they do their work, where they have become merely components in the production system, they have, during their working lives, lost
their identity as individuals. . . . Nobody who has not experienced the effects of years of confinement within the walls of mass production, without
apparent means of escape, can understand the debilitating effects on the
mind, the vocabulary, on the spiritual capacity of human endurance.
Nobody, without this experience, can really understand why men down
tools, when on the surface there seems to be only a pretext, to escape
momentarily from the monotony of an unnatural existence. (3)

Greater Flexibility

There is still much both in the content and the pattern of working
life which is stunting and confining. For while it may be true that
for the majority the most important thing about work is to have it,
the other half of the paradox about work is that many of those in
employment actually wish they had less of it. Thus for example,
research evidence from the Equal Opportunities Commission
suggests that many women would prefer to work part-time or else
use the advances in telecommunications to work more flexible
hours from home, but that their employers were too rigid to experiment with these creative possibilities. (4) Similarly, many older employees would welcome the possibility of a lighter work load in the
years that lead up to eventual retirement. Sandy Cowie, former

Manpower Services Commission Director for Scotland, who has made a particular study of these matters and who believes that work-sharing has a considerable potential within the United Kingdom, comments:

Many workers at all levels feel the strain, as they get older, of full-time work and for health and other reasons would be happy to work for less than a full working week if that course were available to them. In some instances older people are not capable of a full week's work under pressure perhaps due to health reasons. For some too their monetary needs are less as their family has grown up, their house has been paid up and generally they are feeling better off. In these circumstances the compulsion to earn as much as possible is no longer there. On the principle that it is ridiculous at a time of high unemployment that people should be working for longer hours than they wish, it seems a good idea to encourage on a voluntary basis an easier transition to retirement. (5)

In a recent survey of attitudes to retirement conducted throughout the Common Market countries the idea of a transitional period between work and retirement was one which had a wide margin of support in all the member states. About 70 per cent of those polled favoured the idea of a scheme to reduce work in several stages until retirement age was reached thus making the break from full-time paid employment less traumatic. In this country although there are a sizeable number of older workers opting for the Job Release Scheme in their last working year, there are few if any schemes where the transition is eased by the intervention of part-time work for a period before actual retirement takes place. In Denmark, however, a scheme was introduced in 1979 whereby those over 60 can receive an immediate enhanced pension starting at the same level as unemployment benefit and gradually reducing to the general pension level of 50 per cent of unemployment benefit at the normal pension age of 67 and during this time they can work up to 200 hours a year. The Danish scheme is financed by contributions from both employers and employees and has been taken up by one-third of those eligible. (6)

A more radical arrangement is to be found in the Dutch 'Duo-Banen' system where two people share one job, each person alternating between being a wage earner and recipient of social security. Such 'twinning' and even 'trebling' arrangements are some of the most potentially fruitful of the work-sharing measures explored by Sandy Cowie, and recent research by Professor Eduard Gaugler of Mannheim University shows just how effective in productivity terms such arrangements can be. (7)

In twinning or trebling arrangements two or three people agree to cover what would otherwise be one full-time job. The scheme is particularly attractive to married women desiring to combine a certain amount of part-time work with the care of their children. Many women find that if they want to work they often have to commit themselves to more hours than they would really desire because so much of our present work is parcelled up into only full-time packages. Thus in many cases a second best choice has to be made with the parties concerned being away from home for longer than they would personally desire. Again it makes no sense in a time of chronic unemployment for some individuals to be working longer than they really want to when there are so many registered for work who cannot obtain it. Sandy Cowie in recommending the adoption of a greater measure of twinning and trebling arrangements by employers writes: 'There are social problems resulting from the absence of married women when their children are at home—the problems of "latch-key" children, etc. It is suggested therefore that we should encourage an extension of part-time work and also by "twinning" and "trebling"—an arrangement where two or three women agree to cover one job thereby allowing the job to be covered for all the hours necessary while at the same time allowing them to make suitable arrangements between themselves for the care of their children. This would have the advantage for the firm of cutting down absenteeism which can be considerable due to domestic circumstances. Since the recent changes in the National Insurance contributions position no extra charge is incurred by engaging part-time workers. Furthermore, there is some evidence that productivity among part-time workers is higher and in some instances lunch hours are not necessary, while workers, it is said, can concentrate more effectively for shorter periods.' (8) Although Sandy Cowie specifically mentions married women in his report there is no reason why others should not arrange to 'twin' or 'treble' if they so wish. For example a number of husbands and wives might find it convenient to team up in this way. For single parents full-time working presents particular problems and the 'twinning' or 'trebling' option can often be a very satisfactory solution allowing the participants to make a contribution to the world of work while the other party provides caring cover for both sets of children. Another group who might benefit considerably from an increase in part-time and shared jobs are certain categories of disabled persons. In some cases the nature of the disability may be such that it causes them to tire relatively quickly making it impossible to work a full eight-hour day, but not eliminating the wish or their capacity to undertake a shortened week. Research work undertaken by the Multiple Sclerosis Society would indicate that there may be some 100,000 disabled people in the United Kingdom in this category.

One important additional grouping of potential job-sharers needs also to be mentioned here. For in an imaginative attempt to bring some easement to our present chronic youth unemployment problems a number of employers are beginning to experiment with job-sharing as an adjunct to the Youth Opportunities Programme. Particularly important in this field has been the pioneering work undertaken by GEC Telecommunications Ltd. in Coventry. This company has been sponsoring work experience schemes under YOP for several years and has recruited around 50 per cent of the young people on work experience at the end of their programmes. The other 50 per cent were unable to find jobs when their period of work experience with the company ended. This caused a good deal of concern within the company and so it decided to devise—with the co-operation of the trade unions—a job-sharing scheme which would absorb all their former work experience trainees. Under the scheme, the company recruit young people who have completed six months' work experience under YOP to work for $2\frac{1}{2}$ days per week for half pay for a period lasting 18 months. The young people attend a local college one day per week in their own time in order to improve their general education. They receive tuition in life and social skills and job specific training. Their college fees are paid by the Manpower Services Commission as part of the unified vocational preparation programme. This imaginative response to the now pervasive problem of the low recruitment of ex-YOP trainees began in June 1981 and currently involves 32 pairs of youngsters. At the end of the 18 month period full-time jobs within the company will be found for all the young people taken on under the terms of this scheme. By that time they will have had about two years of training and practical experience and will therefore be able to be considered for a range of jobs which would not be open to school-leavers. The scheme does not involve the company in any additional cost and the young people themselves who are obtaining a wholesome mix of work, training and leisure time all seem very enthusiastic about the scheme. Other employers in the Midlands and elsewhere are reported to be watching the progress of the scheme with a good deal of interest because the general format is one which could be very considerably expanded.

For the employer 'twinning' or job-sharing brings two lots of energy and enthusiasm to the job in hand whilst requiring no extra space or equipment. Thus his on-costs are minimal. Further, by restructuring the organisation of work it is sometimes possible to obtain very significant increases in productivity by removing some of the rigidities and restrictions in past working practice. The German research work on 'twinning' arrangements completed in March 1981 is particularly interesting in this regard.

A year-long survey measured the output differences between full-time employees and half-time, job-sharing employees in 35 medium-size companies in the Rhineland. The results indicated output gains averaging 33 per cent per man-day in a variety of occupations. This is all the more startling in a high-productivity economy where *Leistung* and *Technik*—the German concepts of exemplary performance and a production system to back it up—are already prominent features of the industrial landscape. Difficulties arose in some cases. More people wanted to work mornings than afternoons and full social and legal rights had to be maintained at the employers' expense—full-time work is defined as 15 hours a week or more for this purpose in Germany. Other surveys tend to confirm these results. A Norwegian company, Jonas Oglaend, reports absenteeism of 3 per cent among women workers on its three 'mini-shift' system as against 9 per cent for full-timers. In a large American survey of part-time employment nearly three-quarters of all responding firms noted lower overtime payments, while half reported reduced unit costs. (9)

Variations on the Job-sharing theme

Within the British scene the concept of job-sharing is still fairly new, but within the United States such schemes, which effectively split what is normally a full-time job in two, have been operating on a large scale since the mid 1970s. They have also been developing very successfully within the Swedish economic scene opening up opportunities for part-time work in areas which have traditionally been full-time only. Here in the United Kingdom, however, there is a growing interest in the 'twinning' or job-sharing model. A detailed survey of job-sharing has been recently conducted by the Equal Opportunities Commission, who are very interested in its possibilities and the matter is also being investigated by the Policy Planning Branch of the Manpower Services Commission. (10) Already quite a diverse group of jobs have been split in this way as the EOC survey shows. Since the 1960s job-sharing has been used on a systematic basis by the English clearing banks, where a sizeable number of clerical and secretarial jobs have been split into alternate week jobs.

Currently Lloyds Bank says that 200 of its total 42,000 staff work alternate weeks. At Barclays Bank some 2000 of its 50,000 staff work alternate weeks and a few staff work alternate fortnights and, at National Westminster Bank 600 out of its 60,000 staff work alternate weeks. Midland Bank . . . says that the equivalent of 504 full-time posts are split among job sharers. Other organisations where job-sharing occurs on a systematic basis include Sedgwick Forbes, the insurance brokers, where forty employees share jobs; the Lothian Health Board, where twenty doctors share jobs; and the House of Commons library, where ten staff share jobs. (11)

Some jobs are most conveniently split on a week on/week off arrangement. This is the formula most favoured by employees within the English clearing banks because they can then buy a weekly season ticket and so travel to their work more cheaply. However, outside the financial sector the split week is perhaps the more familiar pattern that is emerging within the British scene. This can be organised on a separate $2\frac{1}{2}$ day basis, others are organised so that the job sharers work the same $2\frac{1}{2}$ days; occasionally job sharers split the week into all mornings and all afternoons and at other times jobs are shared by sharing the particular tasks to be completed. Where an alternating pattern is chosen, the job-sharers usually make use of the same desk and although there is seldom need in many tasks for continuity they often leave each other notes for convenience or give their partner an occasional telephone call. In the House of Commons library, where a job-sharing scheme has been running since 1972, both librarians work separate $2\frac{1}{2}$ days but add on an extra $1\frac{1}{2}$ hours to their week on the day they change over in order to exchange information. At Westminster City Council, the two who share the town planning research officer job both overlap one half day a week so that they can meet each other and attend the weekly team meeting.

The attractiveness of the job-sharing model is that in the best practice arrangements that are now emerging, the job-sharer is given the same rate of pay as full-timers. Wherever possible their conditions should be pro-rata that of the full-time employees within the organisation and those entitlements together with adequate provision for both training and promotion written into a properly negotiated collective agreement. Thus the job-sharer's pay, holiday and sick pay entitlement are set at half the full-timer's and provided the job-sharer is working 16 hours or more a week he can qualify for those employment rights which depend on a certain period of continuous service. Again redundancy pay, maternity pay and unfair dismissal compensation will be available to the job-sharer in exactly the same way as to a full-time worker. If these practices are adhered to then the exploitation which has been a significant feature of much part-time working in the past can be countered.

For the employer the job-sharing model offers a number of advantages in comparison to other work-sharing measures. First, the only additional costs will usually be that the employer has to administer two sets of National Insurance, wages, tax, etc. Because National Insurance is paid as a percentage of wages, currently up to a maximum of £10,400, it costs the employer neither more nor less to employ two job-sharers as opposed to one full-time worker up to this wage band. A similar rule applies with respect to the employer's redundancy payment obligations. Below the wage level of £6250 per annum it will cost the employer no more to split what was previously a full-time job into two and instead engage two job-sharers to fill the post. It is these additional on-costs, sometimes totalling as much as 30 to 40 per cent of the basic wage, which can so frequently deter employers from taking on additional labour, but as Adrienne Boyle points out in her excellent detailed guide to the costs and benefits to employers and employees of the job-sharing model of employment, these on-costs can virtually be discounted and are usually more than counterbalanced by the benefits that accrue. (12)

Second, job-sharing has been shown to assist in the reduction of turnover and absenteeism and there can be an increase in both the quantity and the quality of the work done. 'Both in complex and very tedious jobs concentration is difficult to maintain throughout a full working day/week. Working part-time and sharing enables people to stay fresh, energetic and creative during the hours they are working and thus can lead to increased and improved output.' (13)

A third factor is that of continuity. If a full-time person is ill, on holiday or on maternity leave, the whole job generally stops, or a new and unfamiliar replacement has to be found. With job-sharing at least half the job continues. There is also the possibility of one of the partners standing in for the other on a full-time basis in such an emergency. But there are certain other potential benefits which attract employers. The training of certain key workers can be a very costly business and the employer will be loath to lose their skills. Job-sharing offers the possibility of retaining some of the skills of certain key workers who might otherwise have left altogether for family or health reasons, while at the same time giving a new job-sharing recruit the chance to acquire the skills and experience that are needed for optimum efficiency. In this way it is possible to achieve a 'phasing in' and a 'phasing out' of key staff, thereby avoiding the sharp discontinuities of termination and recruitment which attend the normal full-time working system.

Finally, job-sharing has the advantage to the employer of allowing him to get two heads for the price of one. Thus the planning research officer job at Westminster City Council is shared by two people with different, but complementary backgrounds in the field of town planning expertise. Similarly the arrangements at the House of Commons library, which involve job-sharers researching background information for Members of Parliament, allow the post to carry a broader range of skills. Such a benefit can be of particular importance to the employer who is looking for competence in various areas of expertise. Such a broad range of strengths is something that he would be unlikely to obtain if he was dependent only on one person being in the post, but with two carefully matched and complementary job-sharers all facets of a complex task can be satisfactorily covered.

Feminist Patterns of Work

While it has been women workers who have pioneered the increase in part-time working, particularly within the service sector, and it is women who are largely spearheading the experiments with the 'twinning' form of work-sharing, it may be that these feminist patterns of a more flexible approach to working hours become the norm for all in the years ahead. Almost certainly as we come to harness the full potential of the new technology the past patterning of work is going to undergo change. The number employed within the manufacturing sector is likely to continue to come down with an increasing proportion of the working population finding their employ within the service economy. The advances in microtechnology and telecommunications are freeing us from the necessity of doing all our work in centralised factories and offices and are opening up the possibility that more workers could now be home-based in terms of their employment. The trend towards a reduction in the hours of work per week and the numbers of years

worked within one's total life span will not only continue but be ac-
celerated by yet further productivity advances which will follow in
the wake of greater automation. Thus although paid employment
will remain a significant part of our adulthood it is less likely to
dominate our lives and will be allocated a more subordinate role
allowing other aspects of our humanity the time to flourish and
develop.

In this respect the feminist patterns of work which are already
being developed in this country are important as pointers to what
may be the normative patterns for both men and women in
tomorrow's world. If, as many responsible people now suspect, the
present work crisis is not just a temporary phenomenon, then it
may no longer be possible to provide for every member of a working population the opportunity for Full Employment as Beveridge
understood it. The expectation then was that the ideal norm would
be to work a '3 × 48' pattern of 48 hours a week, for 48 weeks of
the year and for 48 years of your life. However, the dramatic increase in the number of married women who have expressed their
desire to work, coupled to the demographic increase in the number
of young people entering the labour market, now makes it impossible in a time of sluggish growth and rapid technological advance to
fulfil that same social expectation in the 1980s. What is within the
bounds of possibility is that we could find a place for everybody,
whether male or female, young or old, if we based our work expectations more closely on female work patterns.

By the end of the 1970s Britain had one of the highest female
employee activity rates in the whole of the Western world, their
presence constituting 39.1 per cent of the total workforce. (14)
Within that female workforce a significant number are part-time
workers. (15) It has been suggested in some quarters that the appropriate, if chauvinist, approach to the growing unemployment
crisis is to bring about a reversal of the social trend which has
brought more and more women into the paid economy. In other
words to view female employees as a reserve labour force which in
our changed economic situation the nation no longer requires and
to encourage married women in particular to return to the home.
Such proposals should be vigorously resisted on both theological
and strategic grounds. There can be no legitimacy within the terms
of the Gospel for according to women less in the way of opportunities for personal advance and self-fulfilment than is offered to
the male members of our society. Such a policy would have par-

ticularly dire financial effects upon many low income families who
are dependent upon the wife's earnings if they are to remain above
the poverty line. Further, the kind of sex stereotyping which sees
women's proper place as being in the home and the man as the
principal breadwinner who supports her, many now find culturally
unsatisfactory and stifling as an expected lifestyle. Many men have
become aware that in the past their lives have missed out on the
convivial, familial and neighbourly aspects of life and recognise
that being a parent is as much a proper male relationship as it is a
female one. The mood of the times is to move towards more
genuinely 'symmetrical' family patterns.

I believe that Sheila Rothwell is absolutely right when she says
that she can see no merit in the argument that the man has the right
to the job while the woman has the duty to stay at home, or that a
woman has no right to 'take away' a man's job in times of unemployment. Decisions about who works, where, for how much and
for how long should be matters of personal and family choice,
which may well vary at different stages of the individual and family
life-cycle. (16)

To submit once again to the propagation of the old Evangelical
ideology of domesticity would be a deeply retrogressive step and
would set back the clock on the advances that have been made by
the feminist lobby to secure equal opportunities in recruitment,
training and treatment within the world of paid employment. (17) A
considerably more creative response would be for us to use the present circumstances of great economic adversity to look again at
some of those sexist assumptions about work patterns and social
role which presently box us in whether we be male or female. There
is a need to challenge some of these inherited beliefs because many
of these images of male and female role are the very antithesis of
Gospel. They stunt and confine, working to restrict personal
choice, rather than opening up life's possibilities in creative directions for humankind whether male or female. This is not an age for
accepting unchallenged the inherited social conventions. They were
framed in a quite different age and in response to a quite different
set of economic realities. There is then, in this whole area, a proper
place for iconoclasms—for breaking and changing some of our
current images as to roles and lifestyles.

What has been gained in the field of female employment is also
important for strategic purposes for, as Sheila Rothwell, Director
for the Centre of Employment Studies at Henley Administrative

Staff College, points out, female work patterns may provide us with useful leads as to how all work may need to be organised in the future. She urges us 'to look at society and where it is going through feminist spectacles for a change. Then we shall see that while it is probably true that "the old pattern of employment, 9 to 5, five days a week from 16 to 65 is no longer with us", it has *never* been true for half of the population and that female life-time and career patterns of mixed full-time, part-time or no paid employment, of breaks for family responsibilities, or for periods of retraining, could well become the *norm* and should at least be the ideal.' (18) Why, she asks, should we search and research for 'new patterns of working life' when the alternative model already lies to hand, in the lifestyles of half the population? In the world of paid work outside the home, shorter working hours and part-time employment offer a more rational pattern for men as well as women. As job opportunities shrink, job-sharing among men, as well as among women, is perhaps the most sensible and humane response to the present crisis. In family terms too it makes sense for both partners to be able to choose a balance of paid work outside the home and unpaid work inside the home. It is a solution, she suggests, which can mean genuine liberation for both sexes.

Alas, however, in the present economic circumstances there is something of an erosion in part-time employment opportunities and the pendulum is, if anything, swinging in the reverse direction to which Sheila Rothwell desires. Because we are now in a recessionary situation part-time workers, in that they usually have few or no rights of tenure and protection, are the first to be laid off. Part-timers are viewed as the most 'expendable' section of the workforce and, because so many of these part-time workers are female, women have been disproportionately affected by the recent round of job losses. In the author's view such a decline in part-time opportunities of employment in the present circumstances is strategically very regrettable. It further reduces the range of choice open to the individual at varying stages of life and puts the clock back in terms of the more flexible approach to working hours which was beginning to emerge in the 1960s and 1970s. What we are needing at the present time is not an increased regimentation of working hours, so that the only options available are full-time working or nothing, but rather a greater range of choice so that a multiplicity of mixes between paid and unpaid work patterns might emerge. As James Robertson points out, 'Part-time jobs enable people—men and women alike—both to earn an income and to spend time on voluntary work, family raising and DIY work in and around their homes.' (19)

It is the prospect of achieving this wholesome mix of paid economy work and what has been called gift economy work, that would allow for a fuller expression of our humanity than our present rather 'workaholic' existence permits, which has of late excited the imagination of a number of our social visionaries. What they are looking for are ways in which we can so structure life that paid work remains a regular part of our daily being and yet there is quite a lot of time left in the week, in the working year, or within the total working span in which to use our gifts and talents in other creative directions. It is a sort of 'flexilife' pattern which extends the 'flexitime' concept by allowing people to choose what suits them best at different periods of their life. There are times when maximising income levels and advancing career patterns are of prime importance. But there are other times within our active adult span when we yearn for a sabbatical break or would welcome some diminution of working hours and would be prepared to trade off potential earnings against increased discretionary time. However, the present rigidities of employment patterns, career structures and the difficulties which arise in trying to mix income sources make such life options virtually impossible for most people. The question that is now being asked is whether we can use this present period of great adversity to so restructure working-time patterns as to allow a greater range of choice and at the same time open up a greater number of part and full-time employment opportunities for those currently unemployed. The ancillary question which also has to be asked relates to costs, profitability and incomes. How much would it cost to effect such changes nationally, individually, organisationally? For however desirable may be the dreams of the social visionaries, if the on-costs are too high, if commercial profitability in a highly competitive world is to be adversely affected and if personal incomes from all sources prove inadequate then we are likely to continue where we are.

Notes and References

1. This figure assumes that it is not realistic to reduce unemployment below 3 per cent because of frictional factors, etc.

2. Engels, F., *The Condition of the Working Class in England*, published in German in 1845. See Panther edition of English translation of 1892 ed., E. Hobsbawn, p. 204.
3. Mr John Newton in his Presidential Address to 1969 Trades Union Congress.
4. Bird, Emma, *Information Technology in the Office: The Impact on Women's Jobs*, Equal Opportunities Commission Report, September 1980, p. 7.
5. Cowie, A.Y.W., An unpublished paper on Work-Sharing, Edinburgh, 1980, p. 5.
6. *Euroforum* 9/80 May 1980, p. 3. A recent report by a French Ministry of Labour working party advocates a flexible approach to retirement with the hours of work being reduced over the years immediately preceding retirement with any fall in income being partially compensated for out of pension rights.
7. *Guardian*, Business Agenda Column, 3 June 1981.
8. Cowie, A.Y.W., op. cit., p. 4.
9. *Guardian*, 3 June 1981, op. cit.
10. Equal Opportunities Commission Report, *Job Sharing: Improving the Quality and Availability of Part-time Work*, Equal Opportunities Commission, July 1981.
11. *Industrial Relations Review and Report*, No. 225, June 1980.
12. Boyle, Adrienne, *Job Sharing: A study of the costs, benefits and employment rights of job sharers*. A comprehensive report examining in considerable detail the feasibility of job-sharing for individual employees and employers. It also assesses costs/savings to the Government by the implementation and promotion of such work arrangements. Available from Job Sharing Project, 77 Balfour Street, London SE 17, November 1980.
13. *Job Sharing: A Guide for Employees*, The Job Sharing Project, May 1981, p. 14, quoting Equal Opportunities Commission, 1980, Survey results.
14. Bird, Emma, *op. cit.* p. 16, quoting Equal Opportunities Commission, *Third Annual Report*, Manchester, 1979.
15. *id.*, p. 20 giving the proportion of females working part-time in 1976 as 40.1 per cent (from *EOC Research Bulletin*, 1.1, 1978–79, p. 44).
16. Rothwell, Sheila, 'Women and Work', article in *Resurgence*, No. 86, May–June 1981, p. 23.
17. The Evangelicals were staunch members of the Church of England who believed in the reform of the Anglican Church from within rather than seceding from the Church and joining with John Wesley and the Methodists. Within the ranks of the Evangelicals there was an inner grouping called the Clapham Sect who were particularly influential in recodifying the place of women in society. The Evangelicals believed that Nature had decreed that all women were first and foremost wives and mothers and that the values of the domestic life should be highly prized. Men and women were not equal; there was a natural division between the sexes and women's special gifts, responsibilities and duties lay within the domestic sphere. Their teaching came to exercise widespread influence in Victorian England and led to the formulation of an ideology of domesticity with regard to women's proper role which still lingers on despite the counter-offensive mounted by the Feminist Movement. See *Fit for Work*, a collection of papers on the Domestic Ideal, ed. Sandra Burman, Croom Helm in Association with Oxford University Women's Studies Committee, 1979, pp. 15–32.
18. Rothwell, Sheila, op. cit., p. 23.
19. Robertson, James, *The Redistribution of Work*, Turning Point, Paper No. 1, Ironbridge, 1981, p. 13.

Chapter 14

WORK-SHARING OPTIONS

In this chapter we are concerned with the 'How?' of the distribution problem raised in earlier sections of this book. Given that it is socially desirable to distribute job opportunities more equitably throughout the social order, what employment mechanisms might assist us in that task? In a rapidly expanding economy one could hope that economic growth would of itself generate the needed jobs. But that is not the present reality. If there were no constraints on public sector borrowing we could buy ourselves out of trouble with a vast programme of public spending. (1) But although this policy may have short-term attractions in a desperate situation, there are considerable limits to its viability in the long term and it is a long-term structural problem that we are dealing with at the present time. (2) Our solutions therefore require to be sustainable solutions. They have to make structural provision for a more adequate number of job opportunities for the remainder of this decade and yet, in trying to formulate our solutions, we must always remain mindful of the hard financial realities which together form the complexities of our present economic milieu. In a sense they also need to be tentative solutions. No one quite knows how employment patterns will work out towards the end of this decade. Will automation bring in a new Leisure Age in which work reduces to yet smaller proportions in our time budget? Or will social and demographic changes at the end of the decade bring about a shift in the so-called 'dependency ratio' causing us to reverse trends and re-expand working hours in order that a proportionately smaller workforce can cope with the needs of an increased body of dependants? (3) Because even our very best attempt to predict the future of work is never a very exact science there is often considerable merit in adopting policies that retain some measure of flexibility. Ideally we are looking for employment policies that will facilitate the transition towards yet further reductions in working time over a person's life, while at the same time allowing us the option of being able to reverse that trend and, if need be, return once again to something approaching our present workload. In this examination of various work-sharing options I want to begin by looking at those employment policies which would reduce the overall labour force size by taking some of those in the most senior and junior age groups out of the paid economy.

Earlier Retirement

The point which I have just made with regard to 'flexibility' has particular relevance when we come to look at proposals to reduce the age of retirement. Briefly there are three reasons why in terms of policy there has been a general reluctance to reduce the labour supply by bringing forward the age of retirement. The first is on the grounds of cost, the second is cultural and the third reflects an anxiety about the permanency of such a measure. Perhaps it might be helpful to look at these issues in reverse order.

A few years ago policy makers were expressing anxiety about the irrevocable nature of taking action over earlier retirement. If, in the face of rapidly rising unemployment, we brought the official age of retirement forward by, let us say five years, would we ever be able to reverse that decision? What if labour became a scarce resource again? Having set a new social bench-mark for retirement would we ever be able to depart from it? The size of the job gap is, however, now so large that there seems little likelihood that we are going to be faced with a general labour shortage during the remainder of at least this decade whatever economic policies are adopted. It therefore makes a good deal of sense to do what is now at long last being proposed which is to start systematically to reduce the size of the labour supply by releasing more and more people from work at the senior end. Mr James Prior, MP, when Secretary of State for Employment, proposed that we now lower the age for the Job Release Scheme from 64 to 63 in November 1981 and to 62 from February 1982 at a cost of about £150 million in a full year. (4) His proposals, as I understand them, give the Government the opportunity to review the provision in a few years' time and to alter or terminate it if in any way it is not having the desired effects. This softly, softly approach with the possibility of regular review built into the proposals makes a good deal of sense as we feel our way forward into new patterns of working time. My only regret is that it has been so late in coming and is as yet, too little. However, it is a move in the right direction. If the social pattern on the Continent is anything to go by, the opportunity to take up the option of early retiral is likely to be welcomed by many men in the 60-plus age band. Positive results have already been obtained in Belgium and Denmark and more recently France has decided to move firmly in the same direction. (5)

What is being advocated here is not compulsory retirement at 62 but the option to move out from work if parties so wish. In other words the range of choice open to individuals is being enhanced. It is an important policy principle to build into not only the early retirement schemes but also into most of the other work-sharing strategies. It takes time to bring about cultural adjustments, and any move towards sudden and compulsory retirement might well bring in its wake certain social and medical problems which could be avoided by a more sensitive framing of the legislation. However, there are many who have worked long and hard within their occupations and who now desire to lay down that burden at the earliest possible moment. They have made their contribution within the paid economy and they would now like to move out while still possessing the health and vigour to make a good transition into the next stage of life with all its opportunities to engage in a range of alternative activities beyond the world of work. The present alterations to the Job Release Scheme are estimated as being capable of freeing some 50,000 individuals in this way but additional proposals by our own Government and the EEC could bring about a quiet cultural revolution throughout Western Europe that would further reduce the labour supply by reducing the working span. We still have quite a long way to go in this respect. For example in May 1980 the *Employment Gazette* noted that there were about a million people above working age who were in some way still included in the labour force. (6) If we could persuade more in the older age groupings to move out of the paid economy and instead make their continued contribution to society in what Peter Cadogan and others are calling the 'gift economy' of voluntary activity and neighbourly care, then we could free a considerable number of part and full-time jobs within the European scene. (7) For the departure of older workers starts off a process of job rotation which can do much to improve the prospects of younger workers and at the same time frees jobs which can be taken up by those currently unemployed. It is in this way that early and voluntary retiral schemes affect employment in a more positive and direct way than virtually any other work-sharing measure.

An alternative policy option would be to bring forward the official date of retirement. Estimates made by the Department of Employment in 1978 indicated that if retirement age for men was brought forward from 65 to 60 years, to bring them in line with women, the impact would be to reduce registered unemployment by nearly 200,000 in the first year of operation, building up to nearly 600,000 eventually. The net cost to the Exchequer at 1978 prices would have been in the order of just over £1000 million. (8)

In the present circumstances I believe that we need to do everything in our power to make an earlier retiral more culturally acceptable. We know that already there is a considerable desire for greater flexibility with respect to retirement and that there is a particularly marked desire for phased arrangements allowing our commitment to work to be reduced in stages. Thus moves in this direction run with the grain of public aspiration. We also know that one of the chief factors determining whether individuals wish to remain economically active is the impact which that withdrawal will have on the household's net income. Thus adequate financial provision for all early retirees is of crucial importance if we wish to obtain maximum participation in any voluntary scheme. Increasing the provision of pre-retirement courses would also help. These need now to be targeted towards the needs of the younger age bands and towards those occupational groups which as yet have not obtained the benefit of being released from work to attend these schemes. Above all greater thought needs to be given to the integration of early retirees into the local community. In attitude, interests and life situation these younger age bands form a quite different group of retirees to those who have been retiring under the previous pension arrangements. The special needs of this younger client group require to be met both in the pre-retirement course syllabuses and in the community. Pensioners, of whatever age, need to feel that they have a place in the community. They, like all human beings, need to feel that they are needed. They need to be made to feel that they still have a precious contribution to make and that their presence counts. For early retirees, many of whom will still be in the full vigour of their late fifties and early sixties, the opportunity to make a satisfying and active contribution to the local community is all important for their sense of self-esteem. It is here that we may see a growing role for the voluntary organisations and the churches, the volunteer bureaux and the skill exchange centres who can help in the task of matching gifts to needs in a range of exciting and imaginative ways. For within this grouping of early retirees is to be found a wealth of talent, experience, technical skill and administrative expertise and a range of agencies need to learn how to effectively tap these human resources and put them to creative purpose for the enhancement of local community life.

There are, of course, a number of actuarial costs involved in bringing forward retiral dates and ensuring that proper financial provision is made for these retirees. The gross costs certainly are daunting. On the other hand, as with a lot of work-sharing measures, there would be a compensating reduction in Exchequer expenditure on transfer payments paid to those currently unemployed. Despite the size of the cost, in the light of other forms of relief being unavailable, it may be a cost which offers us a best choice in the easement of high unemployment rates particularly in the 16–25-year-old age band. Where cost choices have to be made, it would make particular sense to give the option of early retirement to those workers who have been engaged in tasks which tend to be injurious to health. These workers form a particular priority category for early retirement schemes. Thus the move to bring down the age of retirement not only for the physically handicapped, the miners, etc., but for other groupings also, is the sort of humane provision which should be especially encouraged.

Employment Policies Affecting the Youngest Age Bands

As well as siphoning off many older employees from the labour force through the mechanism of the Job Release Scheme and early retirement, it is also possible to reduce the labour supply figures by encouraging the potentially youngest age bands to stay in school, further education and training for longer periods. A well-framed system of grants can have this beneficial effect by providing some inducement to delay immediate entry into the paid economy in order to obtain better qualifications. As I will wish to emphasise in the next chapter, there is an urgent need to do more in this country in the whole field of work preparation and training. Far too many youngsters in Britain are still leaving school with a record of poor academic achievement and ill-equipped for the modern world of work. Whereas in Germany and France a great deal of effort has gone into making more adequate provision for all those entering the labour force, in Great Britain about one-third of our young people leave school without having acquired any academic qualification and virtually a half enter into work without ever receiving any further education and training. (9) In the modern world of work there is going to be less and less place for the totally unskilled and untrained individual and their long-term job prospects are going to become increasingly tenuous. It is therefore imperative, if we are not to build up yet greater unemployment problems in the future, that our young people are given a better start to working life. Ideally this would entail proper vocational preparation for all 16–17 year olds not presently moving on to Further Education. Like the German national training scheme it would offer both 'hands on' working experience within ordinary employers' premises and 'off the job' training. Moves are afoot at the time of going to press to build such a scheme using the assets that we already have to hand in the recently established Youth Opportunities Programme. Here within this national scheme a useful network of links has already been established between employers, the training services, careers staff and further education establishments. If such an ambitious training programme can be put together and funded, then not only will it have the statistical effect of reducing the level of labour supply but, far more importantly, young people in Britain in the lower ability ranges will be given a much better introduction to working life than has previously been available to them. For in the past the provision of a properly planned introduction to working life has only been available to the more able school leaver. In the scheme which James Prior when Secretary of State was so strongly advocating the planned introduction into the adult world of work would become available to all ability groups. Thus the young person on leaving school would either go on to higher education in some form or other, or else move into work. But in moving into work they would do so via a planned traineeship or preparation which would be constructed along the lines of the German national training scheme and which would be likely to include the best of the training features now available in our own Youth Opportunities Programme. Because organisationally such a scheme would grow out of the present Youth Opportunities Programme and the smaller Unified Vocational Preparation Programme, a sizeable portion of its estimated £1 billion cost has in fact already been set aside in the advance Treasury estimates under the heading of youth training costs. (10) Further, such state-funded programmes which are intended to provide training and work experience for the young can qualify for European Social Fund support, thereby reducing the net costs to our own Exchequer very considerably. (11)

A New Shape to Work

The general outline for a possible future shape to work is beginning to emerge out of the old as a result of our examination of some of these proposals and pilot initiatives. That new shape to work would be characterised by a reduced commitment to paid employment over each individual's life span. It would entail a cultural accommodation to expectations of an earlier retiral. Such an earlier retiral date would leave us free to redeploy from the formal economy into the informal and gift economies in the later stages of our active life. (12) In such a forward situation expectations with regard to the termination of working life would come to have a less sharply defined edge. Because some people would be opting to move out of the paid economy, perhaps in their late fifties, while others continued on perhaps in a part-time capacity for a few years longer, the effect would be to blur the present rather sharp divide between the working and the retired. It would make the transitions and adjustments more gradual and the process of parting from work less painful. Rather than there being an abrupt termination of working life, the transition into full retirement would be phased. We would have time to discover new centres of creative interest whilst still retaining some of the old. The whole process of discovering a satisfying alternative rhythm to our lives and a new balance of priorities could take place more slowly, more naturally, more humanely.

At the other end of the age scale we would have constructed a more effective bridge between the world of school and the adult world of work. Our young people would be better equipped, whatever their ability level, to earn their living because they all would have had a planned introduction to the disciplines and demands of work. The hope is that in the process they would be able to acquire a cluster of transferable occupational skills that would give them a certain flexibility in the labour market, and a range of mid-life training provision would enable them to update and enhance their skills in a continuing process over their whole working span. Meanwhile, having thinned the numbers actively engaged within the paid economy in the senior age range and also having removed all the 16- and 17-year-olds from the labour market, an increase in job-sharing or twinning arrangements as described in the previous chapter might prove an attractive option for certain individuals in the middle age bands at particular stages of their working lives. The numbers opting for this lifestyle, especially in mid-life when financial commitments loom large, might not be very great. But it would provide for yet another option. Similarly, the number of organisations able to offer the opportunity for flexitime working, an increase in contract work, short secondments, or those able to build the option of short sabbatical breaks into the working span may be small. But cumulatively all these options, opportunities and variants from the norm are important. It is out of these experiments and innovations that new working patterns for all may begin to emerge. This is the seedbed out of which new social arrangements and new cultural expectations may arise which may be better fitted to meet future needs than some of our inherited work patterns which were formulated in quite different social and economic circumstances.

In addition to all these advantages, these variants and experiments in working patterns would help to break down the present sharp divides between being an *employed person*, a *retired person* or an *unemployed person*, with all the cramping stereotype expectations which attach to those conditions. Instead we would begin to see the emergence of a great mix of life options. Individuals would have a much greater degree of choice as to how much they wished to work for the financial rewards of the paid economy and how much they wanted to obtain other benefits, satisfactions and rewards through a fuller commitment at various stages of their lives to the informal and gift economy.

The Arena of Hard Choices: The Selection of Social Priorities

However, having outlined a number of proposals to reduce the overall number of those men, women and young people actively looking for paid work opportunities, we are still left with a major residual problem. However attractive these variants may eventually prove to be, at this point of time we are still left with a major distributive problem in that we have an excess of claimants and very few job vacancies. In such a situation what mechanisms of distribution are available to us? What policy options are open to us when work is such a scarce resource and we are confronted by the acute needs of so many? Are there any ways in which we could achieve a greater measure of social equity with respect to access to paid employment and its concomitant rewards?

The moral, the technical and the political problems that confront us when seriously attempting to redistribute work are all very sharp in character. Thus in ethical terms, how are we to calculate during a period of work scarcity what is each individual's due? On what basis are our judgments to be made? Should the young take precedence of claim over against the senior age bands who have already experienced steady employment for most of their lifetime with all its attendant benefits? Should sexist solutions to the dilemma over unemployment be allowed to prevail? Is it morally acceptable to treat women as some kind of reserve labour force, having encouraged them to enter work in a time of labour shortage, but now that a period of work scarcity has arisen encouraging their return to the home so that men might have work in preference? Should those fortunate enough to have higher family income be called upon to make the greater sacrifice because in lifestyle they are already so far beyond the poverty line? It is much easier to ask the questions than to find a solid and broadly agreed base for judgement.

In a situation of hard choices, where so many would lay claim to the available work, are there any criteria that would guide us in the framing of distributive policy? For myself I am convinced that sexual discrimination against female claimants to work and its benefits must be resolutely resisted in the search for satisfactory solutions to this most difficult social issue. I would also hold a bias of preference for the young claimant to work and towards the claims of the poor. For the young to miss out on the socialising aspects of the discipline of paid employment would, I suspect, sharpen the divisions between the generations. It would endanger future social cohesion and damage mutual understanding and respect. For the workplace is one of the significant places where the various generations are put alongside each other in a common activity. If the young miss out on that experience in their formative years it is likely to leave a major gap for which it will be hard to find an adequate compensation.

For the poor not to have access to additional finances through work, places unacceptable constraints on present lifestyles. Further, it probably predetermines a life of continued deprivation through into the next generation. Older employees, however, and the more affluent households have, respectively, resources of experience and finance which may better equip them to survive some measure of curtailment in their work opportunities than, say, the young and the poor. On ethical grounds, therefore, when pushed to make hard choices among a variety of claimants for work I would exercise what Professor Philip Wogaman has called a 'moral presumption' in favour of sexual equality, in favour of the young who as yet have had no experience of work and in favour of the poor who have need of adequate financial resources for the living of their lives. (13)

Two other social considerations might also be briefly caught in here. The first is a particular concern for the long-term unemployed. Because of the now well-documented social and psychic damage caused by the experience of long-term unemployment this is a client group which I believe should have a bias of preference with regard to job opportunities. (14) Somehow we need to devise the mechanisms which will ensure that the human experience of long-term unemployment is eliminated from our society. It is such a corrosive condition that every effort must be made to pick up those who have been unable to secure permanent employment after six months and offer them something more constructive than the indeterminate continuance of their enforced idleness. A much stronger social preference needs to be exercised towards these groups in terms of recruitment to normal employment, to government-sponsored training and to a range of national reconstruction projects. Employers and trade unionists, who act as the 'gatekeepers' in our society to the world of paid employment, have a particularly important role in this regard. More than anyone else it is in the hands of employers and the trade unions whether or not those who have been unemployed for some considerable time are re-engaged when the upturn comes. If the long-term unemployed are to get the break that they are looking for, then those who regulate the recruitment process need to play their part in being far more open towards exercising some form of positive discrimination in favour of those who have been locked out of work for a long time. One is reluctant to use the mechanism of fixed quotas and incentive grants to encourage employers and trade unionists towards a more active recruitment of the long-term unemployed, but the social problem is now so large that we may have to consider the relative merits of such 'stick and carrot' devices.

The second social concern relates to the employment needs of the disabled and the availability of suitable work opportunities for those born with low intelligence. The inexorable drive towards greater and greater efficiency within the world of work, whether it be in manufacturing or the service industries, is tending to erode many of the jobs which in more labour-intensive times could be given to those members of the community who had a physical disability or who were of limited intelligence. These two distinct groupings both share the same need for fulfilling work opportunities—for opportunities to become integrated with the rest of the community through shared participation in the activity of work and for opportunities to use their gifts and skills, thus demonstrating their many areas of capability. In attempting to squeeze every ounce of efficiency out of our economic system it seems that we may also be in danger of permanently removing from employment many men and women who have some measure of disability acquired either at birth or by accident in later life, but who are highly motivated to work and who have much to contribute through work. If this is the case then it may be that we should quite deliberately forsake the attempt to win the last half percentage of efficiency in our organisation of work processes, preferring to retain within the economy certain carefully designated labour-intensive and unsophisticated tasks which might be undertaken by those born with lower intelligence who in each generation will need such provision and adopting a policy of retaining a range of other tasks suited to the considerable capabilities of various physically disabled categories.

I have set these preferences down because we are in a hard choice situation with regard to the current availability of work and there needs to be perhaps a greater measure of open debate as to agreed preferred groups. These are not matters in which it is easy to secure definitive positions. We are caught into the realm of uneasy compromise and conflicting claims upon the scarce resource of work. But consideration of these matters is profoundly important if we are genuinely probing for the best human solution to an impossibly difficult situation. For it is as we lay these moral preferences like a template against the existing social arrangements that we begin to see where the thrust of change should be directed.

However much we may desire to bring about some alteration in work patterns in order to meet the demands of both justice and compassion, there is no way in which we can avoid the painful recognition that the practical difficulties are considerable. The practical difficulties of achieving a yet greater measure of work-sharing fall into two principal camps. On the one hand there are the technical organisational problems involved in changing accustomed work practice. On the other hand there are difficult political decisions to be made with regard to the appropriate allocation of concomitant costs.

Let us look at some of the technical problems which we would encounter if we were to decide to move further towards a deliberate policy of work-sharing. The organisation of work in modern industrial societies is a highly complex and sophisticated business. One therefore encounters a wide range of purely technical and pragmatic problems in attempting to reapportion working time in such a way that a greater number can participate in the satisfaction and rewards that paid work brings.

The Vexed Issue of Overtime Working

Let us begin by taking the case of overtime working. A study of the *Employment Gazette* figures for the number of hours of overtime worked within British manufacturing industry reveals that even in a recessionary period an inordinately large amount of overtime is still being worked. From 1977 to 1979 overtime working remained fairly constant at about 15 million hours per week. During this period some 34 per cent of all operatives were working overtime, each averaging about 8.6 extra hours every week. By July 1981 when about three million people were now without any opportunity of work still 26.6 per cent of all operatives in British manufacturing industry were getting regular overtime work. In other words the additional workload was being undertaken by the existing labour force rather than resorting to additional recruitment. Each existing operative who was still engaged in overtime working in July 1981 was averaging 8.3 extra hours a week, a cumulative total within British manufacturing industry of some 9,240,000 hours every week. Further, there are indications as this book goes to press that overtime working looks set to expand and there are grave fears that should there be any upturn in the economy employers will continue to use the overtime device to cope with the additional work generated and that it will really be some time before the economic upturn has a significant impact on the recruitment of those still unemployed. In other words recovery will be overtime led rather than recruitment led.

Prima facie the knowledge that the number of man hours being worked on a premium rate overtime basis remains sufficient to create some hundreds of thousands of extra full-time jobs is, as

TUC General Secretary Len Murray says, an affront to the unemployed. The credibility of fraternity is seriously eroded by the persistence of regular overtime. Yet when one comes to challenge that
state of affairs a barrage of technical excuses for the retention of
the status quo are proffered by both management and the trade
unions. There are the extra costs to be incurred when employing
organisations have to resort to the recruitment of additional labour,
rather than utilising the device of overtime to get the necessary
work done. There are constraints with regard to equipment. If extra
people are taken on, the employer may also need to supply these
additional workers with extra workbench space, tools, machinery,
overalls, etc. There are problems with regard to manpower planning and the sometimes variable flow of work. The extra rush of
work which has triggered off overtime working may prove to be
only short-lived.

From the trade unions there are protests that many low-paid
workers are dependent upon regular overtime working in order to
make something like a living wage. To cut overtime would throw
these very low-paid workers into a position where their net income
for a basic working week was less than that of the unemployed.
(15) But beneath these genuine technical difficulties there is also a
resistence to reform on the grounds of vested interest. For many
workers: 'Happiness is two nights and a Sunday!' The extra
premium payments received through overtime arrangements
become part of the expected earnings pattern and household expenditure rises accordingly. Thus, although often highly inefficient
from the productivity angle and socially undesirable in terms of
health and family life, regular overtime working has become part of
a way of life for many British workers. It has become institutionalised, hallowed in custom and practice and highly resis-
tant to change.

Yet in a time when there is a chronic shortage of job vacancies it
surely remains an affront that some should be working excessive
hours and others in that same community remain totally deprived
of work. Further, the retention of overtime working acts as a major
obstacle when attempting to promote other work-sharing reforms.
The attempts by trade union bargainers to further reduce the length
of the working week towards a target of 35 hours will inevitably be
resisted by the employers who have become persuaded by past experience that moves to reduce the length of the official working
week merely have the effect of increasing the number of hours of

overtime which are then worked at premium or higher rates of pay. This is, of course, counterproductive in terms of industrial efficiency in that it adds to unit costs and in terms of recruitment no benefit accrues to the unemployed.

Although there are sometimes genuine problems in grouping 'lost' overtime hours into part or full-time job units, thereby opening the way to recruit those presently unemployed, there is nevertheless considerable scope for the creation of additional jobs by placing more stringent curbs on overtime working. From an ethical point of view, on the grounds of health and family well-being, and on productivity grounds, I believe that an indiscriminate acceptance of overtime working requires to be challenged. The reduction of overtime is part of the wider move to bring about a general reduction in working time over life. Further, the achievement of local agreements which will have the effect of placing responsible curbs on the number of hours of overtime being worked is strategically an important prerequisite for success with other related measures designed to bring about a shortening of the working week. For as long as there remains recourse to overtime, there tends to be an avoidance of recruitment. In strategic terms, it is recruitment of a greater number into the employment pool, each for a shorter period of time, that work-sharing devices are trying to promote.

One further point might be made here. In terms of employment policies it would be helpful if we could secure some reduction in the present level of contribution made by employers into the National Insurance fund. These employers' National Insurance contributions, which have to be paid out in addition to wages for each person engaged, certainly act as a major disincentive to recruitment and are regarded by many as a tax on employment. If we wish to encourage recruitment rather than overtime, some downward adjustment of these rates might prove a helpful stratagem.

Not all overtime could be eliminated. Companies faced with a fluctuation in their work-flow require some device whereby they can accommodate to spasmodic increases in their workload and overtime is a device which gives that flexibility in manpower planning. Nevertheless, there is a growing consensus within the Common Market that the practice of systematic overtime is undesirable, that it should be examined critically and wherever possible it should be revised downwards. (16) In doing so, particular regard needs to be given to the effect that this would have on the earnings of the lowest paid. However, the scandal of low pay, which currently is estimated to affect some four million adults, is not best dealt with by forcing them to work excessive hours in order to bring their take home pay marginally above the poverty line. (17) Instead action on minimum wage rates, increases in child benefit payments and possibly the introduction of some form of negative income tax, may prove to be a better way of dealing with the very real needs of the working poor. More vigorous action on that front would remove one long-standing obstacle to moving ahead in a strategic assault on systematic overtime working by many others much further removed from the so-called 'poverty line'.

Notes and References

1. *Unemployment: The Fight for TUC Alternatives*, Trades Union Congress, January 1981, *passim*.
2. Harris, Ralph, et alia, *Job Creation—or Destruction*, Six Essays on the Effects of Government intervention in the Labour Market, The Institute of Economic Affairs, 1979, *passim*.
3. The Dependency Ratio is the number of dependants (defined as those below 16 and people over retirement age) per 1000 persons of working age. In 1941 it was only 488, by 1972 it had grown to 679. The 1980s are expected to bring a steep rise in the volume of the working population in EEC countries. But in the 1990s as a result of population trends the numbers of economically active persons in the EEC is expected to drop sharply.
4. *Guardian*, 28 July 1981.
5. *Communication from the Commission to the Council on Worksharing*, Commission of the European Communities, Brussels, 7 May 1979, Part I.
6. *Employment Gazette*, May 1980, p. 498.
7. Cadogan, Peter, *Direct Democracy*, 1 Hampstead Hill Gardens, London NW3, 1975. See also James Robertson, *The Sane Alternative*, James Robertson, Ironbridge, 1978, pp. 52ff.
8. *Department of Employment Gazette*, March 1978, p. 284.
9. *A New Training Initiative*, MSC Consultative Document, Manpower Services Commission, May 1981, Annex 1.
10. The Youth Opportunities Programme which in 1980/81 had the task of providing work experience and training for some 550,000 young people, was allocated a budget of £271 million in November 1980 to which a further £93 million was added in July 1981. The Unified Preparation Programme which has an allocated budget of £2.1 million in 1982/83 rising to £4.5 million in 1983/84 is directed towards those young people who enter jobs where little or no systematic training or further education is provided. The broad aim of this latter programme is to help young people acquire the skills needed to carry out specific tasks at work, to develop attitudes and knowledge which will enable them to play their part in the working community and to improve their job performance. At the present time an expansion of the Unified Preparation Programme is planned so that by 1983/84 at least 20,500 places are available.

11. The Manpower Services Commission has estimated that the gross out-turn expenditure on the 1979/80 Special Programmes would be £176 million. The European Social Fund contribution to the Youth Opportunities Programme portion would be £24 million, while savings on supplementary benefits and unemployment benefits and additional receipts to the Exchequer from taxes both direct and indirect would combine to reduce the actual net cost to the public purse to £71 million. *Review of the Second Year of Special Programmes*, Manpower Services Commission, 1981, 3.10–3.11.

12. 'Gift work' is work we do for love, for ourselves or for others, such as arts and crafts, gardening, growing our own vegetables, do-it-yourself home and car maintenance, or voluntary work where we give time in order to supplement the social services. None of this gift work is priced in our present society, nor is it reckoned with in the economists' thinking, yet it represents a vital sector in personal and social life.

13. Wogaman, Philip, *A Christian Method of Moral Judgement*, SCM Press, 1976, pp. 40ff.

14. See the research work of Dr Harvey Brenner, the American medical sociologist. His American studies have led him to conclude that acute pathological disturbances such as homicide and suicide tend to rise within a year of increased unemployment rates, while deaths from illness such as cirrhosis of the liver or heart disease surge upwards a few years after the unemployment rate increases. Meanwhile the researches of Dr Leonard Fagin, Consultant Psychiatrist at Claybury Hospital, Essex, undertaken for the Department of Health and Social Security in 1980/81 indicate that unemployment over an extended period often causes depression, sleeplessness, drink problems and physical symptoms such as asthma and backache in individuals and stress and conflict within families.

15. *Low Pay—1980s Style*, Low Pay Review 4, Low Pay Unit, March 1981, pp. 4–5.

16. *EEC Commission Proposals on Work Sharing*, 21 March 1978, p. 35; and *Communication from the Commission to the Council on Work-Sharing*, 7 May 1979, Annex 1, pp. 2–3. The Commission of the European Communities, Brussels.

17. Low Pay Review 4, *op. cit.*, pp. 1–4.

Chapter 15

POSITIVE EMPLOYMENT POLICIES

The aim of all work-sharing initiatives is to redistribute the total volume of work in the economy in such a way as to increase employment opportunities for all those wishing to work. A policy of Full Employment is probably no longer politically attainable within the time span of this decade. But a variety of attempts to create a more flexible and fluid approach to employment patterns may help to open up more part-time work and more contract work. I am increasingly convinced that what we should be advocating is a whole package of positive employment measures. These would include a variety of incentives to reduce working time over life. Facilitating earlier retiral dates, part-time working options, sabbatical breaks and making available greater access to education and training throughout the working span would all help to reduce the time that any one individual was actually in work. It would give us time to do other significant things as human beings, whilst at the same time spreading work opportunities more evenly throughout the whole community. However, these changes in working patterns, which would take time to introduce, would need to be complemented by other devices that would give the opportunity of purposeful work to those currently unemployed. In this respect I think that in framing a policy for increased employment opportunities there is a place for a carefully targeted and responsibly financed programme of public works. I am apprehensive about some current proposals just to 'throw money at unemployment', to use Prime Minister Margaret Thatcher's somewhat derisory phrase. However, I am persuaded that a carefully prepared list of priority tasks in the field of industrial regeneration and urban renewal could be drawn up and a very considerable number of worthwhile jobs created around those strategic projects.(1) These could include the development of alternative energy sources, the construction of better port facilities, the electrification of the railways, building projects linked to the urgent task of inner city renewal, the replacement of our crumbling housing stock, sewer systems and prison facilities. These are all urgent maintenance and development tasks and it is incumbent upon the Treasury to find the means of financing them. It is not just that these measures would produce much needed jobs but also that there is a great need to undertake many of these tasks. Prudent expenditure in these areas can in fact often help reduce other costs, as is the case in many energy saving and energy creating projects. Even in the midst of economic difficulty it is still vitally important that we regenerate our industrial base, improve communication networks and rebuild and replace what is now obsolete. Not to do so is as likely to mortgage the future as is a pattern of profligate and unsustainable expenditure. The added bonus would be that a great number of people would be helped, particularly in the construction trades, to find purposeful work in a range of worthwhile endeavours throughout the length and breadth of the land.

Experience within the Common Market has shown that to be an effective instrument work-sharing requires a prudent and diversified approach and that the best results are achieved where there is a careful orchestration of a variety of measures which are then used in combination to achieve movement in a desired socio-economic direction. Work-sharing is not a panacea. It is not a substitute for a proper economic policy. But there are signs that within the EEC member states there is a growing consensus amongst finance, economic and labour ministers that work-sharing and moves towards earlier retirement are instruments that must be more vigorously applied in the fight against unemployment.(2)

Although at the time of writing the British Government has yet to be persuaded of the effectiveness of these measures, such broad agreement among our Common Market partners is of prime importance. For one of the principal fears expressed in the past has been that of taking unilateral action on the work-sharing front and thereby perhaps weakening our international competitiveness. These objections which have been frequently raised at the national level would be substantially overcome if the ten EEC governments can agree to work in consort on this matter. There would of course be the problems posed with respect to competitiveness vis-à-vis non-member countries and as they remain strong rivals in certain sectors it would be necessary to keep the additional cost burdens of the altered work patterns as low as possible. However, unemployment is a growing international problem and any EEC initiative might help considerably towards obtaining corresponding action in other non-member countries.

Assessing and Allocating the Costs

The most powerful argument against the effectiveness of a range of work-sharing measures is the cost burdens that they entail. It is important therefore to look at this feature of the proposals with some care. To do so in depth in this book is not possible, but certain general observations might be helpful. A recent EEC study document identified six areas where the costs of introducing work-sharing might possibly fall.(3) Such measures as we might wish to introduce, in order that work opportunities might be spread more equitably throughout the population, could have an affect on:

Individual incomes.
The tax burden on the working population.
The cost structure of the individual firm.
The competitive position of the sector.
The social security system.
Public expenditure.

Broadly speaking, these financial effects might be subdivided into 'private' and 'public', which as a general rule counterbalance each other. That is, if costs arise on one side, there is usually some easement of a financial burden on the other. For example, the cost of unemployment to the public is enormous. If that public cost is eased by giving to some of the unemployed jobs that have been created through a series of work-sharing measures then the costs of such work-sharing need to be balanced against the costs of unemployment to society if no work-sharing occurs. Even by the financial year 1979/80 when unemployment had not yet reached its present peak some two-fifths of the public sector borrowing requirement (PSBR) was being attributed to the cost of unemployment. This constituted a net financial cost of nearly £4000 million when unemployment stood at only 1.335 million. When commenting on these figures the Manpower Services Commission quite properly reminded those reading their report that these costs could not be totally eliminated, 'but reducing unemployment to the assumed minimum sustainable registered unemployment level of 700,000 would almost halve these financial costs down to £2075 million.'(4) As already indicated, a revised MSC estimate of the current unemployment costs made in November 1981 put the charge to the Exchequer in transfer payments and revenues foregone on the basis of 2.84 million unemployed at £12,447 million. In 1979/80 the MSC had put the total cost to the Exchequer of each additional 100,000 registered unemployed at £300 million. The more recent estimate of £438 million per 100,000 given in a Department of Employment written Parliamentary answer indicates a staggering 46% increase over the previous calculations. The main reason for this very steep increase in the cost of unemployment is that in the last few years a very much larger proportion of skilled and better paid workers have become unemployed. As a direct consequence the cost of the earnings related payments went up as did loss from taxes and national insurance contributions.

These figures clearly indicate that running the economy at high levels of unemployment is exceedingly costly in terms of losses to the Exchequer. Furthermore, it can be seen as a basically negative form of governmental expenditure, being paid out not to create positive and purposeful ends but merely to keep those who are motivated to work in a condition of enforced dependency on the state. The case for trying to save public money by getting Britain back into productive work is overwhelming for economic as well as social reasons. Therefore every creative suggestion that might lead us to that end needs to be actively explored. Even if certain employment creation measures were introduced which did nothing to reduce our overall level of public expenditure, but which nevertheless could be seen to be making substantial inroads into the present unacceptably high levels of unemployment, they would still merit public support. For then at least the expenditure would be being used to more positive account. Instead of the spectacle of men and women wasting away in circumstances of enforced idleness, public monies would be used to enable them to become productive once again. The money would be used to bring hope to those whose lives have been trapped for too long into despair and the creativity of a people would be liberated once again. Thus it is important in all our discussions over levels of expenditure that we bear in mind not just the quantitative amounts but also the broader qualitative end results of such expenditure by examining its impact upon the life and morale of the nation.

Work-sharing does involve costs. The act of sharing always costs somebody something. The question is how much would it cost and how might those costs be reasonably distributed amongst various parties? For example, it may be quite legitimate for the state to bear some of the costs of subsidising work-sharing initiatives if it is going to be making equivalent savings in certain other areas of public expenditure. It might also be claimed that if certain portions of the private sector are able to achieve a marked increase in their profitability through the introduction of labour displacing devices and those who continue to remain in their employ are able to receive enhanced salaries and wages as a direct consequence, that something of those benefits ought to be creamed off by some fiscal means to assist in the future employment of those who have been thus displaced. Obviously such fiscal mechanisms would need to be set in such a way that they would not act as a total disincentive to technological advance. On the other hand, the costs to the state and the loss of a livelihood by those made redundant in such a process cannot be discounted. However, one further cautionary point might be made here. We have seen during this recession a great number of British manufacturing firms 'going to the wall'. Others have manfully struggled through painfully difficult times and have just managed to maintain their viability. For many of these firms additional on-costs imposed on them at this point of time would force them to cease trading altogether. Such a consequence of introducing work-sharing measures would be totally self-defeating. The greatest care therefore needs to be exercised when devising policies for the distribution of costs. We would need to protect those whose profit margins are already precariously low. It is imperative that we do nothing that will inadvertently inflict yet further damage to our vital wealth-creating manufacturing sector and future policy will need to be framed accordingly.

Finally, the individual who opts to transfer from full-time to part-time work and who thereby obtains more leisure, or those who bargain for a reduction in the working week, must expect that there will be attendant sacrifices in either real or anticipated incomes. Staying at the individual level, those parties who are fortunate enough to have high earnings and security of employment in these troubled times must expect to have to bear a considerably higher level of taxation which in part may be used to subsidise work creating and work-sharing measures that will be of assistance to their unemployed brethren who share citizenship of the one nation state. The wealthy and the secure have obligations towards those who have become marginalised and it is a responsibility of good government to ensure that those who have been well favoured in life meet in full measure their social obligations towards the disadvantaged. Careful attention therefore needs to be made to the working of our tax system which can be used either to join or divide a nation in a time of economic difficulty and personal hardship.

Work-Sharing within the Framework of Other Positive Employment Policies

In rounding off my comments on some of the possibilities that lie latent in the realm of work-sharing it might be helpful to say something on the merit of such initiatives within the slightly broader framework of overall employment policies. The great economic determining realities which exercise influence over employment rates in Great Britain are very different from those which prevailed in the 1940s and which exercised the minds of men like Beveridge and Keynes. Escalating energy costs, the introduction of the new technology, Britain's changed place in the global trading scene, the decline of many of our more labour-intensive industries and a fast-moving market for quite new products and services are all changes to which the nation's employment patterns must adapt. If we fail to respond swiftly enough to these realities then economically we perish. But alongside these accommodations to the prevailing economic determinants one can also discern other subtle changes taking place. Changes in the level of expectation with regard to incomes and living standards. A concern about the quality of working life, the acceptable nature of certain tasks, hours of work, holiday and pension entitlements. These pressures, which reflect a desire by employees to be given greater scope for the expression of their humanity both within and beyond the institution of work, also have their moulding effect. They emanate from human aspiration and work themselves out in ways which come to influence job design, wage rates, inflation rates and socially preferred employment patterns. To these pressures of the market and human aspiration a third now has to be added. It comes not from within the world of work but from those who are unable to enter it. For once again, following on the post-war boom, paid employment has become a scarce resource. Jobs are in short supply and the intense demand for job opportunities creates major pressures within the social order with which we also have to contend. As already indicated, our ability to replace men and women with machines and our continued ability to improve the organisational efficiency of our operations has outstripped our ability to create alternative areas of employment for those thus displaced. In the fields of industry, commerce and the public services employing organisations find that as a result of rationalisation they are able to operate very successfully with significantly reduced manning levels. This means that even when the recession 'bottoms out' and the upturn comes, many employers will be in a position to meet their production targets and carry increased workloads without having to engage nearly as many people as were required in the 1960s and 1970s. Extremely high and sustained growth rates are therefore going to be required right through this decade to offset the manpower reducing effects of these productivity gains, let alone stimulate a rate of recruitment that will enable us to reduce dramatically the numbers currently unemployed.(5) The task of achieving such high growth without the danger of triggering off accompanying high inflation is every Chancellor's nightmare and in economic terms the room for manoeuvre is not all that great, so complex are the various constraints. However, failure to achieve these high and sustainable growth rates will have dire consequences for the young and the long-term unemployed for that is where, at the moment, virtually all our strategic hopes have been pinned.(6)

Meanwhile, as the recession proceeds so do the number of casualities continue to mount. For not only has there been a major shake-out of labour in recent years; many employers of labour have had to shut down altogether. These losses, now amounting to hundreds of thousands of jobs, have left some very serious gaps in the employment base of many communities throughout the length and breadth of the land. Factories have been closed which will never open again. The machinery has been stripped out and much of it sold to foreign buyers. Technical expertise has been dispersed and a whole range of occupational skills are now wasting away through disuse.

Job and Wealth Creation

Well-framed national employment policies need to take careful account of all these factors if we are to get Britain back to work again. In the face of the decline that has taken place in many traditional areas of employment a national strategy must be devised which will encourage and direct activity in the fields of research, design and forward investment. In order to make good what has been lost and so that hope can be given back to the people, a strategic series of new employment bases must be secured.

Regional planning mechanisms need to be devised to ensure that a sufficiently adequate portion of this job creation and wealth creation takes place in the geographical locations where it is most needed. Further, these new employment ventures must be encouraged and backed with adequate funds and with an infrastructure of efficient roads, docks and railways. These latter facilities, together with good telecommunications, are of vital importance in giving Britain's industry a sharp competitive edge, allowing for the swift movement and delivery of goods so vital in any major trading nation. The development of a coherent industrial policy which will secure a new employment base for the nation is a task of immense strategic importance. In particular we should seize the opportunities that are now afforded to us by moving swiftly into the fields of micro-electronic appliances, biotechnology, fibre optics, and opto-electronics. All have a very considerable potential for growth.

Education and Training: Investing in People

Accompanying these industrial initiatives parallel provision for the future is also required in the field of education and training.(7) In a progressive society the curricula in schools, colleges and universities require constant monitoring and revision in order to ensure that there is a close match between what is being taught in these institutions and that particular mix of skills and human aptitudes which the new social and economic order is going to require if the life of the community is to be maintained in all its fullness and wholeness. Beyond this equipping of the young in appropriate life skills there is the constant task of attending to the retraining and relocating of those whose previous skills and occupations have now become obsolete. The world of modern work is in a constant state of flux and following in the wake of technological advance virtually every occupational group is now needing to acquire new skills and to gain familiarity with improved working methods. The need to systematically update existing skills and the need to ensure that working competence is increased throughout the whole workforce is of crucial importance if we are to exploit to the full the potential of the new technology in the years that lie ahead.(8) For unless, accompanying our strategic investment in new plant and machinery, there is a parallel policy of equipping our workforce with the appropriate skills, we are going to witness major production bottlenecks and skill shortages in the years that lie ahead and the path to economic recovery will be frustrated. However, the present pervasive uncertainty regarding the economic future and the absence of any clear-cut national plan for British industry mean that both forward investment and strategic planning in the training field remain hamstrung. Without confidence in the future, investment plans will not be implemented. Without jobs to go into at the end of training, the whole process of training remains a bridge that leads to nowhere. In the past Britain has not been particularly successful in achieving a well co-ordinated promotion of all these aspects of its industrial policy. We have been slow to change and adapt and yet that is what we must do in what is now a very fast-moving world. Strategically we find ourselves in a somewhat weak position in comparison with a number of our trading rivals.

Both France and Germany, despite their firm belief in the merits of a free market economy, have nevertheless chosen to adopt a more centralist approach in tackling the problem of achieving key forward investment, training, research and development. Central government in these countries has made sure that despite the adversities of the recession certain very vital strategic objectives were secured. As a result these nations are now in a relatively strong position in what is a highly competitive field. Britain, on the other hand, has in many ways lacked a coherent and positive industrial policy. Because of a lack of business confidence we have seen little in the way of forward investment in many crucial industrial sectors. Both employers and the government in an attempt to save where they could on expenditure have axed their training programmes. This is a very short-sighted policy which will inevitably lead to serious skill shortages in the future. In the field of product innovation we still tend not to move fast enough in that we remain rather poor in bringing our good ideas forward speedily to the all-important stages of production and successful marketing. It is not my intention in this book to explore in detail the complex reasons which combine to create this unsatisfactory position. Nor do I wish to debate here the merits of particular economic and industrial policies which, if adopted, might facilitate economic recovery thereby creating the conditions in which we might hope to see some commensurate increase in the number of jobs. I wish merely to emphasise that these matters are exceedingly important and that if we could only get them right they would undoubtedly make a significant contribution to the resolution of our present unemployment difficulties. It is essential that Britain secure for herself a strong occupational and wealth-creating base if she is to have a sustainable future and all employment policies which might help to secure these vital ends should be encouraged and vigorously pursued.

Interim Solutions

However, having made a plea for more investment in the key growth sectors, for targeted training and for a carefully planned programme of public works that will help improve our infrastructure, I am still not convinced that these policies alone will give us sufficient easement in the face of existent and future unemployment problems. I am not persuaded by all the bland assurances of the party manifestos and the weight of past conventional wisdom that the traditional responses of going for growth are still adequate in the face of our present dilemma over jobs. I say this because in unemployment terms our structural problems are now so severe, the room for economic manoeuvre is so slight and the number out of work for a long period of time is presently growing so alarmingly. Rebuilding what has been lost during the recession is going to be a painfully slow business. Achieving those sustained rates of growth, without triggering off either inflation or a resource crisis, is not going to be at all easy and it is going to take an inordinately long time for market forces on their own to bring those unacceptably high unemployment levels down. And time is what we do not have on our side. The disparities between those who work and those who cannot find work are very great. Toleration is wearing thin, social ills are festering amongst those hardest hit and social cohesion within our democratic society is endangered. Whatever rate of economic recovery can now be achieved will give us a rate of easement which is too slow and too late.(9) The damage to individuals and to the social order is already too great to be acceptable. Compassion demands a speedier remedy than that which the market on its own can hope to deliver. That is the dilemma of our times.

Within such a situation of crisis there is a certain pragmatic legitimacy in devising employment policies that will help to ease the situation by buying a little time. This we have already attempted to do using the temporary employment programmes of the Manpower Services Commission. But schemes of this kind, with which I have been involved at a close personal level since their first emergence, can only hope to hold the line for so long. They are not long-term structural solutions to the long-term structural unemployment problems of our age. Already there are major signs of strain in

many of these schemes. Originally operating at the margins of the
economy and offering some useful measure of work experience and
training to those hardest hit by the onset of the recession, these
schemes are now being required to carry too many for too long.
The answer lies, surely, not in pouring yet more money into temporary employment schemes operating at the margins of the
economy but in seeking the long-term solutions to the serious mismatch between labour supply and labour demand that now
manifests itself throughout Western Europe.

Work-Sharing as a Policy Instrument

It is within this situational context that I believe work-sharing has
its own particular part to play. Work-sharing is not a policy instrument to be pursued as an alternative to going for responsible
growth. Rather it is a policy instrument which is being used by our
European counterparts in conjunction with other programmes for
economic recovery. As an employment policy it has its part to play
in two important respects. First, it can serve as a vehicle for increasing social cohesion during our present difficulties. It can give
democracy a stable base; a condition essential if the nation is to be
governed through difficult times and a prerequisite of economic
growth. The assistance that work-sharing can afford in spreading
work opportunities more evenly across the nation can help give us
that stability within the social order.

Second, work-sharing may be important in the discovery of
lifestyles suited to the long-term future. If in the future a range of
robotised devices are going to undertake more and more of the
routine and repetitive tasks and a new range of diagnostic devices
are able to relieve us of many of our monitoring, testing and fault-
finding chores, then we are all going to have to adjust to a world
where work as we have known it takes a more subordinate place in
our adult lives. The transitions to that kind of society from our present work-oriented society will be made the easier if we all obtain
the opportunity of experiencing during our working span alternative work/non-work modes. Work-sharing, as an alternative way
of organising working life, may therefore act as an important stepping stone to the future. It can provide us with the opportunity, on
the basis of free choice, to experiment with a number of alternative
work/non-work time patterns seeing which best matches our needs
at various stages of our life and career. An active encouragement to
experiment with work-sharing could give us the opportunity to

assess more precisely its cost and its benefits, its impact on employment activity rates and the social scene. These pilot experiments will give us a firmer lead as to which work modes bring in their wake the greatest social and economic good.

Work-sharing can therefore be seen as a policy instrument which in positive terms can assist both the employed and the unemployed. It can help those presently conditioned to know only one mode of working time in their discovery of others. It can help society in its adjustment towards the employment realities of the future where work will have a more subordinate part in our lives. At a personal and a cultural level it is an instrument that can help free us from some of our past bondage to work. Equally important, it also offers a means of release to those who are presently imprisoned into situations of long-term unemployment, whose hope is fading and whose lives are wasting away under the experience of deprivation and enforced idleness. Work-sharing, therefore, has the potential of liberating both those trapped by the bonds of work and those trapped by the bonds of enforced idleness. It is a way forward out of our present predicament which offers us at least a candle of hope in our darkness. As such perhaps it has the potential to be used as an instrument of the Gospel. That is to say, within the world of systems it may offer us a means whereby all may discover a greater life-space, compassion and justice can be given visible expression within the social order and hope can be given to those who previously sat in darkness.(10)

The Ideological Crisis

Reference has already been made to the cultural as well as to the organisational accommodations which are having to be made as we approach the closing decades of this century. For just as there is an organisational crisis over work so, running parallel to it, there is also a cultural crisis which confronts us. Just as our social order is threatened by the crisis over distribution, so also our inherited ideology of work is threatened by the same set of economic, social and technological realities. For there is a failure of congruence between the received work ethic and the actual availability of work. This failure of congruence causes distress among the unemployed who have been culturally conditioned to expect that they will find much of their identity and sense of well-being in work. But this same failure of congruence also creates considerable confusion in the minds of both the general public and the policy makers who have been conditioned by that same work ethic to view those who do not work with unease and suspicion. Because attitudes and perceptions colour policy formation the matter is of some importance to those who are concerned with social policy and social well-being. I therefore propose to devote the whole of the next chapter to the history of cultural attitudes with respect to work and idleness. For although the religious roots of the work ethic have largely withered away and modern man is largely unaware of the reasons why certain cultural attitudes towards work and idleness are held, yet nevertheless, sufficient of the ghost of the work ethic remains to influence social behaviour and to colour social policy.

Lying behind many of our inherited attitudes towards work and idleness and sometimes obscuring our perception of present socio-economic realities, there is a good deal of quasi-religious instruction which in previous eras came to hold considerable sway and formed in the nation's mind a largely unquestioned ideology. Present circumstance is in the process of changing that, for some of the previous exhortations and value systems appear to be singularly unsuited to meet the spiritual and socio-economic needs of the hour. In order that we might shed that which no longer is an appropriate framework of perception and perhaps en route discover a number of helpful insights from a bygone age, I would ask the reader's indulgence to leave aside the pressing immediate scene for a moment and to accompany me back in time in order that we may lay bare the roots of what is called the Work Ethic and its obverse side, our attitudes to idleness. Just as it is sometimes helpful when staring closely at something under the microscope to change the focus of the eye for a moment by glancing away at something more distant, so too, perhaps, our backward glance at what has contributed to the ideology upon which our society is now founded may help us to see more clearly a possible way forward out of our present cultural predicament.

Notes and References

1. *The Reconstruction of Britain*, Trades Union Congress Publications, August 1981.
2. *Guardian*, 12 June 1981, Report on the special Common Market Meeting of senior Ministers to discuss the European jobs crisis.

3. *EEC Commission Proposals on Work Sharing*, The Commission of European Communities, Brussels, 21 March 1978, p. 32.

4. *MSC Review of Services for the Unemployed*, Manpower Services Commission, March 1981, 2.21.

5. Hawkins, Kevin, *Unemployment: Facts, Figures and Possible Solutions for Britain*, Penguin Books, 1979, pp. 89–92.

6. *Jobs—Facing the Future*, A CBI Staff Discussion Document, Confederation of British Industry, January 1980, p. 38.

7. *A New Training Initiative*, MSC Consultative Document, Manpower Services Commission, May 1981, *passim*.

8. The research work undertaken by Professor S.J. Prais for the National Institute of Economic and Social Research indicates that 64 per cent of British employees are completely untrained for their jobs, compared to only 33 per cent in West Germany. *Guardian*, 7 August 1981. See also *An 'Open Tech' Programme*, MSC Consultative Document, Manpower Services Commission, May 1981, *passim*.

9. *MSC Manpower Review 1981*, Manpower Services Commission, June 1981, 3.4 and Diagram 8.

10. See Luke 4.18. In this passage the 'Good News' of the Gospel is presented by Christ as involving a liberation of those whose lives were previously stunted and confined. In this passage God expresses His concern for the poor and Christ indicates that His message and ministry are very much concerned with the continuing task of setting at liberty those who are oppressed.

THE PLACE OF WORK IN OUR LIVES

The Arena of Cultural Attitudes and Expectations

Chapter 16

THE ROOTS OF THE WORK ETHIC AND OUR ATTITUDES TO IDLENESS

Any attempt to piece together in a balanced way a particular society's view of work, and the obverse side, its attitudes to idleness, is fraught with difficulties. Work is a many-sided thing. As an all-embracing word covering a great spectrum of human activity it is elusive of precise and satisfactory definition. (1) When we move on to examine and evaluate our attitudes towards specific tasks and to work in general the descriptive task becomes more difficult still. Our attitudes towards having to engage in a particular task are ephemeral, changing from one moment in time to the next. Work can be both exhilarating and exceedingly tedious. Within the same society it can be something which is capable of absorbing the whole life dynamic of certain individuals, while for a host of others, even within the same employing organisation, work is purely instrumental and one is solely there to earn the money so that the real business of 'living' can begin. As Ferdynand Zweig concludes in his classic post-war account of the British worker, 'There is an element of hate in the most valued jobs, and an element of love in the most hated.' (2)

That combination of love and hate with respect to our own individual occupations and an ambivalence of attitude towards the institution of work itself, as a concomitant of normative adult existence, has probably always been there down through the course of human history. Any attempt, therefore, to encapsulate in a few words how the individuals who make up a given society view work is bound to be inadequate and open to the criticism that evidence of alternative viewpoints was not take into account. In the particular, attitudes to work will be as varied as the nature of the work itself and as varied as human experience itself. Now add to these

he problem of researching back to find what broad at-
ailed with respect to work and idleness in societies long
here the surviving literature is very partial in its nature,
n written not by a representative cross-section of the
orking population but by a small educated élite.

e little or no evidence of how the 'common man' conceived of work in earlier times. The clues that we have to the
various historical meanings of work must be gleaned from the
philosophical and religious writers whose works have survived and
to that extent must be suspect by reason of their partiality.
However, in the fashioning of a prevailing ideology for their day
with respect to attitudes to work and idleness and because the ideas
of such writers often wielded considerable influence when it came
to the formation of what was considered to be appropriate social
policy, they are worthy of very considerable attention. Many of
their ideas have had an extraordinary persistence and linger on to
colour even our own framework or perception many centuries later
on.

But to say that certain ideologies have a persistence is not to take
a static view of our concepts of work. One of the benefits that
comes from taking a longer historical view of work is, in fact, to be
made aware of the subtle shifts and changes, the accommodations
and the accretions which take place over the years. It is salutary
and liberating to discover that value systems do change. Life and
attitudes have not always been like this and indeed are not like this
in certain other cultures. Other modes of living are possible. Men
have not always felt it ncessary to use work as the principal
touchstone of identity and social status, nor have they necessarily
felt themselves to be a total non-person when without it. Thus in an
earlier agrarian economy the village worked, but there was a place
for the 'village idiot' who could not work. Just as in African
societies today where the tribal network still holds people together
in a strong kinship community, it is not what particular occupation
you hold which is important, nor indeed whether you have employment at all. Of far greater social consequence is who your ancestors
were.

Returning to British society it is good to be reminded by
Professor Burnett in his introduction to twenty-seven very precious
autobiographical extracts, illustrating working conditions and attitudes towards work in the nineteenth and early twentieth centuries, that—

[work] was not a central life-interest of the working classes. For most it was taken as given, like life itself, to be endured rather than enjoyed. . . . The picture which emerges from these writings is of men and women . . . who lead lives of hard work but rarely expect to find fulfilment from it, and for whom the family, interpersonal relationships and relationship with God are centrally important. . . . Such happiness and satisfactions as life has to offer are to be found in social contacts within groups—the family, the work-group, the chapel or, for a few, the public house; here meaningful relationships can be made, experiences exchanged, joys and sorrows shared. (3)

Perhaps, taking the long view of human history, that has been the heart of the matter for the bulk of men and women from biblical times until really quite recently. In that case the system of Calvinistic quasi-religious teaching, which has come to be dubbed the 'Work Ethic', and which attempted by means of an unholy alliance between vested business interests and the Church to erect the cult of work at the very centre of human existence, may be an aberration, and not the true norm. To those of us who have spent much of our time in recent years trying to stem the tide of rising un-employment, and wrestling with the seemingly intractable problem of trying to provide jobs for all, such a discovery may come as a blessed release. Perhaps, like all the King's horses and all the King's men, we do not after all have to try to do the impossible thing of putting back together again that order of society which we experienced in the post-war years. Perhaps the way out of the maze is not back the way that we have come, via the door marked 'The Cult of Work', but on to discover a more balanced and wholesome lifestyle, where work has a place, but a more subordinate place, in our system of values.

PERCEPTIONS OF WORK IN THE ANCIENT WORLD

In this chapter we shall be concentrating our attention principally upon those attitudes to work and idleness which had their cradle in the Reformation and which were later developed into a very high doctrine of work. The moral sense of obligation which was at-tached to work at that time was enthusiastically promulgated throughout the land to the point where the activity of work itself, regardless of its ends, became a sort of tribal totem for Western in-dustrialised man, and to be without work in such a work orientated society was perceived as taboo. But in this sub-section I want to start with an earlier period, and to contrast that high doctrine of work which has characterised much of recent Western industrialised life, with the attitude which prevailed in the ancient world among the Greeks, the Jews and the Romans.

Ancient Greece

The Athenian ideas of work are probably more remote from our own contemporary attitude than any other in the history of Europe. 'They are not only remote in time but they represent values that are, in some measure, the reverse of our own. . . . The Athenian outlook is a construct of attitudes of a particular type, a type that contrasts with our own and has had little influence in the economic history of Europe. It is a type, however, which may deserve re-examination at the present time.' (4)

Work was not taken seriously in classical Greece, comments P.D. Antony. 'It was not assigned the moral value which it has gained from twenty centuries of Christianity and the birth of the Labour movement.' (5) Instead the Greeks, through the writings of their philosophers, seem to have taken up a more critical stance with regard to work. Work was not despised. It was seen to be a necessary human activity which had the capability to contribute to things useful and beautiful and enriching to the living of human life. But work was subordinated to these ends. 'An Athenian would have thought it absurd to regard it as an end in itself.' (6)

In contrast to our own culture it was leisure, not work, which was seen to give a man his dignity. Whereas we feel sorry for those 'out of work', they felt sorry for those who did have to work—the 'leisureless'. Sebastian de Grazia, who made a major study of the attitude of the ancient world to leisure, points out that in both Greek and Roman society there was no real equivalent for our word 'work'. (7) *Aschole*, which is the word that the Greeks tended to use, is work expressed as the negative concept of un-leisure, where the *a-* is placed to signify a want or a lack of *schole* (leisure). David Welbourn comments: 'It is interesting how the form of a people's language reveals their basic assumptions. In our culture the negative words are used of the non-work situation—*un*employment, job*less*; even retirement is a sort of negative word, taking its meaning from that which is retired from. For the Greeks it was the other way round; the negative words were used of the work situation, the positive ones being applied to leisure.' (8)

The Hebrew Tradition

There are so many insights from the Judaeo-Christian tradition that I find both pertinent and immensely challenging as we wrestle with the present crisis over the place of work in our society that it would be distracting to set them all down here. I have chosen rather to work in these insights throughout the whole passage of this book, sometimes expressing them in clearly biblical terms and imagery, elsewhere drawing on the deep well of the Christian tradition but voicing those insights about attitudes, values, relationships and purpose in more secular terms. 'Religious truth is normal experience understood at full depth,' wrote Jeffreys. 'What makes truth religious is not that it relates to some abnormal field of thought and feeling, but that it goes to the roots of the experience which it interprets.' (9) It is here that the Hebrew tradition is so rich. Its sharp insights into the nature of man and society again and again have the capability of taking us into the heart of an issue, challenging us to make an appropriate response.

Here, however, I want to restrict myself to making one or two general comments about the way in which work was perceived in the Jewish tradition. First, Professor Robert Davidson does well to remind us that there are very real dangers in trying to extract from the Bible answers to problems which had not yet appeared over the horizon in the biblical period.

There is no biblical counterpart to a society faced with a pool of permanently unemployed or unemployable people. Second, the day is long past when we can speak of the 'biblical doctrine of X' as Alan Richardson does in 'The Biblical Doctrine of Work'. It is far more likely that we shall find in the Bible, both Old and New Testament, a plurality of different attitudes and insights which cannot easily be combined into a unified picture. Further, any approach which argues that there is a Hebrew, and hence New Testament, attitude which can then be contrasted with a Greek attitude is suspect. (10)

Robert Davidson suggests that we must begin by recognising that for the societies we meet in the Bible work is simply taken for granted as a necessary part of life's experience and therefore, by definition, part of the God-given structure of society. Given that work is taken for granted throughout the Bible we may claim that 'work is never given as a definition of human life'. In the Judaeo-Christian tradition, 'life is experienced in its fullness in relationships, in relationships with God and with other people, in "loving the Lord your God with all your heart, your soul and your strength" (Deut. 6.5) and "loving your neighbour like yourself" (Lev. 19.18, Luke 10.27).' In other words in a meaningful sharing of experience with others. Part of the demoralising effect of unemployment, as psychological and sociological studies have shown, is that it is precisely work which provides for men in particular such a sharing of experience. (11) 'Work makes inescapable the realisation that no man is an island unto himself. The organisation and the product of work both imply the interdependence of human beings. Take away this daily experience that efforts must be combined, and the unemployed are left with a sense of uselessness, a sense of being on the scrap heap.' (12)

Again in accord with the biblical tradition we can claim that—

[Our fellow human beings] are never to be valued merely because of their work status. There is no suggestion in the Bible that loss of work assigned to man an inferior status or undermined his self-respect. Man owed his position and his self-awareness to the fact that he was part of a close-knit community, and this community provided the context of concern and caring, which all accepted. . . . Witness the concern for the alien, the widow and the orphan expressed, inter alia, in leaving for them the gleaning of the harvest field, olive grove and vineyard (Deut. 24.19–22). There was no stigma attached to such gleaning. The Book of Ruth asserts that the greatest Israelite of all, King David, owed his existence to the fact of an alien girl gleaning in the fields of a Hebrew farmer. Such gleaning was not charity; it was a social right.' (13)

With regard to the character of work, the multifaceted nature of our occupational activities is well recognised in the Bible. Both the Old and New Testaments abound with brief thumbnail sketches of the citizens of their times busy about their business. The work of the farmer on his land, the fisherman with his nets, the builder, the merchant, the labourers in the vineyard. Such work is generally recognised as wholesome, though both the prophets and the parables of Jesus prevent us ever from giving a blanket benediction to the way in which everyone within the community obtained their income.

There are the passing references to the rich and the powerful taking advantage of the poor, of malpractices in trade, of shoddy workmanship and of poor service. On the positive side there is the joy that comes from working with nature and with others, and from constructing, fabricating and handling the things of this world in order to meet the needs of those who live in township and village. The world as given to man by God is affirmed as being good and in his role as steward over such rich resources there is honour and dignity attached.

Biblical man, especially in the Old Testament, set great value upon the good things of earth which God had provided for man's enjoyment. Hence economic life, which is the system of arrangements whereby these good things are secured and distributed, could no more be looked upon as evil in itself than could the goods themselves. Material abundance was seen as an evil in two situations only: (a) when it led members of the community to a denial of their dependence upon and obedience to their Lord; and (b) when it was gained at the expense and impoverishment of the weaker neighbour. (14).

Two further points might perhaps be made at this stage. The first relates to the linkage between work and what we might call cultural pursuits.

Work is important for the development of all that is meant by the word culture. There can be no paintings or music without paint and canvas and musical instruments. There can be no beautiful cities full of fine buildings without engineers and builders and bricks. There can be no travel to visit other countries and to learn about other cultures without planes and ships and motor vehicles. In the same way, teaching and medicine and other professional work is all dependent on buildings and material objects of all kinds. This has always been true. The ancient Greeks and Romans may have considered that activities such as politics and debate and noble deeds were to be highly desired and esteemed, but they could not have done any of them without a large slave class to perform all the more mundane things for them. (15)

It is here that the Jews again exercise a healthy realism with regard to work. Thus the author of the Book of Ecclesiasticus may have declared that, 'A scholar's wisdom comes of ample leisure; if a man is to be wise he must be relieved of other tasks' (Sirach 38.24 ff). But he immediately goes on to recognise the importance of the ploughman in the field, the master craftsman busy in his workshop, the smith at his anvil and the potter making his tally. Without them, he says, a city cannot be established. They were all necessary if the full and abundant life of the community was to be sustained. It is these skills of hand and brain and eye which 'keep stable the fabric of the world', and without them there could be no freeing of the scholar and others for additional life enhancing activities.

Here, as in many other places, the Judaeo-Christian tradition stresses the essential interdependence of humankind. As Emil Brunner comments: 'The goal of mankind is the Kingdom of God, the perfection of community. . . . Community presupposes reciprocal giving and taking, community is reciprocal exchange and completion.' This is illustrated in the scriptural parable of the human community as a body, an organism. 'Just as every part, every organ in the organism has its own nature and the function corresponding to it, in the body of humanity every man, in virtue of his nature, has his own function, his own service to render to the whole. It is a fellowship of mutual completion by service.' (16) This strong sense of community, of being tied in the bundle of life with others under God and of the responsibilities which are laid upon us one toward the other within such a social setting, is one of the great dominant themes of the biblical tradition. It is a theme which has been central to my thesis.

Finally, a word about one other great biblical theme which must be set down at this point. This is the strength of the Scriptures in voicing concern for the poor, the oppressed and the forgotten. In the great recital of God's dealings with man which lies at the heart of the Judaeo-Christian tradition there is expressed a passionate and fundamental concern for the poor and the unprivileged. The God of whom the Bible speaks is a God who enjoins man to work for the establishment of material justice within the social order and to exercise an active concern for the welfare of his neighbour. The condition and treatment of the poor in any contemporary society is therefore a matter of serious moral concern for those who would align themselves to God's purposes. Further, in man's search to find a sense of meaning amongst the seeming confusion of the historic process (which is the theme that forms the main thread of the biblical material), the clue to understanding is often found to lie within the ranks of the poor and the dispossessed. Again and again in the drama of events the spotlight comes to rest upon the representative of the *am ha-ares*, the common man.

It is through his experiences and from his stance within society that the true significance of what is happening in the world is to be grasped. Again and again in the annals of the Old and New Testaments it is given to the poor, the marginalised and those of low estate to see and understand things about life and God's present purposes. For a variety of reasons these so often seem hidden from the understanding of those other members of the community who are more materially secure and who effectively hold power. I am persuaded that this particular biblical insight is of crucial importance for our age. I believe that it is from the vantage point of those who in a variety of ways find themselves marginalised from today's world, and sharing with them their sense of urgency and anger, that we must begin our interpretation of events and our critique of society if we wish to find a morally valid way through the battery of problems that confront us in the closing decades of this century.

Ancient Rome

Slavery was an integral part of the ancient world but the employment of slaves was probably more extensive and widely organised in the Roman Empire than it had been in the Greek city states. In Roman society 'work was assigned to slaves and foreigners so that gentlemen could avoid the demands it would make on their time and the corruption of its menial character'. (17) A civilisation in which a privileged élite get their most unpleasant and unrewarding tasks done by a system of slaves may at first sight seem even more removed from our own social setting than the world of mirror image values that once existed in ancient Greece. But as the new technology comes to be harnessed it may in fact be that mankind is once again relieved of great tracts of work by an army of sophisticated robotic and self-monitoring devices. How to cope with that social revolution in such a way that both the benefits and the personal sacrifices involved in replacing men with machines are seen to be equitably shared throughout the one community is a major distributive issue of our time.

Let us return for a moment longer to the civilisation of Rome. Mossé noted that the glorification of labour and laws against idleness seem to make their appearance in the Roman literature either 'when slavery was in its very first stages, or when it was declining'. (18) Antony takes up Mossé's observation and comments:

Work begins to be taken seriously as slavery declines. An ideology of work is redundant when the labour force can be conscripted and coerced at will. In conditions of a freer market an ideology has to be developed in order to recruit labour . . . to motivate it by persuading it that its tasks are necessary or noble. In conditions of a free market and chronic shortage of labour, the manufacture and communication of an ideology of work becomes a central preoccupation of society. (19)

The point that Antony makes here is an important one and picks up a theme which he develops in considerable detail in his book *The Ideology of Work*. Antony's thesis is that our ideas about work are not axiomatic, but are ideological in that they are a system of ideas

>osefully inculcated to suit the economic interests of the day.

t process he would argue reaches its highest development in ad-
·...ced capitalism and in state socialism. It is in these societies that
work becomes beatified and assumes an almost neurotic com-
pulsiveness. To the way in which religion was used to sanctify what
the economic system required of men we must now turn.

THE ROOTS OF THE WORK ETHIC
The Secular Task Conceived as Calling

In the monastic tradition prior to the Reformation there was a clear
distinction between those who would serve God in the world and
those called to live the life of a monk or nun.

The latter were 'religious' in a sense which others could not be. A different
standard of morals was enjoined upon them. The general obligations of a
Christian were comprised in what were known as *praecepta evangelica*, or
the morals of the Decalogue, which were in turn practically identified with
natural-law morality. . . . The religious orders, on the other hand, were
obligated to follow the *consilia evangelica*, the higher morality of the
gospels, specially expressed in the vows of obedience, poverty and
chastity. (20)

According to the prevailing teaching of the Catholic Church this
latter morality was impossible of fulfilment in the secular life.

In order to practise it, men must withdraw from the world. 'Come out
from among them and be ye separate', is the motto of monasticism. Thus
what may be called a double standard of morality came to exist within the
church itself. Luther's conception of the secular life as a 'calling' involved
a complete break with this theory. For him no distinction was permissible
between two standards of morality, *praecepta evangelica*, to be performed
within the world, and *consilia evangelica*, which can be fulfilled only apart
from the world. All men are equally obligated to fulfil both the commands
and the 'advices' of the gospel. And this fulfilment is to be accomplished,
not in the cloister, apart from the world, but in the sphere of the secular
life itself. (21)

This change in the conception of 'calling' is perhaps an important starting point for us as we attempt very quickly to sketch in
some of the ways in which the teaching of the Church came to
colour men's view of their work. We start then, with Martin Luther
(1483–1546), who through his writings and preaching helped to
change a way of thinking. His conception of 'calling' paved the way
to a new appraisal of the secular life. Man was to serve God in his

worldly occupation. With Luther, as Max Weber once wrote, the whole world became a monastery and every man a monk.

As he had extended the priesthood of all believers, so likewise he extended the concept of divine calling, vocation, to all worthy occupations. (22)

It is unmistakable that even in the German word *Beruf*, and perhaps still more clearly in the English *calling*, a religious conception, that of a task set by God, is at least suggested. (23)

At least one thing was unquestionably new: the valuation of the fulfilment of duty in worldly affairs as the highest form which the moral activity of the individual could assume. This it was which inevitably gave everyday worldly activity a religious significance, and which first created the conception of a calling in this sense. . . . The only way of living acceptably to God was not to surpass worldly morality in monastic asceticism, but solely through the fulfilment of the obligations imposed upon the individual by his position in the world. That was his calling. (24)

The Teaching of Calvin (1509–64)

Although Luther opened the way for a new appraisal of the secular life by breaking down the Catholic distinction between it and the religious life, he did not himself develop the vast economic possibilities latent in this new appraisal. It was John Calvin, claimed Weber, who supplied the interpretation of calling that was essential to the development of capitalism and has become symbolised in the phrase 'the Protestant ethic' of work.

For our purposes here I want to focus attention on just two aspects of Calvin's influence on our concepts of work. The first is Calvin's teaching that man's chief end is the glorification of God. This aim gives to life its reason, its rationale. Anything which diverts the mind from this one supreme aim is a form of idolatry. Thus one's work in the world takes on a whole new significance.

If God has ordered and arranged this great physical universe for the good of man and through this manifests his glory, it is supremely important to correlate society to the same great end, and this is done through the fulfilment of such duties in our calling as are imposed by the laws of nature. No mere quietistic acceptance of the universe is possible here. The tremendous drive of God's will and God's glory lies back of all work in our calling. The normal result is a tense and ceaseless activity. (25)

It is this sense of drive, of passionate commitment to the single-minded end of bringing the secular within the final aim of life, the glorification of God, and to do this through our work, through our calling, which characterises much of later Calvinism. But providing

additional fuelling to this intense drive towards activity was a
gnawing anxiety arising out of a deep spiritual uncertainty as to
whether one was, in the inscrutable purposes of God, saved or
damned. Williston Walker, Church historian, summarises Calvin's
teaching on this matter thus: 'As originally created, man was good
and capable of obeying God's will, but he lost goodness and power
alike in Adam's fall, and is now, of himself, absolutely incapable of
goodness. Hence no work of man's can have any merit; and all
men are in a state of ruin meriting only damnation. From this help-
less and hopeless condition some men are undeservedly rescued
through the work of Christ.' (26) The doctrine of election, that
some men are chosen for grace and salvation while others are not,
was an important concept for later Calvinists and the Puritan tradition. Election was never assured; a man might be deceived about
himself so that even those who might consider themselves chosen
were still hounded by doubt. As Calvinism developed, the anxiety
fed of not knowing whether one was one of the saved or one of the
eternally damned pressed later theologians to provide some
reassuring word to those who asked: How can I be sure that I am
one of the elect?

Two answers were given. Assurance can be obtained either from the
testimonium Spiritus Sancti, the inner consciousness of the individual that
the power of God is *in* him, or from the ability consistently to perform
good works, the consciousness of the individual that the power of God is
working *through* him. In the first case he is conscious that he is a vessel, in
the second that he is an instrument. While the first method of assurance
was undoubtedly emphasised by Calvin himself and always played, at
least theoretically, a part in Calvinistic theology, the second method
became the more important in practice. (27)

Work Reconceived
These excursions into the religious doctrines which gripped the
minds of those who lived in previous generations are hard for us to
understand who operate within a very different secular conceptual
framework. But perhaps enough has been said to enable us to understand something of the way in which work and idleness were
coming to be viewed as we move into the later Puritan tradition. In
every society man has to work if he wants to live, but as we emerge
into the seventeenth century our commitment to work is beginning
to carry extensive religious and moral overtones. It is a serious
business to which the pleasure or displeasure of God is attached.
Dislike of work is considered a sign that election is doubtful.

Moreover, intermittent work will not do; it must be methodical and disciplined. 'To select a calling and follow it with all one's conscience is a religious duty. Calvinism thus lays the foundation of the tremendous discipline of the modern factory founded on the division of labour—very different from the easygoing ways of the independent artisan.' (28) Everyone, even the wealthy, must work, such is the divine will. Everything secular must be devoted to the glory of God. Thus the cult of work makes its first appearance.

R.H. Tawney, in his book *Religion and the Rise of Capitalism*, expresses very well the subtle shifts that have taken place in our concept of work as a result of Reformation teaching. He writes as follows:

Laborare est orare. By the Puritan moralist the ancient maxim is repeated with a new and intenser significance. The labour which he idealises is not simply a requirement imposed by nature, or a punishment for the sin of Adam. It is itself a kind of ascetic discipline, more rigorous than that demanded of any order of mendicants—a discipline imposed by the will of God, and to be undergone, not in solitude, but in the punctual discharge of secular duties. It is not merely an economic means, to be laid aside when physical needs have been satisfied. It is a spiritual end, for in it alone can the soul find health, and it must be continued as an ethical duty long after it has ceased to be a material necessity. . . . What is required of the Puritan is . . . a system in which every element is grouped round a central idea, the service of God, from which all disturbing irrelevances have been pruned, and to which all minor interests are subordinated. His conception of that life was expressed in the words, 'Be wholly taken up in diligent business of your lawful callings, when you are not exercised in the more immediate service of God.' (29)

ATTITUDES TO IDLENESS

Unemployment seen as a Social Threat: Vagrancy in Tudor England

Because our point of reference with regard to employment patterns tends to be our experience during the post-war period when Britain enjoyed virtual full employment for some twenty-five years, our present experience of large numbers unable to find work appears as a major social abnormality. But periods of high unemployment in Britain are in fact not a new phenomenon, they have a long ancestry, and at this point in our historical survey it might be helpful just to say a word about those groups who found themselves without work in previous generations and how they were treated.

In Tudor times, owing to trade cycles and agricultural change, those without work often had to resort to casual employment elsewhere. Such bands of vagrants were always an unsettling presence in the communities through which they moved. A number were ex-servicemen who had been allowed to keep their arms. Such groups were not averse to obtaining the necessities of life by pillaging the local community as they roamed from village to village, and they were often so strong in number that the local enforcers of law and order were afraid to oppose them. Others were the innocent victims of the economic uncertainties of the times who, having lost their former employment, were forced either to take to the roads and beg or to starve. In bad times the numbers of such vagrants living totally in dependence upon local charity could grow alarmingly and their demands placed a great strain on the ability of the host community to cope. There were also fears that these roaming bands of 'sturdy beggars' might act as agents of social conflict and civic revolt. Thus the unemployed, the masterless man, those without visible means of support, who roamed the roads of England in search of work were both resented and feared in Tudor times. So began an attitude toward the poor and the idle that later came to colour the formation of British social policy.

'The most immediate and pressing concern of government . . . for something more than a century (1520–1640) was with the problem of vagrancy. There is no doubt whatever that vagabondage was widespread, that it was organised and that it imposed on rural and village communities burdens and dangers with which they could not cope.' (30) Professor Jordan's statement may be somewhat exaggerated in its claims, but nevertheless the problem of vagrancy in Tudor England and the poverty that arose through loss of work appears to have been a fairly continuous social problem rising and falling according to local and national circumstances from the end of the fifteenth century onwards.

Poverty and vagrancy were not . . . peculiar to the sixteenth century, despite the frequent protests and intermittent government action during the period. Before the fifteenth century had run its course a number of factors, ranging from the social upheavals following the Black Death to the disruptions caused by the Wars of the Roses, had combined to produce a class of itinerant beggars. Many genuinely sought work which was not available in their own locality. . . . By the beginning of the sixteenth century virtually every corner of England had its share of these professional beggars. They were particularly numerous in the region of the larger towns, and as the century progressed their ranks were swelled still further by a number of events, some of national, some of local importance. (31)

Who were these vagrants and how had they come to be without work? Some were demobilised soldiers and sailors, others were ex-retainers of the great noble households who had been engaged in warfare. Their services were no longer required and Tudor society had a major problem reabsorbing them into their former occupation as artisans. Others were adversely affected by trade slumps in the cloth industry or by failures of the harvest. There were those who had been dispossessed from their land and from their previous mode of living by the enclosure movement. These changes in land use made by landlords with the intention of gaining a better profit from sheep than from arable farming were deeply disruptive to many village communities, forcing a sizeable number into vagrancy. Added to these vicissitudes was the problem of finding enough work for everyone in a period of rising population.

Between 1500 and 1600 the population may have risen by as much as 40 per cent. . . . Unfortunately the rise in population was not matched by a corresponding rise in employment opportunities. The position obviously varied from area to area, but in most districts too many people were pursuing too few jobs. (32)

The picture which emerges from Pound's careful study of Tudor England shows that some of the factors which cause a community to be afflicted by high unemployment have a habit of reappearing down through the centuries. Trade recession, structural change, improved productivity, obsolescent skills, demographic problems caused by a bulge in the birth rate—all have a familiar ring about them. For the families living in the country there was usually some possibility of keeping body and soul alive in times of particular hardship by resorting to what could be found in the surrounding woods and hedgerows or by killing the family pig. For the urban dweller dependent solely upon his meagre wage to buy him sustenance, though, life could be very tenuous. A man who was maintaining himself at one moment might well find himself without any visible means of support at the next, for there was no guarantee of regular employment.

Periods of unemployment could be lengthy and if these coincided with harvest failure or the onset of plague the results could be disastrous. Three-quarters of the sixteenth century had passed before any real provision was made for the able-bodied unemployed, and the government's determination to persecute all but the aged and impotent must, on occasion, have caused very real distress.

The action of the central government was dictated by fear. Every Tudor monarch had to contend with at least one serious rising, and, not insignificantly, every decade from the 1530s onwards saw at least one Act directed towards the relief of the poor and the suppression of vagrancy. Suppression is the key word. Any masterless man was deemed potentially dangerous and the greater the national emergency the more severe were the laws passed against the unemployed. It is not entirely a coincidence that the minority of Edward VI saw the introduction of the most savage vagrancy laws of the century. (33)

Attempts to Suppress the Problems caused by Unemployment

In the earlier part of the sixteenth century the state had come to acknowledge some communal responsibility for those who were unable to work by reason of age, chronic sickness, blindness or lunacy. These so called 'impotent poor' were to receive some measure of institutional relief from the reign of Henry VIII onwards. Thus parishes were authorised to collect money so that the impotent poor were given some basic income and were no longer obliged to beg. But no allowance was made for the able-bodied poor. Those who were unemployed through no fault of their own and who would work but could not had as yet not been distinguished from those who were basically idlers and who could work but would not. The same harsh treatment was accorded to them both. The social history of this period makes fascinating reading because we see both individuals and the state struggling to come to terms with the twin evils of poverty and unemployment. To begin with there was little attempt to make a sustained analysis of the root causes of cyclical unemployment. It was assumed at first that employment for all was available and the government of the day acted accordingly. Any fit person who was found to be without either occupation or income was liable to be subjected to extremely harsh treatment ranging from whipping and branding, to mutilation and death.

If any man or woman, able to work, should refuse to labour and live idly for three days, he or she should be branded with a red hot iron on the breast with the letter V and should be judged the slave for two years of any person who should inform against such idler.

Later laws followed a similar pattern. By an Act of 1572 anyone soliciting alms without a magistrate's licence to beg or, if he came from another parish, who failed to wear 'some notable badge or token both on the breast and on the back of his outermost garment', was to suffer 'burning through the gristle of the right ear'. In 1597 a new provision was added that any 'sturdy beggar' caught should be 'stripped naked from the middle upwards, and be whipped until his body was bloody and sent from parish to parish, the next straight way to the place of his birth'. Both whipping beggars out of the parish and 'badging' the poor, usually with 'blue and yellow bays pinned upon their sleeve and breast', rapidly became popular practices, destined to survive for nearly three centuries. (34) From these contemporary accounts it is clear that it took central authorities a long time to realise that the problem needed to be tackled at its roots and that 'the provision of work was a far greater panacea for ills than the threat of whipping and ultimate death'. (35)

That unemployment and its attendant poverty were grave and recurring social problems which challenged the stability of the nation, all in authority were agreed. That something needed to be done, all were agreed. Failing any better analysis our ancestors responded to unemployment by punishing the unemployed. They tried to drive the problem underground by suppressing all the symptoms of the malaise. Alas, such a response is a recurring response to the problem of unemployment and is not one which was just confined to Tudor times. The same social response makes its reappearance later on in the establishment of the workhouses and the punitive treatment of their hapless inmates. (36) The same punitive streak with respect to the poor and the unemployed makes its appearance today in the public attitudes recorded by Alan Deacon (37) and is a strangely British trait. (38) A deep-seated hostility towards unemployed and the poor lingers on in British society. Public perceptions of the workless continue to be coloured by the suspicion that they are really malingerers. That they are scroungers who could find a job if only they really tried.

Structural Solutions for Structural Problems

Strangely, attitudes towards the unemployed frequently appear to harden at the very time when it is most difficult for them to find a job. The reason why so many people are not working is put down to a belief that they will not work. They will not help themselves. If others are without employment and consequently living in a condition of poverty then it is assumed that these things are so because basically the people involved are lazy. The poor are believed to have brought their condition upon themselves. It is their own fault that they are poor. From such a framework of perception the proposal that any additional material help should be offered to the victims of unemployment is resisted. Such state aid or charity is seen as serving only to encourage idleness. By offering additional assistance one is sapping the will to work. However, the 'blame the victim' response to unemployment is, as we have seen, an inadequate one. It fails to take account of the structural causes which lie at the root of much job loss. It fails in its understanding of the realm of social systems which frequently work in such a way as to trap the unemployed into a situation from which they are unable to escape. Without the understanding and aid of those others who can mobilise the requisite resources and who can help construct a more humane socio-economic structure, the unemployed remain the victims of the system and the cycle of deprivation will continue.

In the Tudor age it was not until the Act of 1572 that central government properly recognised that there were some men who were genuinely unemployed through no fault of their own. Gradually a social transformation took place and responsibility for the maintenance of the poor became a prime function of the state and was no longer wholly reliant upon a personal form of Christian charity. Elizabethan legislation shows that it was becoming more aware of the underlying causes of vagrancy and the Poor Laws came to make a careful distinction between the idler and the unemployed individual genuinely looking for work. In 1576 the concept of 'setting the poor on work' was put into the statute law and it remained there for some three-and-a-half centuries. Thus if the able-bodied required assistance then they had to work for it. The Justices of the Peace were instructed to provide within their communities a stock of raw material such as hemp, and here within these work centres able-bodied beggars were expected to work in return for the relief which they received. Meanwhile children who might be in need of relief were to be apprenticed to a trade so that they could become useful and self-supporting citizens. Finally the persistent idler and those who insisted on taking to the open road instead of working for a living were to be punished in special 'houses of correction'. Thus by the end of the Tudor period we see emerging three different sorts of treatment for three different sorts of pauper. For the impotent poor there was the provision of poorhouses, for the able-bodied genuinely unemployed individual there were the workhouses and for the idler there was the house of correction. Although such a schema probably was never implemented in every community, a genuine attempt had been made using a harsh but effective method to find structural remedies to a persistent range of structural problems.

The Act of 1592 eventually gathered together within the Poor Law the experience which over a century had been gleaned by trial and error as various local communities had struggled to deal with the persistent problems posed by unemployment, poverty and vagrancy. It was noticeable that over this period opinions with respect to the poor and the unemployed had become progressively more humane. Minds became more receptive to the suffering and to the root causes of that suffering. So it was that in the end far greater provision was made for the care of the poor and work was provided for the unemployed. Looking back the legislation that was enacted within the Elizabethan Poor Laws can now be seen as the legislation of a government cautiously groping its way towards the appropriate social mechanisms of remedy. In the end social provision was established that served both to remove the threat of insurrection from the villages and townships and at the same time made a brave attempt to provide in a creative way for all categories of the poor. There is then, perhaps, some element of resonance between the problems which confronted our ancestors in Elizabethan times and our own major social ills. Perhaps like our Tudor ancestors we have to struggle to learn that persistent structural problems require adequate structural solutions. Perhaps also we have to learn that although all in the community have a part in securing more adequate remedies, there is a special role to be played by governments. In every age they have the statesmanlike role of safeguarding the interests of all within the realm, having especial regard for the weak and the poor, framing appropriate legislation in times of crisis and mobilising the requisite resources of assistance.

Idleness as the Object of Moral Censure

In attempting to expose the roots of our attitude to work and to the unemployed we must now return again to the part that past religious teaching had in this process of attitude formation. Religious instruction was, of course, not the sole influence on the formation of that system of beliefs which eventually led to the work-orientated societies of the Western industrialised world. There were enormously powerful economic forces at work shaping an approved way of life, fashioning an ideology that suited a range of vested interests, and these must not be underestimated. In our secular age, where the influence of the Church and its teaching tends to be so marginal, we perhaps forget the great strength of religious sanctions in previous eras of British history. As Max Weber wrote: 'In a time in which the beyond meant everything, when the social position of the Christian depended upon his admission to communion, the clergyman through his ministry, Church discipline, and preaching, exercised an influence . . . which we modern men are entirely unable to picture. In such a time the religious forces which express themselves through such channels are the decisive influences in the formation of national character.' (39) For the purposes of this study I want to look at three specific areas of influence. The English Puritan tradition, the preaching and teaching of the sixteenth- and seventeenth-century Scottish Church leaders, and the educational influence of the Charity and Sunday schools are all worth looking at in our study of work and value systems. Between them they give us something of a picture of the sort of attitudes that were being inculcated into a nation through the agency of the Church.

(a) Richard Baxter and English Puritanism

Richard Baxter (1615–91) was a seventeenth-century English Presbyterian and author of the influential *Christian Directory* and another pastoral work entitled *The Saints' Everlasting Rest*. Weber calls the former 'the most complete compendium of Puritan ethics'. His readership, which was considerable in its day, was constantly exhorted to industry. The saints' everlasting rest is a rest in the next life, not in this one. 'Here it behooves man to work, and ever more to work'. There are two chief motives given for work. Work is still, as it always has been in the Western Church, a means of discipline. It is the best prophylactic against what the Puritan called the 'unclean life', against the sloth and sensuality which riches so often engender. Work in one's calling is Baxter's prescription against sexual temptation as well as against religious doubts. Again, work is to be done because God commanded it, in other words for his glory. This meant that utilitarian motives were disregarded or at least subordinated. So far as this life is concerned, work becomes an end in itself. It gains a meaning beyond itself only when looked at *sub specie aeternitatis*, from a religious and other-worldly point of view. (40)

The *Christian Directory* is dominated by the continually repeated, often passionate preaching of hard, continuous bodily or mental labour. The following extracts from his works give something of the tenor of Baxter's message. It is a call to a bee-like industriousness.

It is for action that God maintaineth us and our activities. . . . It is action that God is most served and honored by.

Be wholly taken up in diligent business of your lawful callings when you are not exercised in the more immediate service of God. . . . Labour hard in your calling. . . . See that you have a calling which will find you employment for all the time which God's immediate service spareth.

God hath commanded you some way or other to labour for your daily bread and not to live as drones off the sweat of others.

Will not wealth excuse [from work]? Answer: It may excuse you from some sordid sort of work, by making you more serviceable to another, but you are no more excused from the service of work . . . than the poorest man. . . . Though they [the rich] have no outward want to urge them, they have as great a necessity to obey God. . . . God has strictly commanded it [work] for all. (41)

(b) *The Scottish Divines of the Sixteenth and Seventeenth Centuries*

The terrific Puritan drive towards intense activity is echoed north of the border in the writings and recorded sermons of a number of eminent Scottish divines. In his book *Presbyteries and Profits*, Gordon Marshall carefully researches the formative influence of the Calvinist tradition within the Scottish cultural and economic scene. What emerges is a picture of the godly life very akin to that delineated by Richard Baxter. The godly work for their meat and are sensitive to the value of time. According to Robert Rollock (1555?–99), idleness is the mark of the reprobate. 'Thou glorifies God in thy doing and labouring; but in idleness thou glorifies not God.' (42) A similar theme is taken up by William Cowper (1568–1619), who was Bishop of Galloway and Dean of the Chapel Royal: 'Idleness was never tolerated by God: even when Adam was in his innocency, he would not have him to live without labour, and therefore appointed him to dresse the Garden of Eden, and laid it as a law on him and on all men; *In the sweat of thy brow shalt thou live.* . . .' (43) To John Abernethy, yet another Scottish divine, sloth becomes one of the deadly sins. 'Men must provide for their families, or else they are worse than infidels.' (44)

The contrast that emerges from this literature as a result of

Marshall's research is the contrast between all who practise a lawful calling on the one hand, and idlers, such as 'gamesters', 'idle vagabonds', 'tricksters', 'wasters', and thieves on the other. Marshall comments: 'The "idleness" that is the object of censure is the idleness of "one without a lawful calling".' (45) Such teaching, emphasising as it does the strong sense of moral obligation with regard to work, also had the negative effect of associating all those who did not work with deviance.

One suspects that the combined effects of the moral censure of the Church and the constant harassment of the unemployed by the civil authorities must have formulated in the public mind certain strong negative stereotype images with regard to those members of the community who did not work. Clive Jenkins and Barrie Sherman put it like this:

It is not surprising that for hundreds of years work has been declared to be 'a good thing'. From the pulpit, the government chamber, the judges' bench, the king's palace, the lord of the manor's house and the factory owner's office, the message has been repeated *ad nauseum*: 'Work is good for you and your soul.' From the Middle Ages onwards religion told us God ordained that the station of most men was to work, and work became associated with such key words as honest, sober, trustworthy. Those who did not work on the other hand, were by implication dishonest, shifty and drunken. (46)

Such stereotype images draw their strength from being simplistic; they are not discriminatory and tend to lump everyone together as being 'all of a kind'. These images also have an extraordinary power of persistence. It is the legacy of some of these images with regard to work and those who do not work, which were formulated in the years under consideration and further reinforced by subsequent indoctrination, which acts as a major stumbling block to the formulation of creative and appropriate social policies for our own times. On the one hand, the legacy of the belief that to work is a good thing *per se* prevents us from being discriminatory as to what kind of work is being undertaken. Whether that work is what Fritz Schumacher called 'good work', that is work which meets real human needs because it is essentially engaged in the production of necessary and useful goods and services. Whether the work in question meets certain ecological criteria in its usage of the earth's resources and in the nature of its products. And finally, whether the work in question meets some of the employee's basic human needs in that there is a sense in which the worker is dignified in the doing of the task. On the other hand, the other principal legacy of belief, that all who do not work in our society are deviant and deserve our moral censure becomes an increasingly anachronistic basis for the formulation of appropriate public policy when for a variety of structural reasons large numbers of people, through no fault of their own, cannot obtain the employment they desire.

(c) *The Influence of the Charity and Sunday Schools*

In this brief historical survey we have been attempting to see how some of our attitudes towards work have been shaped and moulded down through the passage of the years. Alan Fox, the industrial sociologist, suggests that men have no innate, genetically given orientation towards work, rather our attitudes to work are socially and culturally moulded.

Men are taught what to expect and want from work—taught by a variety of socialising agencies. What they learn to want is a social fact of great importance and there will be a variety of institutions and groups eager to do the teaching. If war is too important to be left to the generals, work is too important to be left to the workers. Not only will the state itself implicitly or explicitly encourage certain attitudes to work and discourage others, but so also will social institutions such as industry, business and commerce, religion, and the educational system. Relevant strands in the cultural tradition will exert their influence through education and communications media. The local community, the family and the work group will also contribute their effect. Finally, interested parties such as professional associations, employers' associations and trade unions may seek to consolidate or change the prevailing orientations. Out of all these influences upon different social groups and classes, different orientations to work are created. (47)

Fox's analysis is an important one when we come in this section to examine the role of the Charity and Sunday schools in the process of moulding the minds of the young in accord to the perceived needs of a nation passing through the throes of industrialisation.

Hill sees the problem of the seventeenth century as that of any backward economy—'failure to use the full human resources of the country'. (48). If the country was to begin economic advance an ideology advocating regular systematic work was required. A new discipline of work was needed if those coming from a village agrarian economy were to be engaged in factory employment. Mollie Batten writes:

It was a concern of the early industrialists to recruit men, women and children into their factories and to train them to be a docile labour force. These people in the early nineteenth century had recently come from villages, and others continued to come to the towns in search of a better living and perhaps a fortune. They were used to a life of activity, maybe hard, but containing within the community the whole spectrum from agricultural work, to chores in garden and home, to leisure . . . to idling, to rest, to sleep. In the new industrial towns work had to be a distinctive activity, in a separate place, under constraint, for long hours, made more monotonous by the division of labour. Both conditions of work and conditions of living were conceived in terms of the farm yard and the tied cottage of the country. So the workers had to be taught to be the kind of people who accepted this. The Sunday Schools undertook this moral education and one of the chief articles of this creed was the value of hard and unremitting work. This was God's ordinance for the working man, woman and child. (49)

M.W. Flinn, in his paper 'Social Theory and the Industrial Revolution', makes the same point with regard to the process of indoctrination that was required.

It is unlikely that a society, however vigorously led by entrepreneurs, will advance rapidly and comfortably along the road to industrialisation unless it can at the same time persuade a labour force, hitherto accustomed to the freedom and flexibility of a mainly agricultural, craft, or domestic way of life, to fall easily and unprotestingly into the discipline and rigidity of large-scale industrial organisation. There is, I would suggest, some evidence that an adjustment of this nature was consciously premeditated and vigorously instilled into the labouring generations of the eighteenth century, both before and during the period of the industrial revolution.

Some form of mass education for the working classes first began to be provided at the beginning of the eighteenth century; and throughout this century and into the nineteenth century, the Charity and Sunday Schools were the principal channels through which the middle and upper classes sought to impose their social ideas upon the working class. It might not be too serious an exaggeration to claim that these schools represented the most significant or influential new force being brought to bear on the social attitudes of a large section of the labouring population during the eighteenth century. For this reason, the aims and ideology of these schools may have some bearing upon the undoubted fact of the creation of an industrial labour force which submitted itself peaceably enough to the socially disturbing rigours of urbanisation and industrialisation. (50)

Flinn illustrates his argument by quoting from some of the reports of the governors. As the Committee of the Manchester Sunday Schools expressed it, the Sunday schools 'called in a sense of religious obligation to the aid of industry'. (51) 'That most desirable union,' as Bishop Porteus declared in 1786, 'of manual labour and spiritual instruction.' (52) The role of Charity schools, according to Isaac Watts writing in the 1720s, was 'to impress upon their tender minds . . . the duties . . . of humility and submission to superiors'. (53) Similarly, William Brooke, the organiser of Sunday Schools in Bath, praised 'the advantage [the children] derive from thus being regularly assembled together on a stated day in each week—they become reconciled to confinement and are habituated to behave with silence and respect in the presence of their superiors'. (54)

'It was a willingness and capacity to work hard for long hours that mattered, and the Charity and Sunday schools were geared most directly to meet this need.' (55) 'Industry is the great principle of duty that ought to be inculcated on the lowest class of people', insisted the *Gentleman's Magazine* in the 1790s, and the Charity and Sunday schools responded with endless variations on the theme of 'the Devil finds employment for idle hands'. (56)

The influence of these schools upon the minds of the young must have been strongly formative in establishing that powerful sense of 'ought' that even today is attached to work. Not only 'ought' everyone to bend themselves to work for a living, but that work, however menial, however ill rewarded, should be done well, with enthusiasm, even with devotion.

> How doth the busy little bee
> Improve each shining hour
> And gather honey all the day
> From every opening flower.
>
> In works of labour or of skill
> I should be busy too
> For Satan finds some mischief still
> For idle hands to do. (57)

So sang the children in their Charity and Sunday schools and trickling down into the subconscious of thousands of young minds went the highly formative linking of the image of idle hands with Satan and mischief. 'Grant me industry,' (58) the child was taught to pray, while at the same time the awful consequences of wilful idleness were brought home to the children through the medium of their reading exercises.

John Knight was in the army. He carried a knapsack, and he was no better than *a knave*, for he did not enlist from a wish to serve his King and Country, but because *he did not like work*. After doing many *bad* things he went off, for which *he was whipped*; after a while he went off again, and then *he was shot*. (59)

Again notice in this passage how, through the close conjunction of the words I have placed in italics, the young mind was fed powerful negative imagery which would then be likely to be incorporated into the psyche. From the pulpit and in the Sunday schools a process of formulating moral values with regard to work, and inevitably towards those who did not work, had its part to play in shaping the public mind. As Antony points out, the public's attitude towards those without work is the obverse side of the prevailing ideology of work. 'Once work is dignified, it is a short and almost inevitable step to dignifying the worker, and when work is set up for enthusiastic comparison with idleness it is difficult to avoid admiration for the worker and contempt for the idle.' (60)

We now begin to understand why in a work-orientated society those who do not work are associated in the public mind with negative stereotype images and tend to be stigmatised. It is then but a short step for the unemployed living within such a social setting to internalise these same perceptions of stigma, viewing their own selves with disgust and loathing:

How hard and humiliating it is to bear the name of an unemployed man. When I go out, I cast down my eyes because I feel myself wholly inferior. When I go along the street, it seems to me that I can't be compared with an average citizen, that everybody is pointing at me with his finger. I instinctively avoid meeting anyone. Former acquaintances and friends of better times are no longer so cordial. They greet me indifferently when we meet. They no longer offer me a cigarette and their eyes seem to say, 'You are not worth it, you don't work.' (61)

Where work is raised into an exalted position within a culture, where it is eulogised by influential public figures and the moral imperatives of work are emphasised within the educational system, then those without work are driven out beyond the conceptual framework of those times. That society has no place for them. They are deviants from the norm. That intolerant period of history that was dominated by English Puritanism and Victorian morality had no place for social deviants. Those not in work were the undeserving poor and as such did not merit sympathy or understanding.

Moral condemnation and material deprivation were the sanctions to be applied.

The Gospel of Work

'For the architects of modern society, work was the real substance of life. It was exalted to the position of an absolute and made a value in itself. . . . Eulogies of work may be found in abundance in the philosophical writings and in the general literature of recent centuries, . . . in wide circles in Western Europe and America the belief in work as a supreme value persists.' (62) So wrote J.H. Oldham describing the heights to which work came eventually to be elevated. The acceptance of such a high doctrine of work, however, though pervasive, was not absolute. Significantly it was the working classes, our modern equivalent of the Hebrew's '*am ha-ares*', who long rejected the advocacy of the establishment that the new cult of work should be erected into the centre of human existence. According to Professor John Burnett, they found it an 'unpalatable and alien notion'. (63) Among the ranks of the common man there was a strong undertow of resistance and scepticism with regard to this so-called 'Gospel of Work'. In part it was perhaps a scepticism born of wondering whose real interests were most served by the rigorous pursuit of the capitalist economic process, and in this regard I am always reminded of the highly perceptive Haiitian proverb which muses, 'If work were a good thing the rich would have found a way of keeping it all to themselves.'

The working classes also resisted the subordination of all things to work because they valued convivial relationships, and the cult of work, particularly as it was manifested in the factory system, was disruptive of them. The factory system and the process of centralised production broke up the old patterns of communal living where 'almost the whole of life, including work, had gone forward within the circle of the family; increasingly, as the nineteenth century progressed, though much less quickly than is commonly supposed, work became separated from family and the home'. (64) The process of industrialisation tended to separate a man from his wife and children by separating work from the home sphere. It imposed on the worker, through the rapacious demands of the factory system, a diminution of free time for family and friends. Further, those precious opportunites for recreation and festivity that had previously helped to bind people together within the village and had given expression to communal joy were also severely curbed. Involvement with other people outside of work as well as in it, time to be with family and neighbours, time for convivial group activities, visits to fairs and markets, to village sports, excursions into the countryside or simply walks with friends, these things were all precious to the common man from time immemorial. They formed part of the rich fabric of life and understandably the worker was loath to part with these expressions of wholesome communal and family life in order to appease the demands of the new factory system.

However, bit by bit the process of indoctrination came to take root. The vested interests of business and the state were advanced by demanding from all individuals a total and passionate commitment to their work. Antony comments, 'Work has always been important, but its organisation, motivation, and control in conditions of industrialization demanded a wholesale commitment to its values and a concerted attempt to achieve it by ideological and other means.' (65) This Gospel of Work, as William James described it, became the prevailing ideology amongst large sections of Victorian England and something of its ghost still lives on. Whether the work to which so many assiduously came to bend their hands and minds always justified or deserved such total human commitment is another question. However, perhaps sufficient has been said in this brief historical survey to indicate some of the key changes that have taken place in the way of attitude formation. In particular I have drawn attention to the post-sixteenth century over-emphasis on work. The influences here I believe were initially religious in origin. Later, other key groupings took certain religious concepts and shaped them into a convenient ideology because such attitudes of diligence and wholehearted commitment towards daily work suited commercial and industrial interest. I have also drawn attention to the way in which prevailing attitudes and perceptions exert an influence over the shaping of social policy. Often social policy in Britain has been hostile to those who were without work. Those in authority have viewed the unemployed with mistrust, seeing this marginalised group as a potential threat to established interests. At times the response of those living in comparative affluence to the workless and the poor has been to interpret their condition as one which was self-inflicted. That is to say, their unemployment could be attributed to sloth, social deviance and lack of personal motivation. However, within the historical record there also runs the strand of enlightenment and social concern and this too I have tried to identify. At best the state and the community have recognised their collective responsibilities towards those trapped into situations of persistent poverty and enforced idleness and have broken out beyond the bounds of egocentric self-interest in an attempt to make structural provision for what were fundamentally structural problems. Public perceptions have been shown to be susceptible to modification. Inappropriate and unhelpful attitudes have been shed and a greater measure of understanding has emerged.

These two strands, the punitive and the compassionate, can be traced back through the centuries in terms of the public response to unemployment and poverty. At times one strand has appeared to be more dominant; at times the other. At times both are twined together giving rise to a strange ambivalence of social response. It is precisely these same problems of attitude, public perception, social acceptance and state policy with regard to the plight of the unemployed that require careful scrutiny in our own times. In the midst of the present very deep economic crisis it is important that we all embark upon a re-evaluation of our inherited value systems, perceptions, attitudes and social policies, all of which were framed in a previous era. Are they appropriate and serviceable within a social order where approximately three million are unemployed or must these things and with them our lifestyles change if there is to be a true congruence with present realities? In the next chapter I want to pursue this discussion further and attempt to sketch out what I have termed a 'contribution ethic' which may provide a better basis for future lifestyles.

Notes and References

1. The Oxford English Dictionary defines work as 'The expenditure of energy, striving, application of effort to some purpose'. But I have found Sylvia Shimmin's article on 'Concepts of Work' (*Occupational Psychology*, October 1966) more helpful. She writes, 'Work is commonly regarded as a clearly defined area of life and a definable activity.' In an attempt to identify certain criteria which would help us clarify this definition further, she suggests the following: (i) that work is a purposeful activity, (ii) that it is instrumental, (iii) that it yields income, (iv) that it entails the expenditure of effort and (v) some element of obligation and/or constraint.
   See also Parker, Stanley, *The Future of Work and Leisure,* Paladin, 1972, especially Chapter 2, 'Problems of Definition'.
2. Zweig, Ferdynand, *The British Worker*, Penguin Books, 1952, p. 104.
3. Burnett, John, *Useful Toil: Autobiographies of Working People from the 1820's to the 1920's*, Penguin Books, 1977. The whole of this Preface merits careful reading. The extracts are from p. 15 and p. 18.

4. Antony, P.D., *The Ideology of Work*, Tavistock Publications, 1978, p. 15. My thinking has been greatly influenced by Antony's lucidly argued thesis. I have drawn heavily on his work in this section.

5. Mossé, C., *The Ancient World at Work*, Chatto and Windus, 1969, p. 25.

6. Antony, P.D., 1978, *op. cit.*, p. 19.

7. De Grazia, Sebastian, *Of Time, Work and Leisure*, Twentieth Century Fund, New York, 1962, p. 4.

8. Welbourn, David, 'New Attitudes for a New Age', Unpublished Paper prepared for a Conference in Sunderland, February 1979.

9. Jeffreys, M.V.C., *Glaucon: An Inquiry into the Aims of Education*, Pitman, 1950, p. 118.

10. Davidson, Robert, 'Work and Unemployment—a Biblical Approach'. An unpublished working paper for the Scottish Unemployment Theology Group, 1980.

11. *Ibid.*

12. Jahoda, Marie, 'The Psychological Meanings of Unemployment', *New Society*, 6 September 1979, p. 495.

13. Davidson, Robert, 1980 op. cit.

14. Wright, G. Ernest, *The Biblical Doctrine of Man in Society*, Ecumenical Biblical Studies, No. 2, SCM Press, 1954, p. 144.

15. *Work and the Future: Technology, World Development and Jobs in the Eighties*, A Report from the Industrial Committee of the Church of England General Synod Board for Social Responsibility, Final Draft, p. 3.

16. Brunner, Emil, *Justice and the Social Order*, Lutterworth Press, 1945, pp. 43 and 45.

17. Antony, P.D., 1979, *op. cit.*, p. 25.

18. Mossé, C., 1969, *op. cit.*, p. 29.

19. Antony, P.D., 1978, *op. cit.*, p. 22.

20. Fullerton, Kemper, 'Calvinism and Capitalism: An Explanation of the Weber Thesis', *Harvard Theological Review XXI*, 1928. This helpful guide to the teaching of Luther and Calvin is contained in a collection of papers entitled *Protestantism and Capitalism: The Weber Thesis and its Critics*, Ed. Robert W. Green, D.C. Heath and Co, Lexington, U.S.A., 1959, p. 10.

21. *Ibid.*

22. Bainton, Roland H., *Here I Stand: A Life of Martin Luther*, Mentor Books, Abingdon Press, 1950, pp. 180–181.

23. Weber, Max, *The Protestant Ethic and the Spirit of Capitalism*, Allen and Unwin, 1978, p. 79.

24. *id.*, p. 80.

25. Fullerton, K., 1928, op. cit., p. i3.

26. Walker, Williston, *A History of the Christian Church*, T. & T. Clark, Edinburgh, 1959, p. 351.

27. Fullerton, K, 1928, op. cit., p. 13.

28. Tilgher, A., *Work through the Ages,* NOSOW and FORM, 1962, p. 19. These form extracts from an earlier study, *Work: What it has Meant to Men Through the Ages*, Harcourt Brace, New York, 1930.

29. Tawney R.H., *Religion and the Rise of Capitalism*, Penguin Books, 1948 ed., pp. 240–241. Closing quote from Richard Baxter, *Christian Directory I*, 1678 ed., p. 336b.

30. Jordan, W.K., *Philanthropy in England*, Allen and Unwin, 1959, p. 78.

31. Pound, John, *Poverty and Vagrancy in Tudor England*, Longman Group, 1971, p. 3.

32. *id*, pp. 5–6.

33. *id*, p. 81.

34. Longmate, Norman, *The Workhouse*, Temple Smith, 1974, p. 14.
35. Pound, John, 1971, *op. cit.*, p. 82.
36. Longmate, N., 1974, *op. cit.*, *passim*.
37. Deacon, Alan, 'The Scrounging Controversy: Public Attitudes towards the Unemployed in Contemporary Britain', *Social and Economic Administration*, 12.2, Summer 1978.
38. *The Perception of Poverty in Europe*, Commission of the European Communities, Brussels, March 1977, p. 80.
39. Weber, Max, 1978 ed., *op. cit.*, p. 155.
40. Fullerton, K., 1959, op. cit., p. 16.
41. Baxter, Richard, *Christian Directory I*, pp. 108ff., 336f. and 375f.
42. Marshall, Gordon, *Presbyteries and Profits: Calvinism and the Development of Capitalism in Scotland 1560–1707*, Clarendon Press, Oxford, 1980, p. 69. Quote from Robert Rollock, *Paul to the Thessalonians, Epist I*, pp. 71f. Robert Rollock was Regent, then Principal or First Master of the University of Edinburgh (1583) and in 1587 Professor of Theology.
43. Marshall, G., 1980, *op. cit.*, p. 78. William Cowper, *The Anatomy of a Christian Man* in *Workes*, p. 349.
44. Marshall, Gordon, 1980, *op. cit.*, p. 83.
45. *id*, p. 70.
46. Jenkins, Clive, and Barrie Sherman, *The Collapse of Work*, Eyre Methuen, 1979, p. 16.
47. Fox, Alan, *A Sociology of Work in Industry*, Collier–Macmillan, 1971, p. 2.
48. Hill, C., *Society and Puritanism in Pre-Revolutionary England*, Secker and Warburg, 1964, pp. 124–125.
49. Batten, E.M., *The Changing Meaning of Work Today*, Preliminary Paper, Industrial Committee, General Synod Board of the Church of England, June 1967.
50. Flinn, M.W., 'Social Theory and the Industrial Revolution', contained in *Social Theory and Economic Change*, eds. Tom Burns and S.B. Saul, Tavistock Publications, 1967, pp. 14–15.
51. Wadsworth, A.P., 'The First Manchester Sunday Schools', *Bulletin of the John Rylands Library*, 33.300, 1950–51.
52. Porteus, Beilby, 'A Letter to the Clergy of the Diocese of Chester concerning Sunday Schools', 1778, p. 11.
53. Watts, Isaac, *An Essay Towards the Encouragement of Charity Schools*, 1728, p. 14.
54. Brooke, William, *Short addresses to the children of Sunday Schools*, 7th ed., 1811, p. 78.
55. Flinn, M.W., 1967, op. cit., p. 17.
56. *Gentleman's Magazine*, LXVII, 1797, p. 820.
57. Watts, Isaac, *Divine and moral songs for children*, 1869 ed., p. 38.
58. Kennet, White (Bishop of Peterborough), *The Christian Scholar*, 1811, p. 46.
59. Trimmer, Sarah, *The Charity School Spelling Book Part II*, new ed., n.d., p. 24.
60. Antony, P.D., 1978, op. cit., p. 44.
61. Zawadski, S., and P. Lazarsfeld, 'The Psychological Consequences of Unemployment', *Journal of Social Psychology*, VI, 1935, p. 239, quoting a statement made by a 43-year-old unemployed mason in Germany during the Depression.
62. Oldham, J.H., *Work in Modern Society*, SCM Press, 1950, p. 18.
63. Burnett, John, 1977, *op. cit.*, p. 19.
64. *id*, pp. 18–19.
65. Antony, P.D., 1978, *op. cit.*, pp. 299–300.

Chapter 17

NEW ATTITUDES FOR A NEW AGE

A man's work is one of the more important parts of his social identity, of his self; indeed, of his fate in the one life he has to live.

Everett C. Hughes *Work and the Self* (1951)

When I first saw unemployed men at close quarters, the thing that horrified and amazed me was to find that many of them were *ashamed* of being unemployed. . . . The middle classes were still talking about 'lazy idle loafers on the dole' and saying that 'these men could all find work if they wanted to', and naturally these opinions percolated to the working class themselves. . . . They simply could not understand what was happening to them. They had been brought up to work, and behold! it seemed as if they were never going to have the chance of working again. In their circumstances it was inevitable, at first, that they should be haunted by a feeling of personal degradation. That was the attitude towards unemployment in those days: it was a disaster which happened to *you* as an individual and for which *you* were to blame.

George Orwell *The Road to Wigan Pier* (1937)

I set these two very striking quotations at the head of this chapter because of their usefulness as social bench-marks with regard to value systems and attitudes held earlier this century. They are indicators of the way in which work and its obverse condition, idleness, came to be regarded. Religion had succeeded in helping to make a sacred duty of work and a sin of idleness. Attitudes have moved on somewhat, but although in the process of secularisation the original theological supportive roots of the Work Ethic have withered and become forgotten, with regard to the necessity to work still something of the old moral imperative lingers on. The strong sense of moral obligation so powerfully engendered by the Work Ethic has a sort of half-life which continues to influence us. The Work Ethic as a complete system of values by which to live may be dead, but something of its ghost remains within our culture to trouble and haunt those who find themselves without employment. Such culturally inherited attitudes are hard to shake off even when the social circumstances change and the stance adopted is no longer appropriate. But if the Work Ethic no longer fits the needs of the hour, then what value systems remain? What are we able to affirm and what can we no longer affirm with any degree of integrity?

With respect to our value systems and the place of work in our lives we are in a state of some confusion. Some disturbing cracks have appeared in the previously imposing facade of work and we are no longer so sure that we can put our belief in the things to which our forefathers so wholeheartedly committed their lives. Instead there is a pervasive uncertainty. As there is uncertainty with regard to appropriate economic policy, so there is perhaps an even greater uncertainty within the nation with respect to a sustainable ideology of work. The ideology of work that we have inherited is crumbling just as the ideal of Full Employment is crumbling. They are two strands of the same crisis over the place of work in our lives.

Although in my profession I move constantly in the world of work and part of my role is to try to assess what is happening there, like everyone else in our age, I am a child of the same confusion. There is no clear cut, coherent picture of what is happening. I seem to be able only to catch glimpses of what the future perhaps holds with regard to a new ideology of work. I cannot speak with confidence about the future. I am filled with many uncertainties as to the precise direction in which we will move following on the demise of the Work Ethic. But there are just a few things of which I am becoming increasingly convinced which I would like to share in this chapter. They emerge for me in the form of four basic affirmations which perhaps may come to act as guides for us as we step into an unknown darkness. While not acquiescing to the social injustice which is a feature of our present unemployment scene I believe that we need to become more accepting of the victims of economic adversity. But in addition to this social acceptance of the unemployed, which emerges from an affirmation of the indefeasible dignity of all men and women, we need also to continue to affirm that work which is socially useful. My third affirmation concerns what I have called a Contribution Ethic. The last affirms the preciousness of those other realms of human life which lie outside the arena of work. These four affirmations I have set out as the subsection titles of this chapter and I would want to say a fuller word about each.

1. *The Social Affirmation of the Unemployed*

A consideration of our value systems and our inherited social attitudes are important because they have the tendency to affect both personal behaviour and also the shaping of policy. First, the attitudes that we have inherited from the past help to condition the way in which we relate to those who are unemployed when we encounter them in a variety of informal social settings. Second, they affect the way the unemployed as a group are treated by those who man our benefit offices and those who provide services and facilities for the unemployed. Third, they subtly influence public sympathy within the electorate, senior Civil Servants and Government Ministers and this will help set the priorities when formulating economic and social policy. (1) For all these reasons it is therefore important that we examine current public perceptions and root out of our society the unhelpful negative stereotypes and myths inherited from the past which still attach to those who are unemployed.

The negative image of the unemployed as a social group is well illustrated in this recorded interview conducted by Jeremy Seabrook in Blackburn in 1969.

Most people on the dole could find work if they wanted to. If you look in the paper at any time, there's loads of jobs going.

They used to have to go and queue up for it, but now it's sent through the post.

There's plenty of jobs going, mostly simple jobs, driving, labouring. Anybody can do that, you don't have to be of superhuman intelligence to do that.

One case I know, I don't know him personally, but I've heard of him, he does a job for a few days, then he gets the sack so he can go back on the dole. Because if you're sacked, you can draw the dole; but if you leave of your own accord, you don't get it. That's why most of these people want to get sacked.

Governments should give them one month. One month to get a job, then no dole.

They could be put to work building motorways.

You'll always get some who want something for nothing these days. It's that kind of world now.

Are people on the grab?

Definitely. Look at the unemployment figures. . . . There must be a percentage of that figure born idlers, scroungers.

They don't want to work, they're lazy.

They can get as much off social security as they can in a job.

That's what socialism does for you.(2)

Even in the midst of the recession similar attitudes are being expressed today. These very negative perceptions of the unemployed, which are almost completely dismissive of the structural causes and which still equate unemployment with voluntary idleness, are deeply distressing to those who genuinely cannot find work. The stigma of being associated in the public mind with the work-shy loafer remains very painful to them. A sense of shame still attaches to their condition and the defensive response is one of social withdrawal. The general public for its part still seems more concerned to hunt down the social security scrounger than to encourage the setting up of an appropriate range of social provisions for this growing client group. Still the ill-informed will blame the victim attributing their continued unemployment to lack of personal motivation. The general cultural climate in which the unemployed live, move and have their being remains ambivalent towards those who have no work, and relationships between those in work and those who are without work are uneasy. There is a sense in which the unemployed remain the pariahs of our social system (viz. the entitlement of the long-term unemployed to only the lowest levels of supplementary benefit rate), and such social provisions as are made are still often offered in a cautious, half-resented fashion. The unemployed are quick to discern these things and in their hypersensitive state they tend to shrink yet further into their inner shell of shame, passivity and housebound isolation.

It is important that the social order is purged of these unhelpful and accusatory attitudes towards those who, try as they might, cannot secure work at this point of time. Such cultural attitudes serve to inhibit and destroy the last vestiges of initiative, creativity and self-respect within the unemployed who are caught into a situation not of their own making. Instead as a nation we must affirm in both personal relationships and social action that those who are without work in this time of economic crisis have as legitimate a place within the social order as the sick, the young, the retired or the employed. In their social distress they hunger for the life-affirmative word. We need to say in effect to those who cannot find work in our society: 'You are a child of the universe. You have a right to be here.'(3) Whether or not at this point of time they are able to make a contribution to society through the medium of the paid economy, they are entitled to an adequate place within the social order. For each man and woman, as a child of God, has a value, dignity and worth that is absolutely independent of their utility within the economy and social arrangements must reflect this.

That adequate place for every citizen within the social order entails not only the provision of some means of adequate income but also the cultural conditions of social acceptance. For in its own way the absence of social acceptance can be as damaging to human fulfilment as the absence of the material necessities of life. The existential problem of trying to live out my life in a society which insists on treating me as a non-person is almost as acute as the problem of living in a society where I am in receipt of an income that is too low to allow me to enjoy life like everyone else. Both an adequate income and social acceptance are essential ingredients of a civilised existence. Alas, in most cases the unemployed as a social group are condemned to live lives that suffer from a relative shortage of both. If we are genuine in our desire to secure for our neighbour and our neighbour's child the dimensions of a civilised existence then we must address ourselves both to the task of devising the means that will lift the burdens imposed by relative poverty and at the same time we must concern ourselves with the task of lifting the remaining burden and curse of social stigma which still attaches to those who are not in paid work. I suspect that both objectives can only be achieved as a result of securing a redistribution of both work opportunities and incomes which will serve to reduce some of the present sharp divides and give us lifestyles which have more in common.

2. *The Affirmation of that Work which is Socially Useful*
The social affirmation of the unemployed is one side of the problem which confronts us, living as we do in the wake of the Work Ethic with its strictures against idleness. I now want to put work under the spotlight. It may be considered a subversive question but

nevertheless it is one which must be asked by the radical theologian. To what extent are we able to affirm work in modern society?

In the previous chapter I pointed out the difficulties that confront us when trying to describe how a particular historical culture views work. Individual attitudes towards work vary enormously and there is no definitive position. Rather we find that attitudes towards work form a continuum, stretching from those who virtually invest all their drives, energies, time and feelings of inner significance in the world of their work, to those groupings, like the 'hippies' and the 'drop-outs', who would wish to sit exceedingly loose to the world of paid employment and who would instead find their fulfilment in the contemplative life, simple living and convivial relationships. Similarly, the number of individuals who now approach their vocation as a task wholly undertaken to the greater glory of God would be few. Even within the ranks of the Christian Church I personally know many who find it hard to endow their particular occupational activities with meaning and significance. Whether it be the assembly worker putting together he knows not what for a customer he will never see, or the administrative employee busily sending papers and forms to someone else so they can send them back to him, or the professional employee caught in the endless treadmill of meetings and travel, there is a terrible lack of the sense of achievement and real purpose in many people's working lives. In such a situation it is impossible to sustain a high doctrine of work. The reality of being engaged in tasks that are without evident significance falls too far short.(4) Here then is a problem which is quite distinct from the burning problem of unemployment. The unemployment problem is basically a quantitative problem which has to do with an insufficiency of work opportunities. But what we are touching upon here is a problem with work itself. It is a qualitative issue which asks deep and searching questions about the ends of work. The locus of this problem lies within the ranks of the employed and in the operation of the prevailing economic system. For within the institutional economy in a wide range of occupations there are a great number of people who have no strong conviction about the importance and worth of what they are actually doing week in and week out.

In Britain today there is a good deal of questioning with regard to what is going on in market economics. Is the good of all mankind really being served by our present economic system or are

its benefits only very patchily distributed? Does the system merely
serve itself? Are the real needs of our own people let alone the
Third World actually being met or are we missing the mark? At the
personal level also there is a feeling of unease both with respect to
the organisation and the ends of work. As one moves among a wide
range of occupations there is a disturbing lack of real personal
commitment. There is an emptiness; a feeling of futility at the
centre of far too many work lives. We have already noted many of
the signs of alienation in the lives of those who are workless. The
lack of a sense of purpose and belonging, the feeling of no longer
being in control of one's life and that awful sense of inner
emptiness. But feelings of alienation and purposelessness arise in
the lives of many working individuals also.(5) Here we touch upon
an uncertainty with regard to the affirmation of work which
manifests itself in many industrial societies. It is a malaise which
saps the will to work because we do not know whether what we are
doing in our working time is really worthwhile. Our forefathers who
so wholeheartedly embraced the Work Ethic presumably never
allowed themselves to entertain such doubts, but we in our age find
it very hard to be entirely rid of them. Is life really being enhanced
and enriched by all our endeavours? What is being achieved as a
result of all our combined labours? *Cui bono*? Whom does it serve?
To what end is all our work directed and is it in all cases work that
really deserves to be done? Some of it appears so meaningless and
trivial.

Other features of the social scene seem to indicate that we have
got our priorities all wrong. Thus for example, throughout the
world over three million highly qualified scientists and engineers are
busily engaged in further refining the killing capacity of our missile
systems and yet the most urgent task of providing safe and cheap
power is neglected in comparison.(6) The world, as we know,
is faced by a shortage of several essential resources and yet our
strategic deployment of manpower into the vital tasks of more
efficient design and repair, recycling and renovation activities
remains shamefully small. We remain a 'throw-away society' and
are prepared to mortgage our children's future with a profligate
pattern of consumer consumption that threatens future supplies.
We find profit in making junk products while the Third World
starves. We press on eagerly in the production and marketing of
products which we know are not good for our health and yet a
whole range of primary health care and life-enhancing tasks go un-

attended for lack of the requisite finance. There is an ugly imbalance of priorities. 'On the scales of justice and humanity we see one pan weighed down with massive investment in human and material resources of potential and real death and destruction. In the other pan the meagre resources devoted to the elimination of poverty and the enhancement of life for all humanity.'(7)

The simple slogan 'All Work Good, Idleness Bad' is an inadequate guide to life. It does not ask the radical and qualitative questions which must always be put whenever we are reviewing human endeavour. Perhaps those who so whole-heartedly embraced the Work Ethic were not sufficiently discriminating about ends. But if we cannot give a blanket endorsement to all that provides scope for paid employment what can we affirm as a fit activity for man in his capacity of *homo faber*? It is here that the concept of 'good work', to use Schumacher's phrase, or 'socially useful products', to use the Lucas Aerospace Shop Stewards' phrase, may be helpful to us.(8) The initiative of the Lucas Shop Stewards' Combine Committee in this regard is a very interesting one. Faced by the prospect of future redundancies the shop-floor workers, the *am ha-ares* of the British Aerospace industry, went to their management with an alternative plan which suggested that they should redeploy their skills and energies into the development and production of a range of socially useful products. One hundred and fifty such alternative products were identified. The difficulties which they encountered in trying to achieve a change of direction in company policy forms a long, sad and continuing saga. But in the creative ideas that were forthcoming in these and other alternative plans, vital and radical questions were being asked about both the organisation and the ends of industry.

How can we combine our skilled human resources, our technical and capital resources in such a way that both worthwhile employment is created and through our labours the real needs of the global village come to be met? That is a key organisational issue for our age. For any society which cannot affirm the importance and worth of the central activity by which it lives is a society with a hollowness at its economic centre which cannot be concealed. In such a flawed society the institutionalised economy may attract large numbers of people because of the financial rewards that can be obtained there. But their relationship towards work will be principally instrumental. It will be unable to command their whole-hearted commitment and it will fail to unleash their fullest potential until it is able to offer them humanly significant things to do within the paid economy.

3. *The Affirmation of a Contribution Ethic*

'The entire experience of mankind demonstrates clearly that useful work, adequately rewarded in some combination of material and non-material things, is a central need of human beings, even a basic yearning of the human spirit.'(9) Is Schumacher right? Does man have these two great basic needs? First, the craving to belong and to have *citizenship:* the felt need to be part of a meaningful community. Second, the desire to be wanted: the need as a human being to be given the opportunity to make some kind of contribution to the ongoing life of that community and for that contribution to be recognized. We are speaking here of a yearning for the opportunity to give expression to that which is within us by doing something that will in some way enhance and enrich the lives of others. Is that what work at its best is really all about? Making some kind of contribution to the community of which we are an integral part? Doing something for others and in doing so breaking out of our ego-centredness?

The act of making a contribution to the community of which we are an integral part does not have to be conceived as being confined to what we do within the paid economy in our occupational role. That is certainly a very important sphere giving us a structured situation in which we can do things with others and for others and for which we receive some compensating financial reward. But that is not the only human forum in which we are given the opportunity to make a significant contribution to life. Perhaps out of the ashes of the Work Ethic, which is seriously challenged by the loss of the ideal of Full Employment, there will emerge the concept of a Contribution Ethic—a belief that our humanity does find fulfilment in doing things for others. That God is glorified through our being of service to our fellows whether that be through employee/customer relationships in the paid economy or whether that service, that giving of ourselves, is manifested in some way or other quite outwith the paid economy.

Both to be able to give something of self and to receive from the hands of others is an essential part of the reciprocal nature of community. Should that delicate balance of relationships ever be altered so that we find that we are given no satisfying opportunities to contribute, or if we appear to give and give but receive no expression of social recognition in return, our equanimity is disturbed and the wholesome balance and equity of community life is endangered. A Contribution Ethic recognises that an element of reciprocity is essential in healthy social arrangements. It is disturbed when there are inadequate rewards and it is concerned when men, women and young people have no adequate opportunities to make their own valid contributions to the society of which they are an integral part. But a Contribution Ethic recognises that what is done for others outside the forum of paid employment can be as precious and as important as that which is done in our occupational capacity. The important thing is that an enriching contribution is made to life and its worth is recognised, not that we are paid for it. The concept of a Contribution Ethic is perhaps easier to affirm in our age than the old Work Ethic whose arena for significant action was more tightly drawn. It is an ethic which has a universality about it being available to the waged and the unwaged, the employed, the young, the retired or the unemployed, the sick, the healthy, the retarded or the handicapped. All have a contribution to make. What is required is the recognition and the encouragement of that contribution.

4. *The Affirmation of the Preciousness of Life Beyond Work*

We are engaged then in the reassignment of certain values. The new ethic still holds that all which happens within the arena of employment is deeply significant with regard to the shaping of the created order and the meeting of the needs of mankind. But the new ethic would also wish to affirm with vigour the sacred preciousness of all the other aspects of community life and human activity. The deployment of skill and energy by men and women in their occupational role towards ends that are socially useful does have ultimate significance. But both man and God are served by equally precious and valid contributions made in a host of other ways quite outwith the arena of the paid economy. It is this strong affirmation of the sacred nature of all that which lies beyond work, as well as work itself, which is the distinctive feature of this whole life, or Contribution Ethic. It is an ethic which will not permit us to set boundaries on what is precious and significant. It is an ethic which will not allow us to allege a degree of unimportance to certain social groups. It embraces the whole of life and all possible categories of people. It asserts the worth of all people and the significance of all actions.

The Contribution Ethic recognises the workplace as a forum in which we can exercise our energies and skills and that work when properly directed supplies us with a wide range of opportunities to provide those goods and services which will enrich and enhance the lives of others. But it takes issue with the Work Ethic, which had the tendency to so invest value in the institution of work and commerce that it failed to keep in healthy balance the significance of other human spheres. Thus part of the heresy of the Work Ethic was to emphasise the importance of the occupational at the expense of the informal, the convivial, the world of family and friends, the spheres of festivity and recreation, the blessedness of unstructured time. These other spheres were subordinated almost to the point of extinction in the frenzied exhortations towards the activity of work. Little time was permitted to explore the full dimension of being. The call was always to be doing. The Contribution Ethic in contradistinction would wish to assert that these other expressions of our humanity merit strong affirmation. They are integral aspects of what it is to be human and must never be allowed to become totally eclipsed by work. The fullness of our God-given humanity is such that it requires adequate opportunity for its expression and development in these other areas also. Work alone cannot contain all that we have to give. The convival, festive and family occasions also provide us with many rich opportunities to be with others, to share common experiences and to give something of our essential selves to the enhancement of those about us. Here within the family circle and amongst friendship groups, in the gift economy of voluntary work and ordinary neighbourly relations, another set of skills and graces can be fruitfully exercised. Here an extra depth of human needs can be met and lives enriched and sustained in a way quite different from that which transpires when the relationship is founded on a contractual relationship involving the transfer of money. I speak here of the gift relationship and of the preciousness of such relationships within the social order. These gift exchanges, in which we do things for others out of love, affection and concern, are exceedingly important in the bonding process. These interactions and activities of the gift economy create and sustain the sense of community and of genuine care within the social order. As such they give a human face both to family life and to the local neighbourhood scene. The Contribution Ethic recognises these things. Unlike the Work Ethic it is not threatened by uncommitted time, by our human sexuality or by recreational pursuits. Whereas the champions of the Work Ethic saw these things as potential snares that would entice us away from man's true end, the new ethic desires that all should be afforded the opportunity in life to explore the full reach of our humanity and within its compass work, leisure, home and community life, human sexuality, contemplation and relaxation all have their valid place. The concern of the new ethic is that there should be the opportunity to obtain a wholesome balance. That those who are unemployed have available to them opportunities for access to the satisfactions and rewards that work brings and that those who are overburdened by work should have access to the blessings to be found in having time for family and friends, relaxation and recreational pursuits. For the abundant life is to be found in achieving a healthy mix and a wholesome social order provides the freedoms and the resources that enable all its members to attain these things.

Notes and References

1. Sinfield, Adrian, *The Long-Term Unemployed—A Comparative Survey*, OECD Report, 1967, p. 62.
2. Seabrook, Jeremy, *City Close-Up*, Penguin Books, 1973, pp. 186–187. The comments come from three young married couples and an engaged couple. Seabrook comments: 'When asked for their views, these tended to constitute a catalogue of received ideas, culled at random on an *ad hoc* basis out of thin air. The fallowness of their social sense ensured that the only ideas that could exist were windblown cliches and commonplaces.' *id.*, p. 184.
3. From *The Desiderata*, trad.
4. Goulder, Alvin W., 'The Unemployed Self'. An essay contained in *Work 2: Twenty Personal Accounts*, ed. Ronald Fraser, Penguin Books, 1969, pp. 346ff.
5. Blauner, Robert, *Alienation and Freedom: The Factory Worker and his Industry*, University of Chicago Press, Chicago, 1964, *passim*.
6. Ward, Peter, *The Cutting Edge or the Slippery Slope? Workers Alternative Plans for Industry*, TASS–AUEW Paper, October 1979.
7. *id.*
8. Schumacher, E.F., *Good Work*, Jonathan Cape, 1979, p. 3.
9. Schumacher, E.F., Unpublished paper, 1976. Quoted in *Thinking Mission* 31, Summer 1981, ed. Margaret Dewey, United Society for the Propagation of the Gospel.

Chapter 18

PASSING THROUGH CHANGE

One last brief comment perhaps requires to be made upon our subject matter. I have looked at the current crisis over work and unemployment from a number of angles. At times, quite purposively, I have wanted to focus attention on particularities, because the particularities of how the crisis is experienced within the personal realm of specific social groups is very important for us to appreciate and understand. At other points I have been more concerned with general trends, policies and principles. But in this chapter I want to pan back, rather like a television camera and take a last look at the present crisis over work in long shot. I am concerned here to try to make some sense of the present turn of events. For we are all caught up in the midst of painful change and accommodation. The old familiar touchstones of our socio-economic life no longer have their former stability. The traditional wise men of state no longer seem to have the answers. The conventional wisdom appears to be inadequate to meet the needs of the hour. Life as we have known it is in disarray. No one is any longer sure what the future holds. As a people we are passing through change and it is bewildering, confusing and not a little frightening to find our lives caught in this situation.

Because the world of work has played such a significant part in our lives, major changes in that sphere are deeply disturbing to us. We have become so used to having work at the centre of our lives that we would feel very ill at ease without it. The loss of the ideal of Full Employment is a serious challenge to our inherited value systems. We have grown up both expecting to work and expecting that all those who really wanted to work could work. As we have seen, an acute labour shortage in the post-war years served to feed and confirm those beliefs. But now the prospect of failing to be able to provide work for all presents us with a major social problem. It is the problem of a failure to achieve congruence between expectation and reality. The cultivated expectation and the social realities with regard to work no longer tally. In such a situation we find it very difficult to adjust. From the past we carry in our minds certain images of what ought to be and yet it is not so. Personal accommodations to the new situation are difficult enough. But where these attitudes and expectations with regard to work have become incorporated into the very structures of our institutions, where our working practices and public policies have been formulated in the belief that full employment is normative, then the problems of failing to achieve congruence are greater still. Because of the time-lag which always affects the accommodation of large institutional bodies to the new realities we find ourselves without the support of adequate structural arrangements in the new situation.

Just as in 1939 the nation found herself ill-equipped to fight a war, so too in 1982 we find ourselves ill-prepared to cope with a major crisis over work. There is inadequate provision for the casualties and the necessary reorientation and mobilisation of resources to handle our situation in a more satisfactory way is only slowly coming about. It is as though our work-based society finds herself false-footed by the turn of economic events. Over the years we have carefully established our structures, our policies and our collective life around one premise—that there would be work for all who wanted it. We now find ourselves caught into a situation where this is not so. Indeed, if some predictions are correct, the previous social patterns with regard to work may never return again.

Such mismatches and contradictions of expectation are symptomatic that a paradigm shift is taking place within the contemporary scene. (1) Our constellation of beliefs and inherited assumptions with regard to work and the unemployed are having to change. Further, the structures of our society are having to change with them. But to change direction from being a work-orientated society to one whose ethos has a different centre is a cruelly painful business. For the weaker and poorer members of society such times of major cultural transition are filled with danger. In their inability to influence events and without recourse to the material defences which come from having ample financial resources the young, the weak, the poor, the immigrant, the handicapped and certain sections of the aged are all particularly vulnerable. In the human scramble, which occurs when the old order has to be abandoned and territories within the new order are secured, there is great danger that these social groups are left behind. Insufficient life-space is left for them. There is no substantial future for them in attempting to remain where they have been because the old order is in the process of slow decay and collapse. But in power terms they do not possess sufficient muscle to be able to stake out their legitimate claim to an adequate life-space within the new socio-economic order. A time of change is therefore a time when the weak are particularly liable to get hurt. It is a time when all the vulnerable groups particularly need our succour. It is a time when the compassion and solidarity of a nation is tested.

At a time of major social change it is in the adequacy of the social provision made for the more vulnerable groups within the community by the collective whole that the moral credibility of that society is to be assessed. Is protective legislation sensitively framed to protect their interests? Is sufficient regard given to ensure that the social mechanisms work in such a way that their opportunities of attaining to full and satisfying lives are not diminished? For how we choose to treat each other as we pass through difficult times is not just a matter of the weak being the objects of our compassion and magnanimity. The whole calibre of our living, the whole quality of the social order is being weighed in the balance, and in these things, the Christian would say, we are ultimately answerable to God.

As well as being a time of danger for those in vulnerable social categories, a time of cultural crisis is also often a time of opportunity. A time of social disturbance can sometimes be a time when the breakdown of the old order sets us free to establish a different foundation for the new order. The old industrial order of the developed nations has enjoyed many strengths and has brought to its people many benefits. In particular it has brought in its wake a high standard of living for the vast majority of her people. But the old order in which we have been raised also has many flaws and weaknesses which have been the subject of growing concern. The persistent gross disparities of income between individuals within the one nation, the neglect of the poor by those living in conditions of comparative affluence, the contrast in living standards between the central and the peripheral regions of the EEC, not to mention the even grosser disparities which exist between the various nation states of the one global village—these are all deeply disturbing features of the present national and global scene. They point to a failure of solidarity between man and his neighbour while at the same time pointing to the inadequacy of the distribution mechanisms. Meanwhile on the resource front there is equal concern over our stewardship of the earth's resources and mounting moral criticism of a mode of living which makes such heavy demands on energy and mineral supplies. There are sharp questions being raised with regard to the impact of advanced technology not only upon the environment but also upon social lifestyles and a call to exercise a greater discrimination with regard to identifying the most appropriate technologies that will enable us to meet a range of human needs. Finally there is a concern over issues of democracy and the degree to which ordinary people can participate in the process of decision-making in what is an increasingly complex social scene. Taking the radical stance there are many things that it would be good to change. It is in that sense that the present crisis over work, the economy and the social order provides an opportunity. It can open the way to a deeper public debate about social goals. It perhaps gives us the opportunity to ask deep questions about the quality of life, the balance of priorities and the overall direction of our economic activity. It opens the way to a reassigning of values and to a re-evaluation of what contributes to the making of the good life, both within the social and personal realms.

What will the future of work be? No one knows for certain the precise shape of the social arrangements that might be attained a decade hence. In that voyage of discovery both within the biographical sphere and in the creating of a new socio-economic order there are no maps. We sail uncharted waters. It is hard to live our lives amid uncertainty. But perhaps we have to live a little longer with confusion. We may have to make do with rather a large number of provisional arrangements. But as we experiment and gradually grope our way forward I am fairly confident that the outline of a defensible future will emerge. We are in transit. We are engaged in the search for those stepping stones that will lead us towards a more acceptable future social order. We are searching for a system of social arrangements which will enable all citizens of our society to secure the dimensions of a civilised existence and which will preserve a proper respect for them as human beings. Such a new world of work and non-work has not as yet come fully into being. It lies in our hands to influence its construction, ensuring that it has adequate life-space not only for ourselves and our children but also for our neighbour and our neighbour's children.

Our present problems are great but I am confident that all is not lost. At least the outline for a worthy future can be discerned even now. The task is to flesh it out and to give substance to our most promising visions. Out of adversity may yet come good. We have felt ourselves boxed in and unable to advance economically in the direction we had originally intended and in consequences our work-centred world has been thrown into crisis. But perhaps there is another way out of the dilemma of work and unemployment. In the words of the ancient Greek dramatists:

> 'The end men looked for cometh not,
> And a path is there where no man thought.' (2)

Notes and References

1. Kuhn, T.S., *The Structure of Scientific Revolutions*, University of Chicago Press, Chicago, 1970, *passim*.
2. Euripedes, *The Bacchae,* Gilbert Murray translation.

CONCLUSION

I have argued in this book that there are two primary issues which lie embedded within the present somewhat confused debate over unemployment and the future of work. The first is in essence a cultural issue and has to do with accommodations in values, expectation, attitudes and lifestyles in the face of the new employment realities. The second relates to the distribution of work and income within the social order and is concerned with issues of equity, opportunity, sustainability and fraternity. Essentially these two great issues, the cultural and the distributive, demand that an adequate response to be made by all within the nation state. Our analysis is flawed if we merely see them as the personal problems which, alas, confront and afflict those currently unemployed. The problems posed by the loss of the reality of Full Employment raise sharp moral issues for all of us who are still in employment and the corporate solidarity of the nation is tested as we pass through these difficult economic circumstances. I have argued that *all* should share in the accommodations and personal adjustments that are having to be made in the face of the new realities. Not to do so leads to deep and bitter cleavages appearing within the social order and amid the persistence of those injustices we live as two nations and not as one. Further, there is much that could be gained in human terms from now seizing the opportunity to strike a new balance between paid work and gift work, between the organised economy and the informal economy, between occupational concerns and convivial relationships. It is not just that much personal and social pain would be diminished if all shared in the accommodation of lifestyle and working practice. It is that there is so much richness to be found the other side of change. The discovery of an alternative, sustainable and wholesome lifestyle is therefore something that we search for not just because we are driven by necessity out of the old lifestyle but perhaps more so because we are drawn by human hope. Similarly, we set ourselves over against the perpetuation of injustice within the social order not primarily because we fear its imminent material collapse and tremble at the message delivered to us by the prophets of civil doom. Injustice has demonstrated down through the annals of history that it has very considerable powers of survival. No, rather we are led by the firm conviction that there is a better way for human beings to live together within community. One that is more joyous, more confident and in every way qualitatively richer than that of the social order founded on the two nation principle.

Achieving Justice within the Social Order

The discussion in much of this book has centred around the distributive problems which arise when labour supply exceeds labour demand to the extent that millions find themselves without the opportunity to work. How is the available work to be distributed among so many claimants? What principles should apply with regard to the allocation of work opportunities within a nation? Above all how can equity and compassion be incarnated into the structures and the world of systems in a free and democratic society so that social justice can be actualised? These are issues which should properly concern all men and women of goodwill in these present troubled times for there is a fundamental injustice in expecting a minority of people to bear the majority cost as we pass through our present economic difficulties. People want some purposeful activity to shape their living around. They all have need of certain basic economic resources. They quite rightly want the opportunity to meet and share with other people and as we have seen work is in many ways a bridge to the attainment of those human goals. The equitable distribution of work opportunities is therefore a key social issue in our time and the appropriate social mechanisms that will enable us to achieve that more equitable distribution need to be found. The health and wholeness of the nation is at stake for the persistence of gross injustices in the distribution of opportunity between the generations, between the geographical regions and between a range of occupational and ethnic groups will serve to destroy social cohesion and acts as a breeding ground for envy, bitterness, alienation and civil strife. Thus in the words of Archbishop William Temple, 'We are challenged to find a social order which provides employment, steadily and generally and our consciences should be restive till we succeed.'(1) We may not be able in the present economic circumstances to resecure Full Employment in the short or even mid-term. But we can and should promote active policies to increase employment opportunities particularly for the young, the handicapped, the ethnic minority groups and the long-term unemployed whose lives are currently so frequently characterised by a sense of futility and frustration. That is to say, a policy of work redistribution must accompany our policies of job generation.

The issue of how we can bring about some sharing of work opportunities within the one community, however, inexorably leads us on to face up to the other problems to which Work-Sharing is linked. Principal among them is the problem of income. As someone has said to those who would advocate the policy of Work-Sharing: 'I am only too happy to have someone else share my work. It is my income I am not prepared to share.' It is here that vested interest is most directly challenged for in our society it is exceedingly difficult for the individual to separate issues relating to work from issues relating to income. If we are to fashion a social order which is to provide the dimensions of a civilised existence for all its members then we shall have to examine not only the place of work in our lives but also the working of our fiscal systems and the operation of the income provisions of the Welfare State. The problem of wealth redistribution across the nation goes hand in hand with the task of redistributing work opportunities. In the face of persistent high unemployment it becomes increasingly clear that our present system of state benefits is failing to meet the real income needs of very many of its citizens. The need for a rigorous review of all the components which go to make up income is urgent for it is the functioning and patterning of these arrangements which combine to mediate the level of justice and compassion to be found in any given community. As such they must form the object of our constant and critical scrutiny if our neighbour concern is to be given adequate expression. However, the detail of the discussion of precisely how our system of incomes might be changed is far too large and complex an issue to be taken up in this particular work and must be left to others to pursue elsewhere.

I have argued throughout this book that we are our brother's keeper with regard to our neighbour's opportunity to secure employment. I have argued that the collective community has a responsibility towards those who desire a place in the paid economy but who cannot obtain it. I have also urged that this collective responsibility should entail a willingness to accommodate in our present working practices, that more might share in the available work, and a readiness to bear the concomitant costs. I am quite convinced that the structural dislocation of employment patterns, particularly amongst the young, the unskilled and the long-term unemployed, are now too severe to somehow right themselves automatically when the economic upturn comes. We now have in quantitative terms exceedingly serious employment mismatches within the British scene and the longer these problems remain unattended the more intractable do they become. *Laissez-faire* policies and market forces will not rid us of the malaise of our present two-nation society where some continue to reap the benefits that paid work brings and others remain locked out of work. We will need positive and radical policies if we are to do anything more than merely tinker with the problem that now stares us in the face.

The call to all men and women of goodwill must be to convert their concern into the formulation of policies that will express once again the collective responsibility of the whole community towards the weaker members who are caught into a situation not of their own making and from which they cannot escape. Inevitably such policies as will obtain any real purchase upon the difficulties that now confront us will be costly. Caring for others always was costly, as the Cross and the mark of the nails in Christ's hands and feet must always remind us. Man constantly shrinks from living in reciprocity with his fellow-man because *agape*, or 'other concern', inevitably makes its demands upon us and challenges our chosen lifestyle. But we need to remember that our failure to accommodate a little and our refusal to bear any of the cost to set things right makes life even more painful and costly for those whose lives are caught between the upper and nether millstones of our present economic order. Those who presently bear those costs are those whose services have been dispensed with in recent years and increasingly they are our own sons and daughters. Failing to care and to share is costly in terms of the damage which is occurring in the lives of our young people when we deny them the opportunity of entering the adult world of work. Failing to care perpetuates a wasting away of life. As such it is the antithesis of the Gospel vision in which Christ's declared purposes are that men and women 'might have life, and that they might have it more abundantly' (John 10.10).

The more I spend time with those who cannot find work, the more I study the social distribution of unemployment in our society, the more convinced I become that there is a deep wrong in the way in which we are handling our present predicament. That is not a narrowly political statement. It is something deeper. For what I see in the present situation constitutes a fracture of fellowship, the re-creation and perpetuation of an underclass in the midst of otherwise comparative affluence. Above all, as one who loves this country and her people, I am deeply saddened by the failure of community and the collapse of solidarity in the face of our present economic difficulties. Instead of sharing the wealth of the nation and the work of the nation with some measure of equity across the whole spectrum of the community we have abandoned others to their fate and have allowed the burden of the pains and the sacrifices to be borne, in power terms, by a weak minority—the young, the less qualified, the ethnic minorities, the disabled and those in the peripheral regions. These we have let fall by the wayside and we have made no adequate alternative social provision for them.

Perhaps the greatest of the sins is the sin of *acedia*, the sin of not caring, the sin of not getting involved in the resolution of the issues. For not to care is the polar opposite of Christian love. But how is our love, our care, to be expressed? If Christian love, to use C.F. Andrews' definition, is 'the accurate estimate and supply of someone else's need', how is it to be expressed amid the complexities of the economic and social order? It is not enough to feel for others, to be sensitive to their plight, to have concern for them. Moral purpose must become incorporated into appropriate policies and adequate social mechanisms. The unemployed do not want sympathy. They want results 'in the form of arrangements which will ensure them the essentials of a civilised existence and show a proper respect for their dignity as human beings'.(2) That fire in the belly, that desire to see right prevail, that burning neighbourly concern that we call Christian love must be converted into what Emil Brunner called 'the coin of justice, since that alone is legal tender in the world of systems'.(3)

The present state of affairs with regard to the way our economic ills are borne across the nation and within local communities is very far from just. The overall distribution of the sacrifice as it works itself out in individual lives and in group circumstances is not just. It is for this reason that I would argue that the persistence of

the high level of unemployment which we are presently experiencing is both morally unacceptable and unnecessary. It is unacceptable because our corporate handling of the prevailing adverse
situation manifests gross inequities within the social order and for
that we must all bear some responsibility. It is unecessary in that
there is, I believe, a social and economic alternative. We have
chosen not to share the costs and the accommodations in personal
lifestyle and working practice as we might have done. We have let
the weak go to the wall while the rest of society has continued to
enjoy all the benefits that work brings. Thus for most of us life continues to go on very much as before. We have let the market
mechanisms work but with respect to the social order we have been
tardy in making a moral critique of what was happening as a direct
consequence of our non-intervention.

Profitability and market demands are of course exceedingly important criteria for judgment within this present world order. But I
would affirm that over and beyond them there are other even more
significant criteria to be applied to which the world of economics
must forever remain subordinate. I speak here of the realm of
moral preferences and the arena of ultimate goals. It seems to me
that there is a frame of reference greater and more ultimate than
that which is normally chosen as a criterion of judgment within our
mixed economy. It has to do with our vision of the good society,
the calibre of social relationships and the opportunity for all to enjoy sufficient life-space to experience the height and breadth and
depth of our humanity in a life of wholesome fellowship and community. Different groups will articulate their vision of the good
society in differing ways. For the Jews it was the concept of
shalom, which in the Hebraic tradition has many rich connotations
including the concept of a community where within the framework
of God's purposes there is harmony, where mutual responsibility is
exercised and where there is unity and solidarity of purpose and
caring concern within its membership. '*Shalom*,' says Pederson,
'expresses every form of happiness and free expansion, but the
kernel in it is the community with others, the foundation of life.'(4)

For the Christian the pointers to the nature of the good society
come both from the rich Hebraic tradition with its strong concepts
of justice and righteousness within the social order and also from
the teaching of Jesus about the nature of the Kingdom of God, the
calibre of right relationships and God's particular concern for the
poor, the oppressed and the dispossessed. For Professor Halsey, as

we have seen, it is the concept of the fraternal society which is his guiding principle embodying the fundamental values of liberty, equality and fraternity and he would assert that it is the extent to which we have succeeded in embodying these into the social order that societies should be judged.(5) For the World Council of Churches in conference it is the concept of a Just, Participatory and Sustainable society.(6) For St Paul it was his vision of the mutuality of fellowship that exists within the Body of Christ. The good society perhaps cannot ever be precisely and finally described. As its attainment always just eludes us, so too perhaps does its absolute definition. Although there is a certain haziness about its exact outline, and differing parties will wish to express their vision using a different set of words, nevertheless I believe that sufficient insights have come to us down through the ages to provide us with certain consensus points when drawing up a frame of reference that will act as a guide to socio-economic policy. It may not give us a blueprint which if followed in all particulars will usher in the new Jerusalem. But at the very least it can provide us with something of a template which when laid against the existing social order will show us where serious mismatches are occurring and where change in structures, systems, lifestyle and practice must be initiated. We must concern ourselves with combating the cycle of deprivation that long-term unemployment brings. We must concern ourselves with the shaping of the appropriate mechanisms that will ensure a fuller and more equitable distribution of employment opportunities. We must address ourselves to the task of so directing the energies of our economic system that its rich resources can be geared to meeting the real needs of the global village and the relief of want and suffering the world over. These must remain forever high on any political and social agenda for they are all part of the process of creating an open space for Man. They are necessary if we are to advance in the construct of the good society in which all citizens of this global village may have the opportunity to fulfil their potential and attain to the full stature of their humanity. I believe that all men and women of goodwill have a role in that corporate purpose. For part of our humanity is to be creatively involved in the reform of the institutional patterns in which we live, responding creatively and imaginatively to the social order around us and attempting in company with others to bring into being a good that does not as yet exist in actuality.

It may not be that we can devise the perfect social and economic mechanisms to achieve our aims of the Just, Participatory and Sustainable Society for, in the words of the World Council of Churches' statement, 'No society—past or present—has achieved this goal in its fullness. . . . But we are capable of more profound justice, fuller participation and greater concern for sustainability than we now know and practise.'(7)

Notes and References

1. Temple, William, *Christianity and the Social Order,* Penguin Books, 1942 p. 21.
2. Tawney, R.H., *The Attack and Other Papers,* Allen and Unwin, 1953, p. 91.
3. Brunner, Emil, *Justice and the Social Order,* Lutherworth Press, 1945 p. 116.
4. Pederson, J., *Israel I–II*, Oxford University Press, Oxford, 1946, p. 313.
5. Halsey, A.H., *Change in British Society*, Oxford University Press, Oxford, 1978, p. 160.
6. *Faith and Science in an Unjust World, II* Report of the World Council of Churches Conference on Faith, Science and the Future. World Council of Churches, Geneva, 1980, *passim.*
7. *id.*, p. 149.

BIBLIOGRAPHY

Please note that London is the place of publication except where indicated.

Employment Trends

Association of Professional, Executive, Clerical and Computer Staff, *Office Technology: The Trade Union Response*, First Report of APEX Word Processing Working Party, March 1979.

Association of Scientific, Technical and Managerial Staffs, *Technological Change and Collective Bargaining*, ASTMS Discussion Document, 1979.

de Benedetti, Franco, *The Impact of Electronic Technology in the Office*, Olivetti, 22 March 1979.

Central Policy Review Staff, *Social and Employment Implications of Microelectronics*, November 1978.

Clarke, Roger, *The Microprocessor Revolution*, Church of Scotland Church and Industry Committee, 121 George Street, Edinburgh, 1979.

Employment Gazette, 'Labour Force Outlook to 1986', April 1981.

Equal Opportunities Commission, *Information Technology in the Office: The Impact on Women's Jobs*, Manchester, September 1980.

Hawkins, Kevin, *Unemployment—Facts, Figures and Possible Solutions for Britain*, Penguin Books, 1979.

Hines, Colin, *The 'Chips' Are Down: The Future Impact of Microprocessors and Computers on Employment in Britain*, A Discussion Paper, Earth Resources Research Ltd, April 1978.

Jenkins, Clive, and Barrie Sherman, *The Collapse of Work*, Eyre Methuen, 1979.

Manpower Services Commission, *Labour Market Quarterly Report*, May 1981.

Manpower Services Commission, *MSC Manpower Review 1980*, May 1980.

Manpower Services Commission, *MSC Manpower Review 1981*, June 1981.

Manpower Services Commission, *Plan for Scotland 1980–1984*, May 1980.

The National Computing Centre and AUEW (TASS), *Computer Technology and Employment*, 1979.

National Economic Development Council, *Microelectronics: Challenge and Response*, Memorandum by Secretaries of State for Industry, Employment and Education and Science, 1978.

Raison, Timothy, ed., *Prospects for Employment—A Tory View*, Conservative Political Centre, 1972.

Sawdon, Andrew, and David Taylor, *Youth Unemployment: A Background Paper*, A Youthaid Publication, July 1980.

Sleigh, Jonathan, Brian Boatwright, Peter Irwin and Roger Stanton, *The Manpower Implications of Micro-Electronic Technology*, HMSO, 1979.

Smith, David J., 'Unemployment and Racial Minority Groups', *Employment Gazette*, June 1980.

Stonier, Tom, *Materials Production Labour Requirements in Post-Industrial Society*, A Working Paper commissioned by Central Policy Review Staff (Cabinet Office), Bradford University, 10 November 1978.

Trades Union Congress, *Employment and Technology: A TUC Interim Report*, April 1979.

The Transport and General Workers' Union, *Microelectronics: New Technology—Old Problems New Opportunities*, June 1979.

Williams, Roger, ed., *Tomorrow at Work—Essays on the Future Patterns of Work and Leisure*, BBC Publications, 1973.

Wright, Michael, *The Microprocessor and Job Displacement among Clerical Workers*, London School of Economics, n.d.

Economic Considerations

Beckerman, Wilfred, *In Defence of Economic Growth*. Jonathan Cape, 1974.

Bleakley, David, *In Place of Work—The Sufficient Society*, SCM Press, 1981.

The Brandt Report, *North South: A Programme for Survival*, Pan Books, 1980.

Church of England, *The Ends and Means of Industry and Our Attitudes to Them*, Working Papers 4, Industrial Committee of the General Synod Board for Social Responsibility, February 1978.

The Club of Rome Report, *The Limits to Growth*, Pan Books, 1974.

The Second Report to the Club of Rome, *Mankind at the Turning Point*, Hutchinson, 1975.

Galbraith, John Kenneth, *The Affluent Society*, Hamish Hamilton, 1958.

Galbraith, John Kenneth, *Economics and the Public Purpose*, Andre Deutsch, 1974.

Galbraith, John Kenneth, *The New Industrial State*, Penguin Books, 1969.

Hirsch, F., *The Social Limits to Growth*, Routledge and Kegan Paul, 1977.

Robertson, James, *Policy Alternatives to Full Employment and Economic Growth*, Paper for the Anglo-German Foundation for the Study of Industrial Society, June 1976.

Schumacher, E.F., *Good Work*, Jonathan Cape, 1979.

Schumacher, E.F., *Small is Beautiful*, Blond and Briggs, 1973.

Stewart, Michael, *Keynes and After*, Penguin Books, 1972.

Wickham, E.R., *Inflation—A Christian Comment*, A Working Paper produced for the Industrial Committee of the Board for Social Responsibility, Church of England, 1974.

Sociology of Unemployment

Bakke, E.W., *The Unemployed Man*, Nisbet, 1933.

A Bristol Broadsides Booklet, *Fred's People: Young Bristolians Speak Out*, Bristol Broadsides (Co-op) Ltd, Bristol, 1980.

The Churches in South Manchester, *The Shock of No Work*, Manchester, 1980.

Daniel, W.W., and Elizabeth Stilgoe, *Where Are They Now? A Follow Up Survey of the Unemployed*, PEP Survey XLIII, 572, October 1977.

Daniel, W.W., 'Why is High Unemployment Still Somehow Acceptable?', *New Society*, 19 March 1981.

Field, Frank, ed., *The Conscript Army—A Study of Britain's Unemployed*, Routledge and Kegan Paul, 1977.

Gould, Tony, and Joe Kenyon, *Stories from the Dole Queue*, Temple Smith, 1972.

Harrison, Richard, 'The Demoralising Experience of Prolonged Unemployment', *Department of Employment Gazette*, April 1976.

Kemp, Fred, Bernard Buttle and Derek Kemp, *Focus on Redundancy*, Kogan Page, 1980.
Liebow, Elliot, 'No Man Can Live With The Terrible Knowledge That He Is Not Needed' *New York Times Magazine*, 5 April 1970.
Manpower Services Commission, *A Study of the Long-term Unemployed*, February 1980.
Manpower Services Commission, *Young People and Work*, Manpower Studies 19781, HMSO, 1978.
Markall, Graham, *The Best Years of Their Lives: Schooling, Work and Unemployment in Oldfield*, William Temple Foundation, Occasional Paper 3, Manchester, 1980.
Moylan, Sue, and Bob Davies, 'The Disadvantages of the Unemployed', *Employment Gazette*, August 1980.
Newcastle-upon-Tyne Centre for the Unemployed, *On the Stones*, Newcastle, September 1980.
The Pilgrim Trust, *Men Without Work*, Cambridge University Press, 1938.
Showler, Brian, and Adrian Sinfield, eds., *The Workless State: Studies in Unemployment*, Martin Robertson, Oxford, 1981.
Sinfield, Adrian, *The Long-term Unemployed: A Comparative Survey*, OECD Report, 1967.
Sinfield, Adrian, *What Unemployment Means*, Martin Robertson, Oxford, 1981.
Stevenson, John, and Chris Cook, *The Slump: Society and Politics During the Depression*, Quartet Books, 1979.

Sociology of Work

Abram, Philip, ed., *Work, Urbanism and Inequality: UK Society Today*, Weidenfeld and Nicolson, 1978.
Fox, Alan, *A Sociology of Work and Industry*, Collier–Macmillan, 1971.
Jephcott, Pearl, *Married Women Working*, Allen and Unwin, 1962.
Klein, Viola, *Britain's Married Women Workers*, Routledge and Kegan Paul, 1965.
Mackie, Lindsay, and Polly Pattullo, *Women at Work*, Tavistock Publications, 1977.
Parker, S.R., R.K. Brown, J. Child, and M.A. Smith, *The Sociology of Industry*, Allen and Unwin, 1972.

Attitudes to Work and Idleness

Antony, P.D., *The Ideology of Work*, Tavistock Publications, 1977.
Arendt, Hannah, *The Human Condition*, University of Chicago Press, Chicago, 1958.
Ball, Colin, and Mog Ball, *Fit for Work?—Youth, School and (Un)employment*, Writers and Readers Publishing Co-operative, 1979.
Batten, E.M., *The Changing Meaning of Work Today*, Preliminary Paper for Industrial Committee of General Synod Board for Social Responsibility, Church of England, June 1967.
Berger, Peter L., *The Human Shape of Work*, Macmillan, New York, 1964.
Blauner, Robert, *Alienation and Freedom: The Factory Worker and His Industry*, University of Chicago Press, Chicago, 1964.
Brett, Paul, *Work and the Theologians*, Working Papers 3, Industrial Committee of the General Synod Board for Social Responsibility, Church of England, February 1979.
Burman, Sandra, ed., *Fit Work for Women*, Croom Helm, 1979.

Burnett, John, *Useful Toil: Autobiographies of Working People 1820s to 1920s*, Penguin Books, 1977.

Carter, Michael, *Into Work*, Penguin Books, 1966.

Cohen, J., 'Ideas of Work and Play', *British Journal of Sociology*, 4, 1953.

Cotgrove, S., and Stanley Parker, 'Work and Non-Work', *New Society*, 41, 11 July 1963.

Cox, Sarah, and Robert Golden, *Down the Road*, Writers and Readers Publishing Co-operative, 1977.

Deacon, Alan, 'The Scrounging Controversy: Public Attitudes towards the Unemployed in Contemporary Britain', *Social and Economic Administration*, 12.2, Summer 1978.

Deacon, Alan, 'Spivs, Drones and Other Scroungers', *New Society*, 28 February 1980.

Firth, Raymond, *Human Types*, Sphere Books, 1970.

Flynn, M.W., 'Social Theory and the Industrial Revolution', contained in *Social Theory and Economic Change*, Tom Burns and S.B. Saul, eds., Tavistock Publications, 1967.

Fraser, Derek, *The Evolution of the British Welfare State*, Macmillan, 1975.

Fraser, Ronald, ed., *Work 2: Twenty Personal Accounts*, Penguin Books, 1969.

Fromm, Erich, *The Fear of Freedom*, Routledge and Kegan Paul, 1966.

Fullerton, Kemper, 'Calvinism and Capitalism: An Explanation of the Weber Thesis', contained in *Protestantism and Capitalism: The Weber Thesis and Its Critics*, ed. Robert W. Green, D.C. Heath, Lexington (USA), 1959.

Goldthorpe, J.H., D. Lockwood, F. Bechhofer and J. Platt, *The Affluent Worker: Industrial Attitudes and Behaviour*, Cambridge University Press, 1968.

Harvie, Christopher, Graham Martin and Aaron Scharf, eds., *Industrialisation and Culture 1830–1914*, The Open University, 1970.

Herzberg, Frederick, *Work and the Nature of Man*, Staples Press, 1968.

Hughes, Everett C., 'Work and the Self', contained in *Social Psychology at the Crossroads*, John H. Rohrer and Muzafer Sherif, eds., Harper and Row, New York, 1951.

Klein, Lisl, *The Meaning of Work*, Fabian Tract 349, October 1963.

Longmate, Norman, *The Workhouse*, Temple Smith, 1974.

Marsden, D., and E. Duff, *Workless—Some Unemployed Men and Their Families*, Penguin Books, 1975.

Marshall, Gordon, *Presbyteries and Profits: Calvinism and the Development of Capitalism in Scotland 1560–1707*, Clarendon Press, Oxford, 1980.

Meakin, David, *Man and Work: Literature and Culture in Industrial Society*, Methuen, 1976.

Mills, C. Wright, *White Collar: The American Middle Classes*, Oxford University Press, 1953.

Mossé, Claude, *The Ancient World at Work*, Translated from the French by Janet Lloyd, Chatto and Windus, 1969.

Pound, John, *Poverty and Vagrancy in Tudor England*, Longman, 1971.

Orwell, George, *The Road to Wigan Pier*, Penguin Books, 1981.

Seabrook, Jeremy, *City Close-Up*, Penguin Books, 1971.

Seeman, Melvin, 'On the Meaning of Alienation', *American Sociological Review*, XXIV, 1959.

Shimmin, Sylvia, 'Concepts of Work', *Occupational Psychology*, 40, 1966.

Tawney, R.H., *Religion and the Rise of Capitalism*, Penguin Books, 1948.

Tilgher, A., *Work: What it has Meant to Men Through the Ages*, Harcourt Brace, New York, 1930.

Troeltsch, Ernst, 'The Economic Ethic of Calvinism', contained in *Protestantism and Capitalism: The Weber Thesis and Its Critics*, ed. Robert W. Green, D.C. Heath, Lexington (USA), 1959.

Weber, Max, *The Protestant Ethic and the Spirit of Capitalism*, Allen and Unwin, 1976.
Wesker, Arnold, *I'm Talking About Jerusalem*, Penguin Books, 1960.
Williams, R., and D. Guest, 'Are the Middle Classes Becoming Work-Shy?' *New Society*, 1 July 1971.
Zweig, Ferdynand, *The British Worker*, Penguin Books, 1952.

Psychological Insights

Bowlby, John, 'Processes of Mourning', *The International Journal of Psycho-Analysis*, XLII, Parts 4–5, 1961.
Brown, J.A.C., *The Social Psychology of Industry*, Penguin Books, 1954.
Clinebell, Howard J., *Basic Types of Pastoral Counselling*, Abingdon Press, New York, 1966.
Cohen, Stanley, and Laurie Taylor, *Psychological Survival: The Experience of Long-term Imprisonment*, Penguin Books, 1981.
Goffman, Erving, *Stigma—Notes on the Management of Spoiled Identity*, Penguin Books, 1968.
Hayes, John, and Peter Nutman, *Understanding the Unemployed: The Psychological Effects of Unemployment*, Tavistock Publications, 1981.
Hill, John, 'The Psychological Impact of Unemployment', *New Society*, 19 January 1978.
Jahoda, Marie, 'The Impact of Unemployment in the 1930s and the 1970s', *Bulletin of the British Psychological Society*, 32, 1979.
Jahoda, Marie, 'The Psychological Meanings of Unemployment', *New Society*, 6 September 1979.
Lowe, Gordon R., *The Growth of Personality From Infancy to Old Age*, Penguin Books, 1972.
Marris, Peter, *Loss and Change*, Routledge and Kegan Paul, 1974.
Murray-Parkes, Colin, *Bereavement—Studies of Grief in Adult Life*, Penguin Books, 1975.
Pincus, Lily, *Death and the Family: The Importance of Mourning*, Faber and Faber, 1976.
Ross, Donald, *Psychological Effects of Redundancy*, Church of Scotland, Church and Industry Committee, 121 George Street, Edinburgh, March 1980.
Ruddock, Ralph, *Roles and Relationships*, Routledge and Kegan Paul, 1972.

Poverty and Inequality

Atherton, John R., *Religion and the Persistence of Poverty: A Challenge to British Social Democracy and the Churches,* William Temple Foundation, Manchester, 1980.
British Council of Churches, *Understanding Inequality*, Britain Today and Tomorrow, 1, 1977.
Burghes, Louie, *Living from Hand to Mouth: A Study of 65 Families Living on Supplementary Benefit*, Poverty Pamphlet 50, A Joint Family Service Unit and Child Poverty Action Group Publication, December 1980.
Burghes, Louie, *So Who's 'Better Off' On The Dole?: Myths and Facts about Unemployment,* Poverty Fact Sheet, Child Poverty Action Group, February 1980.
Child Poverty Action Group, *Poverty—What Is It*? Poverty Fact Sheet, Child Poverty Action Group, n.d.
Commission of the European Communities, *The Perception of Poverty in Europe*, Brussels, March 1977.
Department of Health and Social Security, *Which Benefit*? DHSS Leaflet, November 1980.

Employment Gazette, 'Pattern of Household Spending in 1979', November 1980.
Field, Frank, *Inequality in Britain: Freedom, Welfare and the State*, Fontana, Collins, Glasgow, 1981.
Holman, Robert, *Poverty—Explanations of Social Deprivation*, Martin Robertson, Oxford, 1978.
Jordan, Bill, *Paupers—The Making of the New Claiming Class*, Routledge and Kegan Paul, 1973.
Low Pay Unit, *Low Pay—1980s Style*, Low Pay Review 4, March 1981.
Supplementary Benefits Commission, *Annual Report for 1978*, HMSO, 1979.
Supplementary Benefits Commission, *Annual Report for 1979*, HMSO, 1980.
Townsend, Peter, *Poverty in the United Kingdom*, Penguin Books, 1979.

Retirement

Atchley, Robert C., *The Sociology of Retirement*, Schenkman Publishing Co., Cambridge, Massachusetts, 1976.
Employment Gazette, 'An Increase in Earlier Retiral for Men', April 1980.
McGoldrick, Ann, and Cary L. Cooper, 'Voluntary Early Retirement—Taking the Decision', *Employment Gazette*, August 1980.
Tournier, Paul, *Learning to Grow Old*, SCM Press, 1972.
Townsend, Peter, *The Family Life of Old People*, Penguin Books, 1957.

Leisure

Bridge, David, *Looking at Leisure*, Epworth Press, 1978.
de Grazia, Sebastian, *Of Time, Work and Leisure*, Twentieth Century Fund, New York, 1962.
Parker, Stanley, *The Future of Work and Leisure*, Paladin, 1972.
Roberts, Kenneth, *Leisure*, Longman, 1970.

Employment Policies

Addison, John, et alia, *Job 'Creation'—or Destruction: Six Essays on the Effects of Government Intervention in the Labour Market*, Institute of Economic Affairs, 1979.
Beveridge, William H., *Full Employment in a Free Society*, Allen and Unwin, 1944.
Boyle, Adrienne, *Job Sharing: A Study of the Costs, Benefits and Employment Rights of Job Sharers*, Job Sharing Project, November 1980.
British Youth Council, *Youth Unemployment: Causes and Cures*, Report of a Working Party, March 1977.
Carter, Charles, and David Eversley, *Why Unemployment? What Can We Do?* Religious Society of Friends, London Yearly Meeting, March 1981.
Confederation of British Industry, *Jobs—Facing the Future*, CBI Staff Discussion Document, January 1980.
Brett, Paul, *Unemployment—What Can Be Done?* Working Papers 11, Industrial Committee of the General Synod Board for Social Responsibility, Church of England, February 1981.
Clarke, Roger, *Sharing in Work*, Church of Scotland, Church and Industry Committee, 121 George Street, Edinburgh, Autumn 1977.
Commission for Racial Equality, *Youth in Multi-Racial Society: The Urgent Need for New Policies*, March 1980.
Commission of the European Communities, *Communication from the Commission to the Council on Work-Sharing*, Brussels, 7 May 1979.

Cowie, A.Y.W., An unpublished Paper on Work-Sharing, Edinburgh, 1980.

Department of Employment Gazette, 'Measures to Alleviate Unemployment in the Medium Term: Early Retirement', March 1978.

Equal Opportunities Commission, *Job Sharing: Improving the Quality and Availability of Part-time Work*, Manchester, July 1981.

Euroforum, 'Retirement: Time for a Change of Attitude', 9/80, 25 May 1980.

European Economic Community, *EEC Commission Proposals on Work Sharing*, EEC Commission Documents, Brussels, 21 March 1978.

Industrial Relations Review and Report, 'Two People One Job: An IR–RR Review of Job Sharing', 225, June 1980.

Jackson, Michael P., and Victor J.B. Hanby, eds., *Work Creation: International Experiences*, Saxon House, Farnborough, 1979.

The Job Sharing Project, *Job Sharing: A Guide for Employees*, 77 Balfour Street, London SE17.

Koller, Martin, and Lutz Reyher, *Working Time Over Life: Participation in the Labour Market and Economic Growth*, Commission of the European Communities, Nuremberg, February 1980.

Manpower Services Commission, *An 'Open Tech' Programme*, A Consultative Document, May 1981.

Manpower Services Commission, *A New Training Initiative*, A Consultative Document, May 1981.

Manpower Services Commission, *MSC Review of Services for the Unemployed*, March 1981.

Manpower Services Commission, *Review of the Second Year of Special Programmes*, 1981.

Manpower Services Commission, *Securing a Future for Young People*, Coombe Lodge Report 11.4, Papers from MSC Study Conferences, 1978.

Manpower Services Commission, *Training Needs of the Eighties*, Text of a Lecture delivered by Sir Richard O'Brien, Chairman of MSC at the Scottish Council for Educational Technology, 15 April 1981.

Melville, Joy, 'How the Jobless Can Help Each Other', *New Society*, 23 July 1981.

Mukherjee, Santosh, *There's Work To Be Done: Unemployment and Manpower Policies*, HMSO, 1974.

Mukherjee, Santosh, *Through No Fault of Their Own: Systems for Handling Redundancies in Britain, France and Germany*, PEP Report, Macdonald, 1973.

National Economic Development Council, *The Social Background to Some Economic Problems*, 29 May 1974.

Robertson, James, *The Sane Alternative—Signposts to a Self-Fulfilling Future*, James Robertson, Ironbridge, 1978.

Rothwell, Sheila, 'Women and Work', *Resurgence*, 86, May–June 1981.

Scottish Trades Union Congress, *Scottish Convention on Unemployment: Base Paper*, Glasgow, 8 December 1980.

Tripartite Steering Group on Job Satisfaction, *Making Work More Satisfying*, HMSO, 1975.

Trades Union Congress, *The Reconstruction of Britain*, August 1981.

Trades Union Congress, *Services for the Unemployed: Unemployed Workers' Centres*, Bulletin 1, March 1981.

Trades Union Congress, *Unemployment: The Fight for TUC Alternatives*, January 1981.

Turning Point, *The Redistribution of Work*, Turning Point Paper 1, Ironbridge, 1981.

Ward, Peter, *The Cutting Edge or the Slippery Slope? Workers Alternative Plans for Industry*, TASS–AUEW, October 1979.

Weir, Molly, ed., *Job Satisfaction—Challenge and Response in Modern Britain*, Fontana Collins, 1976.
Wilson, N.A.B., *On the Quality of Working Life*, Manpower Papers 1, HMSO, 1973.

Theological Reflection

Atkinson, Michael, and Paul Brett, eds., *Mission in Industrial Society*, Industrial Committee of the General Synod Board for Social Responsibility, Church of England, July 1978.
Autton, Norman, ed., *From Fear to Faith: Studies of Suffering and Wholeness*, SPCK, 1971.
British Council of Churches, *Employment and Unemployment: Britain Today and Tomorrow Report*, October 1977.
Brunner, Emil, *Justice and the Social Order*, Lutterworth Press, 1945.
Chenu, M.D., *The Theology of Work—An Exploration*, M.H. Gill, Dublin, 1963.
Church of England, *Work and the Future: Technology, World Development and Jobs in the Eighties*, A Report from the Industrial Committee of the General Synod Board for Social Responsibility, Church Information Office, 1979.
Church of England, *Work or What? A Christian Examination of the Unemployment Crisis*, Church Information Office, 1977.
Church of England, *Work in Britain Today—A Christian View*, Church Information Office, 1969.
Cone, James H., *Black Theology and Black Power*, Seabury Press, New York, 1969.
Cone, James H., *God of the Oppressed*, Seabury Press, New York, 1975.
Conway, Martin, *Through the Eyes of the Poor*, British Council of Churches, August 1980.
Cox, Harvey, *The Feast of Fools: A Theological Essay on Festivity and Fantasy*, Harper and Row, New York, 1972.
Cox, Harvey, *On Not Leaving it to the Snake*, SCM Press, 1968.
Cox, Harvey, *The Secular City*, SCM Press, 1966.
Craig, Robert, *Social Concern in the Thought of William Temple*, Gollancz, 1963.
Cramb, Erik, *The Contribution of Liberation Theology to a Christian Response to Mass Unemployment*, Unpublished Paper produced for the Scottish Theological Development Group on Unemployment, September 1980.
Davidson, Robert, *Work and Unemployment—A Biblical Approach*, An Unpublished Paper produced for the Scottish Theological Development Group on Unemployment, University of Glasgow, March 1980.
Davies, J.G., *Dialogue With the World*, SCM Press, 1967.
Duncan, Robert, *What is the Question Please?*, Unpublished Paper produced for the Scottish Theological Development Group on Unemployment, Glasgow, November 1980.
Elliott, Charles, 'Vision and Utopia', *Theology*, May 1978.
Fisher, Paul, *Not Yet Utopia: Microelectronic Technology and its Implications*, British Council of Churches, 1979.
Fletcher, Joseph, *Moral Responsibility—Situation Ethics at Work*, SCM Press, 1967.
Gill, Robin, *Theology and Social Structure*, Mowbrays, Oxford, 1977.
Gustafson, James M., and James T. Laney, eds., *On Being Responsible: Issues in Personal Ethics*, SCM Press, 1969.
Industrial Mission Association Theology Development Group, *The End of Work? Papers on Theology and Technological Change*, William Temple Foundation, Manchester, 1980.
Jenkins, David E., *The Contradiction of Christianity*, SCM Press, 1976.

Jenkins, David E., *Human Rights and Industry*, William Temple Foundation, Occasional Papers 1, Manchester, 1979.
Jenkins, David E., 'Putting Theology to Work', *Theology*, March 1978.
Kane, Margaret, *Theological Development*, William Temple Foundation, Occasional Papers 2, Manchester, 1980.
Kane, Margaret, *Theology in an Industrial Society*, SCM Press, 1975.
Kennedy, Francis, *Shafts of Hope: An Investigation of the Development of the Work Ethic*, Unpublished Paper produced for the Scottish Theological Development Group on Unemployment, Glasgow, February 1981.
Koyama, Kosuke, *The Crucified Christ Challenges Human Power*, Document 4.01, World Council of Churches Conference on World Mission and Evangelism, Melbourne, Australia, 1980.
MacQuarrie, John, *An Existentialist Theology*, SCM Press, 1955.
Moltmann, Jürgen, *Theology and Joy*, SCM Press, 1973.
Northcott, Michael, *Sociology, Analysis and Theology*, Unpublished Lecture Notes, Certificate in Religious Studies Residential Week-end, University of Manchester and William Temple Foundation, 15 March 1980.
Oldham, J.H., *Work in Modern Society*, SCM Press, 1950.
Outka, Gene, *Agape: An Ethical Analysis*, Yale University Press, New Haven and London, 1972.
Phipps, Simon, *God on Monday*, Hodder and Stoughton, 1966.
Preston, Ronald H., *Religion and the Persistence of Capitalism*, SCM Press, 1979.
Quaker Social Responsibility and Education Journal, I.3, November 1979.
Richardson, Alan, *The Biblical Doctrine of Work*, SCM Press, 1963.
Robinson, John A.T., *The Body: A Study in Pauline Theology*, Studies in Biblical Theology 5, SCM Press, 1952.
Robinson, John A.T., *In the End God*, Fontana Collins, 1968.
Sheffield Industrial Mission, *Church and Industry—A Continuing Debate*, Sheffield, 1977.
Schrey, Heinz-Horst, Hans Hermann Walz and W.A. Whitehouse, *The Biblical Doctrine of Justice and Law*, Ecumenical Biblical Studies 3, SCM Press, 1955.
Sleeman, John F., *Economic Crisis: A Christian Perspective*, SCM Press, 1976.
Temple, William, *Christianity and the Social Order*, Penguin Books, 1956.
Tillich, Paul, *The Boundaries of our Being*, Fontana Collins, 1973.
Tillich, Paul, *The Courage To Be*, Fontana Collins, 1962.
Tillich, Paul, *Love, Power and Justice*, Oxford University Press, 1954.
Welbourn, David, *New Attitudes for a New Age*, Unpublished Paper, Sunderland, February 1979.
Welbourn, David, *Creative Living in a New Age*, Incorporating material from Keith Argyle, Unpublished Paper, Sunderland, 1979.
Welbourn, David, *Creator Man: A Re-examination of the Genesis 1–3 Theology of Work*, Unpublished Paper, Sunderland, n.d.
Wickham, E.R., *Encounter with Modern Society*, Lutterworth Press, 1964.
Williams, Colin, *Faith in a Secular Age*, Fontana Collins, 1966.
Wogaman, J. Philip, *A Christian Method of Moral Judgement*, SCM Press, 1976.
World Council of Churches, *Christian Social Thought in a Future Perspective*, Anticipation 26, Geneva, June 1979.
World Council of Churches, *Faith and Science in an Unjust World*, Report of the World Council of Churches' Conference on Faith, Science and the Future 2—Reports and Recommendations, ed. Paul Abrecht, Church and Society, World Council of Churches, Geneva, 1980.
Wright, G. Ernest, *The Biblical Doctrine of Man in Society*, Ecumenical Biblical Studies 2, SCM Press, 1954.

Wright, G. Ernest, *God Who Acts: Biblical Theology as Recital*, Studies in Biblical Theology, SCM Press, 1952.

General

Bainton, Roland H., *Here I Stand: A Life of Martin Luther*, Abingdon Press, New York, 1955.

Disraeli, Benjamin, *Sybil* or *The Two Nations*, Oxford University Press, 1981.

Fromm, Erich, *To Have or To Be?*, Abacus, 1979.

Gaventa, John, *Power and Powerlessness: Quiescence and Rebellion in an Appalachian Valley*, Clarendon Press, Oxford, 1980.

Halsey, A.H., *Change in British Society*, Oxford University Press, 1978.

Jeffreys, M.V.C., *Glaucon: An Inquiry into the Aims of Education*, Pitman, 1950.

Kuhn, Thomas, S., *The Structure of Scientific Revolutions*, Foundations of the Unity of Science, II.2, University of Chicago, Chicago, 1970.

Mills, C. Wright, *The Sociological Imagination*, Penguin Books, 1970.

Tawney, R.H., *The Attack and Other Papers*, Allen and Unwin, 1953.

Titmuss, Richard M., *The Gift Relationship: From Human Blood to Social Policy*, Allen and Unwin, 1970.

Walker, Williston, *A History of the Christian Church*, T. and T. Clark, Edinburgh, 1959.

INDEX

activity rates, 89, 119, 151

alienation, 74, 75, 194, 206

Baxter, Richard, 176-177

bereavement, job-loss as, 24, 79-80, *see also* mourning

Beveridge, William H., 3-4, 6, 9, 11, 32, 119, 145

boredom, unemployment experienced as, 51, 53, 81

Brandt Report, 93

calling, concept of, 166-169

Calvin, John, 167-168

Calvinism, 169, 177, *see also* Scottish divines

Charity schools, *see* Sunday schools

Child Poverty Action Group, 40, 42, *see also* poverty lobby

community, concept of, 25, 70, 162, 163-164, 196-197, 209-210, *see also* fraternal society

Contribution ethic, 185, 190, 196-199, *see also* 25

convivial relationships, 111, 120, 183-184, 193, 198, 205

costs, financial, of early retirement, 112, 125, 127-128
of job-sharing, 113, 117 and Chapter 13 Note 12
of labour, 101, 137-138
of recruitment as opposed to overtime, 136
of unemployment, 90, 142-143
of a vocational preparation programme, 129 and Chapter 14 Notes 10 & 11
of work-sharing, 122, 142-144, 150-151, 208

democracy, democratic society, 9, 11, 21, 70, 75, 105, 149-150, 203, 206

dependency, economic, 23, 28, 29, 33, 36, 49, 143, 170

depression, subjective experience of unemployment, 29, 30-31, 53, 59, *see also* Chapter 14 Note 14

Depression, the, patterns of work and unemployment, 4, 5, 15, 67, 73-74, 76, 94-95, *see also* Chapter 7 Notes 1 & 2

despair, experience of, 4, 29-31, 76, 78, 82, 143

disabled, 5, 34, 49, 95, 113-114, 133-134, 197, 201, 207, 209

disorientation and disorganisation, experience of, 81, 82-83

distribution of work opportunities, xviii, 32-33, 72-74, 87, 92, 94-95, 131-132, 140, 192, 205-206, 211

early retirement, *see* retirement

earnings related supplement or benefit, 37-39, 47, 67, 81, 95-96

equality or equity, general, 70-71, 92, 205-206, 211
of job opportunities between the sexes, 119-120, 132-133

ethnic minorities or immigrants, 5, 11, 34, 49, 72, 74-75, 95, 201, 207, 209

factory system, formative influence of, 110-111, 180-181, 183-184

family tensions, resulting from unemployment, 59-60, 81 and Chapter 14 Note 14

fear, 66, 68-69, 106, 172

female work patterns, 5, 7, 113, 120-121

financial aspects of unemployment, 35, 37-49, 53, 57, 59, 66-68, 81, 84-85, 90, 96